ERIE'S
GREAT MAUSOLEUM MYSTERY

GHOULS,
GRAVE ROBBERS
& EXTORTION

JUSTIN DOMBROWSKI

THE
History
PRESS

Published by The History Press
Charleston, SC
www.historypress.com

First published 2024

Manufactured in the United States

ISBN 9781467156615

Library of Congress Control Number: 2024930900

Notice: The information in this book is true and complete to the best of our knowledge. It is offered without guarantee on the part of the author or The History Press. The author and The History Press disclaim all liability in connection with the use of this book.

CONTENTS

ACKNOWLEDGEMENTS

The fulfillment of this book could not have been possible without many people.

J. Banks Smither, my managing editor, helped guide this project to completion and supported it since its earliest stages. Abigail Fleming, senior editor, helped provide critical notes in her edit of the manuscript.

Research was also assisted by the staffs of The Cleveland Public Library, The National Archives at Kansas City, The National Archives at Philadelphia, The Indianapolis Public Library, The Prothonotary's Office of Erie County and the staff for Gannon University.

Betsy Mackrell and the Erie Cemetery Association helped corroborate information about the Scott mausoleum and its construction. The Erie County Historical Society at the Hagen History Center again allowed unfettered access to their archives, which provided rich, supplemental photographs and information that has complemented the narrative of this book.

Descendants of both Charles Franklin and Gilbert Perkins were both warm and welcoming throughout the writing process, contributing additional facts and particulars about both men and their involvement in this bizarre case.

William "Hammy" Oldfield, the great-great-grandson of Inspector John Frank Oldfield, has been more than gracious in assistance, including his wealth of knowledge about the U.S. Postal Inspection Service and legacy of Inspector Oldfield. In the end, I have gained a valuable friend whose passion for history is just as momentous as the pertinacious work of Inspector Oldfield himself.

Those who have also provided support and historical insight and support through this journey include fellow historians such as Anita Breitweiser, George Deutsch and Jonathan Burdick; many friends and colleagues; and countless family members, including my parents and, perhaps, the most important: my wife and my children.

INTRODUCTION

When the family mausoleum of former congressman and mayor William L. Scott was horribly desecrated in Erie, Pennsylvania, in 1911, what ensued was an outlandish parable of sensationalism. Colossal headlines, saturated in ink, were flowered across the sheets of thousands of newspapers, from the banks of the Penobscot River in Bangor, Maine, to the booming metropolis of Los Angeles, metastasizing like a wrathful inferno.

"GHOULS ROB FAMILY VAULT" trumpeted the *Bangor Daily News* on page 12. "GHOULS BREAK INTO MAUSOLEUM; BODY TAKEN HELD FOR RANSOM?" queried the scandalized *Los Angeles Times*. "COUNTRY-WIDE SEARCH FOR TOMB DESECRATORS" roared the *Buffalo Evening News*.

Millions of Americans were swiftly subjected to news emanating from the Gem City. Dozens of newspaper correspondents, thrill seekers and amateur sleuths converged on Pennsylvania's third-largest city, aspiring to furnish every miniscule detail to a public waiting to devour the latest exclusive.

The hunt for those responsible, labeled by the press as "ghouls" and "vandals," was conducted by hordes of operatives from rival detective agencies as they roamed the city's streets, alleyways and darkest corners, unrestrained, in their quest for prestige in deciphering the ghastly goings-on.

Letters, crude in their delineation, were mailed to Charles Strong. Purportedly written by the infamous "Black Hand," such letters were not uncommon during the Progressive Era. At that time, families, rich and poor, were frequent victims of extortion and, in some cases, murder.

The attempted extortion, through the U.S. Mail, precipitated the intervention of the country's most powerful law enforcement agency: the U.S. Postal Inspection Service. Under the leadership of the vociferous and shrewd Postal Inspector John Frank Oldfield, a squad of government agents accumulated evidence and arrested those responsible for the threatening letters, resulting in one of the country's most sensational criminal trials in 1911.

Following the trial, the case lapsed into legend.

At least this is how the story is remembered, regurgitated every autumn when thousands of leaves gravitate to the earth, drenching Erie's alleys and cemeteries into purveyors of wickedness and fright, morphing the true story of the desecration of the Scott mausoleum into a multifaceted fable never fully scrutinized.

Until now.

This narrative, freed of falsities and restored with research, divulged for the first time, includes reproductions of two of the original Black Hand letters and source material from other correspondences, memoirs, newspaper articles, court records and unpublished manuscripts, revealing an assemblage of colorful characters from bygone days, consigned to oblivion.

Many newspaper articles and statements included within are presented in their original format for clarity, including noted spelling errors. The City of Pittsburgh, Pennsylvania, for example, is often referred to by its then original spelling of "Pittsburg" before the federal government agreed to formally return the -h to the city's name in July 1911.

Although a century has passed since the desecration of the Scott mausoleum, the hunt for the nefarious ghouls has commenced once more.

PROLOGUE
THE RED HOUSE

I t was just after 4:15 a.m., on January 27, 1911, as Louis Wadlinger shuffled along the snow-covered sidewalks of West Nineteenth Street in the city of Erie. The owner of a small confectionery store and milk depot, Wadlinger braced against the stabbing cold air as he ventured from his milk cart, performing his customary route.

Wadlinger detested the devilish routine, especially during the early morning hours, as those throughout the city at such an hour were likely to be accosted by drunks and delinquents. Wadlinger's family, mindful of the dangers that lurked along Erie's darkened streets, greeted each return from his audacious sojourn with repose. Passing from one porch to another, Wadlinger's feet chomped against the ice and snow as he neared the corner of West Nineteenth and Chestnut Streets, where he perceived the shape of a man nearby.

Wadlinger halted in his step, a lump forming in his throat as he prepared for the worst.

A thick, damp stillness suspended in the air as the stranger inched closer, his features emerging under the luminosity of a streetlight, revealing a man short in height with the frayed appearance

Louis Wadlinger. *From the Erie Daily Times.*

of a railroad laborer, his facial features concealed under a coating of dirt and grime.

"You have a match?" the stranger asked, shaking.

Wadlinger fished a small matchbook from his pocket and handed it to the stranger, who nodded in a gesture of gratitude. Striking a match against his thigh, the stranger ignited a cigarette dangling from the corner of his mouth, soon exhaling into the night before motioning to the iron gates of the Erie Cemetery behind him, admitting he had lingered around the vicinity for nearly an hour, watching as four men transported something from the cemetery. "A corpse!" the stranger uttered, his eyes wide with exhilaration.

Wadlinger's gaze turned to the cemetery's gated perimeter, straining beyond the gloomy silhouettes of tombstones and stripped tree limbs, fused together in an expansive abyss.

When the stranger described a black-topped wagon illuminated by the dim flame of a lantern halting against the curb, Wadlinger's curiosity

West Nineteenth Street facing east near where Louis Wadlinger was approached by the stranger on January 27, 1911. *Author's collection.*

intensified. He had observed this very wagon earlier that morning. Wadlinger's attention remained attuned to the stranger's animated features as he described the men exiting the wagon with the corpse.

"They carried it into the red house," the stranger stammered.

With the hour growing late, and dubious of the eerie tale, Wadlinger exchanged a farewell with the eccentric stranger. As he stood near the corner of West Nineteenth and Chestnut Streets, Wadlinger looked over his shoulder, watching the stranger vanish into the frigid darkness. Looking back into the cemetery, Wadlinger heard nothing except the flutter of his own breath.

It was only twelve days later that Louis Wadlinger would realize the significance of the stranger's story, and his imagination at once returned to the Red House.

Darkness slithered through the city of Erie as Amelia Hertwig and a female acquaintance strolled among the tombstones inside the Erie Cemetery on the evening of February 8, 1911. Despite the brittle, unsettled and chilly weather punctuated by sharp winds, Amelia had enjoyed some much-needed fresh air. Through the slivers of trees and granite she could barely distinguish the faint illumination of nearby houses and decided it was time to return home.

As she traipsed over a rise on the narrow cemetery road, Amelia's attention was lured to the towering, Gothic marble and granite edifice of the Scott mausoleum. The influence of the Scott family was well known in Erie, forever intertwined with the city's history reaching as far back as 1851. Admiring the crypt's large dome and beautifully stained glass, Amelia's gaze became transfixed on the pair of solid bronze doors at the mausoleum's entrance.

Something was awry.

A pall of uneasy tranquility settled over the cemetery, amplified by the absence of once noticeable wildlife. Ascending the stone slabs leading to the pillared portico of the mausoleum, Amelia came face-to-face with the bronze doors and found them slightly ajar, the edges of one of the panels of the inner door chipped and damaged. Thrusting her arm through the iron bars, Amelia brushed her hand against the panel, causing it to topple to the ground with a loud clang.

The entrance of the Scott mausoleum. *Author's collection.*

Amelia whipped around, her eyes widening as she looked to her friend, and her heart throbbed as she swallowed nervously before pushing against one of the bronze doors.

A spectral groan fizzled from inside the crypt with a sight that filled Amelia Hertwig's stare with pure horror.

Stumbling backward, nearly collapsing, Amelia retreated down the front steps as fast as her feet could carry her, with her friend in quick pursuit. Through the trees, Amelia detected the residence of the cemetery's superintendent.

Amelia Hertwig needed to reach a telephone.

The four-story mansion dominated the corner of West Sixth and Peach Streets, the edge of Millionaire's Row, in downtown Erie. With its generous windows and blue sandstone exterior, the mansion was beautifully accentuated with rustic yellow Pompeian brick, terra-cotta ornaments and slated roofing capping numerous slopes and porches. Plumes of smoke billowed from innumerable chimneys against the last vestiges of another cold February evening.

Consisting of forty-six rooms and costing nearly $480,000 following its completion in 1896, the home exuded sheer affluence. Its owners, Charles and Annie Strong, hosted lavish parties and celebrations, making ostentatious displays of power and wealth.

A pair of lions, etched in stone, guarded the main entrance on West Sixth Street as visitors were often ushered through colossal solid oak doors that opened into a regal great hall. Assisted by butlers, callers were announced to the Strong family on their arrival as they stood under gleaming crystal chandeliers suspended from delicately carved ceilings.

A massive ballroom on the eastern wing of the first floor was planted under hand-painted ceilings featuring cherubs peeking through voluminous clouds. Next was the reception room, enhanced with a well-stocked library and sumptuously furnished with fourteen-karat gold leaf. The formal dining room on the western end of the home could billet up to forty guests at its massive dining room table, its walls decorated with hand-woven tapestries. Branching off was the family's private dining room, extensively trimmed with plush mahogany and luxuriant artwork.

The second floor accommodated Annie Strong's bedroom in the eastern annex, with adjacent sitting rooms affording an open view of

The Strong Mansion. *Erie County Historical Society at the Hagen History Center.*

Central Park and a private bathroom. Charles Strong, while lodging at the home, occupied a similar pair of rooms on the western annex with three bedrooms and private bathrooms for guests. The third and fourth floors were reserved for roughly thirteen servants, and the basement housed the kitchen and servants' dining room along with a sizeable wine cellar, separated from the floor above with thirty-three inches of steel, wire mesh, concrete and oak flooring.

That evening, inside the family's private dining room, Charles Strong was joined by his wife, Annie, and their daughter, Thora, as they ate dinner and swapped local gossip, with Charles, as always, chiming in on news both local and from around the world.

As president of the Erie County Electric Company and owner of the *Erie Dispatch* newspaper, Charles Strong was the wealthiest businessman in Erie. His wife, the daughter of former congressman and Erie mayor William L. Scott, owned the *Erie Evening Herald* newspaper and was widely recognized by its rival, the *Erie Daily Times*, as "Erie's social dictator."

Together, the pair had formed a dynamic union, becoming Erie's first true "power couple."

Around 7:30 p.m., the piercing ring of a telephone shattered the ambience of the dining room.

Discreetly sponging her mouth with a napkin, Annie Strong excused herself as she walked to the phone, cradling the receiver against her ear and pressing the transmitter near her mouth. Charles Strong reclined, exhaling smoke from his cigar as he eyed his wife, immediately discerning something was wrong.

Annie became ashen, her eyes moist and mouth quivering. Charles hastened to his wife's aid, seizing the transmitter and receiver as Thora cried out for their servants. Charles strained to listen as a frantic Amelia Hertwig excitedly related her discovery at the cemetery. Annie, supported by her daughter and servants, sat at the table clutching the edge with growing distress.

Charles nodded firmly, imploring Hertwig to take her time as she recited what she witnessed in the cemetery. It was then Charles learned that the mausoleum of Annie's family had been ransacked and horrifically desecrated.

1

GHOULS

I n January 1911, an increase in criminal activity kept the City of Erie Police Department busy.

During the early morning hours of January 29, 1911, Erie's bayfront was rocked by the immense explosion of the Pennsylvania Railroad Coal Trestle. The blast was felt throughout the city's First Ward, as it smashed windows and rattled homes. Officers immediately converged on the waterfront and were faced with a smoldering mass of twisted steel and splintered wood. The explosion of the trestle, targeted by nitroglycerine, miraculously caused no fatalities.

On the morning of February 7, 1911, two employees of the Perry Iron Works ambled along a path north of the Pennsylvania Soldiers & Sailors Home and were passing through the soldiers' cemetery when they discovered the frozen body of a man, lying face down, his face and body disfigured by bullets. The man was later identified as Giovanni Baptiste Arrechi, and letters found on his person indicated involvement with the "Black Hand" crime syndicate.

That night, around 11:45 p.m., restaurant proprietor Sam Newgreen phoned police and informed them a man entered his establishment and claimed to have shot somebody. Officers and detectives later learned Benny Hall, shooting craps in his home on German Street, was shot and killed after an argument ensued over money. The shooter, identified as Thomas Callens, fled and was later found in the basement of Newgreen's saloon, arrested and charged with Hall's murder.

At 7:40 p.m. on February 8, Chief of Police Edward Wagner received a phone call from Charles Strong with information he received indicating the Scott mausoleum had been broken into and damaged. Wagner informed Strong he would have officers meet him at the cemetery and immediately detailed Detective Sergeant John "Jack" Welsh and Patrolman Harry Robinson to the case.

A native of Waterford, Ireland, Welsh, a former chief pressman at the *Erie Morning Dispatch*, joined the department as a patrolman in June 1897 and became one of four men assigned to the rank of detective sergeant when the position was created. Primed to become chief in 1905 following the reelection of Mayor Robert J. Saltsman, Welsh suffered a humiliating setback when an inexperienced

Detective Sergeant John "Jack" Welsh. *Author's collection.*

patrolman, Edward Wagner, was appointed to the position. Tasked with investigating some of Erie's most infamous cases, Welsh merited respect from his brother officers and the public for his principles and humility.

As Detective Sergeant Welsh and Patrolman Robinson ventured into the cold, black night, across the street, inside the warmth of the Strong mansion, a frantic Annie Strong labored nervously beside the telephone following the departure of her husband and daughter.

Navigating the myriad streets, Welsh and Robinson eventually passed through the main gates of the cemetery. After greeting Charles Strong and his daughter, they proceeded to the mausoleum. At the crypt's entrance, Detective Sergeant Welsh inspected the lock and chain, once secured against the doors, now lying on the ground under the glow from a lamp held by Charles Strong.

Extracting his revolver, Welsh banked his weight against the doors. Inside, the mausoleum's interior trembled against flickering shadows, revealing the mutilated marble slabs of several crypts. Near the altar on the western side, palms and potted plants were "swept aside, as if with fiendish glee the intruders sought to further desecrate the stately structure."[1]

The *Erie Daily Times* laid out a detailed report of the damages:

The grave robbers evidently knew the lay of the land well before they accomplished their purpose, for of the many crypts on the north and south sides of the mausoleum, only those in which bodies reposed were molested. In the north side, three crypts were broken into, one on the extreme west end of the lower tier, and the two middle crypts of the second tier. The marble slab had been broken in pieces, the robbers evidently not taking time to release the seal. The end of the metallic casket had been cleanly

Top: Chestnut Street entrance to the Erie Cemetery. *From* Erie Cemetery: A Hand Book.

Bottom: The Scott mausoleum as it would have appeared in 1911. *From* Erie Cemetery: A Hand Book.

19

cut out, permitting the withdrawl [sic] *of the inner casket. The casket enclosing the body was broken in pieces, and several of the larger of these had been thrown into the yawning recess. The remaining pieces littered the floor, together with the broken slabs of marble.*

The caskets were all sealed in the wall and a chisel was used in removing the copper from the crypts that contained the bodies of Mrs. [Mary Matilda] *Scott, Mrs.* [Anna] *McCollom* [sic], *Mr.* [John Van] *McCollom and Mr.* [Richard] *Townsend. In the other two cases, big holes were made and the copper pressed back, until the grave robbers could make holes in the caskets large enough to see what they contained.*

The marble seals of the two upper crypts had been bodily removed, but the contents had not been disturbed other than the copper casing punctured, to permit a view within. Both metallic caskets contained holes large enough to admit a hand, and the cloth covering of one of the inner caskets was torn in several places.

Drawing of the interior of the Scott mausoleum based on descriptions of the damage by *Times* cartoonist Walter Kiedaisch. *Erie County Historical Society at the Hagen History Center.*

The City of Erie Police Department photographed in front of City Hall. Chief Wagner is visible in the front row with Captain William Detzel to his left. *Erie County Historical Society at the Hagen History Center.*

The crypt containing William L. Scott's coffin exhibited minimal attempts to gain entrance. On the lower tier, a marble slab was broken, and the coffin containing the remains of Annie's mother, Mary Matilda Scott, was deposited against one of the front doors, its casket lid missing and the decomposed corpse exposed.

Thora Ronalds, peering inside, shrieked before falling into the arms of Patrolman Robinson. Detective Sergeant Welsh crouched against the ground, picking up discarded pieces of copper, inspecting the edges. Under the faint glow of Charles Strong's lamp, Welsh discovered the edges were covered with a layer of dust, indicating the damage was not recent.

Only the crypt containing the body of Anna Townsend, Annie Strong's infant niece, remained intact.

Behind Mary Matilda Scott's coffin, Strong's attention was drawn to an empty casket inside an open vault on the lower tier of the northern side. Puzzled, he called out to Detective Sergeant Welsh, telling him a body was missing.

Welsh tiptoed through the debris.

"Who was buried here?" Welsh asked.

Strong surveyed the crypts and their corresponding bodies before telling Welsh he believed the crypt held the remains of Anna McCollum, Annie's aunt. Outside, a heavy gust of wind whistled against the mausoleum walls. Charles Strong had seen enough and exited. Welsh followed, assessing the scene, telling Strong he believed the crime occurred ten or more days earlier, with some marks indicating use of a chisel.

Welsh scanned the cemetery grounds, unable to observe the nearest nearby residence. In the distance, the shrieking wail of a locomotive echoed into the night as it thundered along the New York Central railroad line, whose tracks traversed the middle of West Nineteenth Street.

To Welsh, the isolation of the mausoleum guaranteed those who engaged in its violation could have done so virtually unmolested.

Welsh and Robinson remained at the mausoleum while Charles Strong and his daughter returned home and confirmed the dreadful news to Annie Strong, who then phoned attorney John W. Sterling, a trustee for her father's estate in New York City. Sterling assured Annie he would immediately dispatch private detectives to Erie.

Receiving confirmation the mausoleum had been breached, Chief Wagner tasked Detective Sergeant Edward Liebel and several patrolmen to inspect all railroad stations, depots, freight houses and routes of escape from the city. Auxiliary detectives and patrolmen gathered at the Erie cemetery and branched out through the adjoining neighborhood of "Little Italy" north of West Nineteenth Street, under orders to arrest any suspicious persons.

As Annie fielded a flurry of phone calls late into the night, Charles Strong phoned undertaker Alured P. Burton, one of the few persons familiar with the mausoleum's interior, and asked him to proceed to the cemetery. On his arrival, Burton was informed by Annie Strong that no entry was allowed until the arrival of private detectives.

Eventually, John Sterling apprised Annie Strong that detectives from the William J. Burns Agency would arrive on Friday, February 10. Firm in her desire for an expeditious response, Annie decided to hire a closer agency and immediately dispatched a wire to the Perkins Union Detective Agency in Pittsburg. Harry Perkins hastily responded by wire and informed her he would arrive in Erie on February 9, the next day.

Efforts to keep Annie away from the mausoleum failed when she traveled to the cemetery to witness the carnage firsthand. There she confirmed the missing corpse was her aunt Anna McCollum and dictated directives for police to guard the mausoleum.

Annie insisted to Detective Sergeant Welsh that the department's actions must be as discreet as possible.

Annie Strong's father, William Lawrence Scott, was born in Washington, D.C., on July 2, 1828. Raised by his widowed mother, Scott attended the Hampden Academy near Richmond, Virginia, until the age of thirteen, when he was hired as a congressional page in the U.S. House of Representatives. Attracting the attention of Charles M. Reed, a former congressman from Erie, Scott worked as a shipping clerk in the warehouse for one of Reed's businesses in Erie.

At twenty-three, Scott formed a partnership in the lake and canal trade before forming a coal and shipping partnership with local businessman John Hearn through John Hearn & Company, laying the foundation for what would become Scott's colossal financial empire. In time, Scott controlled coal fields in Pennsylvania, West Virginia, Illinois, Iowa and Missouri, accumulating seventy thousand acres of land while employing twelve thousand laborers.

On September 19, 1863, Scott married Mary Matilda Tracy, daughter of local railroad entrepreneur John Tracy and granddaughter of Daniel Dobbins, a sailing master who oversaw the construction of ships later commanded by Oliver Hazard Perry in the American victory at the Battle of Lake Erie in 1812. The marriage produced two children: Mary, known

Left: Mary Matilda Scott. *Erie County Historical Society at the Hagen History Center.*

Right: William Lawrence Scott. *Erie County Historical Society at the Hagen History Center.*

as "Winnie," in 1854, and Annie Wainwright Scott, born on January 15, 1859, in Erie. As Scott's family ascended the city's social circles, his business opportunities expanded when he partnered with his brother-in-law, John F. Tracy, constructing an extensive railroad network amassing nearly twenty-two thousand miles.

Following an unsuccessful campaign for mayor of Erie in 1863, Scott was elected in 1866 following ruthless opposition from the *Erie Weekly Gazette*, which sought to label him a "Copperhead." After declining a second term in 1876, Scott instead ran for Congress as a member of the Democratic Party. Following an unsuccessful campaign there, he was elected to a second term as mayor in 1871.

In time, Scott rapidly became one of the wealthiest men in America as his railroad partnership created the Chicago, Rock Island & Pacific Railroad, the first to connect the East Coast to the Missouri River, and the New York, Philadelphia and Norfolk Railroad. A stockholder in the Lake Shore Railroad, Pennsylvania Central and New York Central Railroads, Scott complemented his financial empire with the purchase of thousands of acres of farmland, owning only the best breeds of cattle.

Scott's passion for Thoroughbred horse racing also led to the construction of the Algeria stud farm in Millcreek Township, consisting of a one-mile racetrack and accommodations to breed and winter thirty-five racing horses, with his most notable purchase being a stallion named Algerine.

When the City of Erie announced plans to extend its trolley services to the peninsula, Presque Isle, Scott protested, claiming the streetcars would spook his horses, and his staunch opposition forced trolley passengers to exit at West Eighth and Pittsburgh Avenue and travel on foot to the peninsula—even funeral processions, traveling to the neighboring Trinity Cemetery, which frustrated the public. Criticism was also leveled at Scott's engagement in construction projects beyond the city limits to circumvent higher taxes and water rates.

In Erie, Scott's social and economic influences inflated when he became president of Second National Bank, Erie's largest bank, in 1874. The following year, he constructed a four-and-a-half-story building known as the Scott Block on the northwest corner of East Tenth and State Streets. In 1878, he purchased the *Evening Herald*, a local newspaper, and in 1886, he established the Edison Electric Light & Power Company.

In 1875, the Scott family moved into the John Tracy home on Peach Street between West Seventh and Eighth Streets, modifying the house into a blend of Greek Revival and Italianate detailing, while entertaining family

Scott Block as it appeared on the corner of State and West Tenth Streets. *Erie County Historical Society at the Hagen History Center.*

and friends. The following year, Scott became a member of the Democratic National Committee. Scott also held this post in 1880 and 1884, and while serving on the committee, he became a close friend and advisor to President Grover Cleveland, even contributing $50,000 to his campaign. There were even rumors Scott was considered a candidate for the U.S. secretary of the treasury in Cleveland's administration.

In 1884, Scott won the first of two elections to the U.S. House of Representatives, and in 1887, when Grover Cleveland toured western and southern America, Scott used his influence with industrialists Cornelius Vanderbilt and George Pullman to "ensure the best finest cars and safest routes."[2]

On September 8, 1881, Scott's daughter Annie married Charles Hamot Strong in a ceremony unifying two of Erie's wealthiest families. Attendees, numbering just over one hundred, created a steady progression of carriages cycling before the front door of the Scott home hours before the ceremony. Wedding attendants, wrote the *Erie Morning Dispatch*, "drifted from the carriages only to be lost to view in the spacious hallway of the Scott home." Rooms in the home "thronged with a brilliant party, the rich and elegant toilette of the ladies, in pleasing contrast with the black broadcloth of the gentlemen, making a brilliant picture."

After 8:00 p.m., the bridal party assembled before Reverend J.T. Franklin inside the Episcopal cathedral of Saint Paul. Annie Scott, clothed in a striking dress of cream-colored satin, embroidered in pearls and trimmed with Duchesse lace, wore a traditional bridal veil down the aisle.

"Annie," local reporters raved, "had never before looked so lovely."

After the ceremony, guests were treated to a wedding banquet prepared by the world-famous Delmonico's of New York, with every delicacy served by a

Annie Strong on her wedding day. *Erie County Historical Society at the Hagen History Center.*

corps of well-trained waiters. Presents for the bride and groom consisted of numerous gems, silver and gold, paintings, vases, bric-a-brac and everything wealth could acquire.

Valued at roughly $500,000, among the gifts were a magnificent set of gold knives and forks with handles made of turquoise and a set of pearl jewelry complete with tea service of solid silver from Annie's parents. Annie and Charles later departed for their honeymoon, and on their return, they would move into an elegantly furnished home on Peach Street. In one night, Annie and Charles Strong became one of the wealthiest young couples in America and were well respected within the social circles of New York City; Washington, D.C.; and London, England.

Charles Hamot Strong was born in Erie on March 14, 1853, to Landaff Strong, a respected local physician, and Cecilia Hamot. Like his wife, Strong was a descendant of one of Erie County's most prominent families. His paternal grandfather, Martin Strong, arrived in Erie County in 1795, settling in Summit Township. His other grandfather, Pierre Simon Hamot, a French émigré, settled in the county in 1802, and after his death in 1846, the Hamot Homestead was donated by the family for use as a general hospital, which opened in 1891.

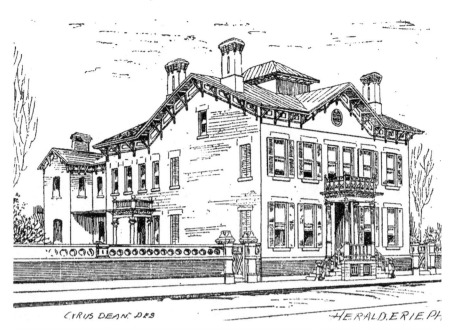

Top: Home of Charles and Annie Strong after their wedding, at 810 Peach Street. *From* Erie, Penn'a, Illustrated.

Bottom: The home of William L. Scott on the northwest corner of West Eighth and Peach Street. *From* Erie, Penn'a, Illustrated.

An early photograph of Charles Strong and his daughter, Matilda "Thora" Strong. *Erie County Historical Society at the Hagen History Center.*

A graduate of Yale University, Strong returned to Erie and practiced law but was soon unimpressed with the work. He then worked as a bookkeeper and shipping clerk with the Mt. Hickory Iron Works, later becoming president there before serving as president of the Union Coal Company of Shamokin, vice-president of Youghiogheny River Coal Company of Illinois and president and director of the Erie and Pittsburg Railroad.

On June 24, 1882, Annie gave birth to a daughter, Matilda Thora Wainwright Strong. In her youth, Thora could be seen mounted on her pony within the family's fenced-in property or with her parents at "The Head," where summer days consisted of swimming, picnics, dances and the presentation of the first moving picture show in Erie.

Strong, who co-founded and served as president of the Edison Electric Light and Power Company with his father-in-law, was also president of the W.L. Scott & Company.

Meanwhile, Annie fashioned "Erie's first society"; dances were the excitement of the city's social circles, with assembly balls at Scott Hall at East Tenth and State Streets. Ducats, at a cost of three dollars per couple, included the services of a carriage, which transported parties to the hall, and included a light meal of chicken salad and ice cream. Women were served punch as the men slipped out to mingle at Colonel Carney's bar, the only electric-lit saloon in town, for a "snort" (smokeless tobacco).

Charles and Annie Strong, immensely fascinated with technology, owned several Packard automobiles, and Thora, accompanied by her chauffeur, was seen driving around town. At times, Charles Strong sometimes traversed Erie's streets on his bicycle.

On April 12, 1888, the first edition of the *Erie Daily Times*, manufactured by nine former printers from the *Erie Evening Herald*, went to print following an ongoing labor dispute. Facing competition from five local newspapers, the *Times* found itself in a tumultuous competition in a war of words and reporting.

On November 25, 1889, William Scott announced the construction of a mausoleum valued at $35,000. Edward L. Pelton, a well-known marble and granite cutter, served as contractor, taking inspiration from the mausoleum of John Baptiste Ford in Pittsburg. The mausoleum, although similar to Ford's, was accentuated by Scott's taste and opulent innovation; it would be, the *Erie Daily Times* raved, "an imposing edifice" that would rival those "erected by the Messrs. Vanderbilt, Gould and Stewart."

The *Times* published further details about the construction:

> *The mausoleum will be built of granite and will cover about 1,000 square feet, and from the ground to the top of the dome will be about 50 feet. The general design of the structure will be gothic; it will be built in the form of [a] Greek cross and will face the east. The approaches from the street will be made of granite and the approach to the interior of the mausoleum will be covered by a portico supported by polished pillars or columns.*
>
> *There is not to be a piece of wood about the entire structure, but it will be of granite exclusively so far as the exterior is concerned. The walls of the mausoleum will receive strength from buttresses placed at the corners and which will stand seventeen feet high. The walls will be built with rock-faced ashlar from the Hallowell quarries and will require about 500 tons. The wings of the mausoleum will be finished with Gallic panels. The structure above the buttresses will rise in layers of granite slabs which recede one from other till they reach the dome or lantern of the mausoleum.*
>
> *The dome or lantern is an exquisite design and each side has two Gothic niches or windows with polished columns. The finish of the dome is in pyramidal shape and slopes up in receding layers with a finely-executed cross-shaped finale [sic]. The beautiful exterior has 22 polished columns about its base and at the top of the structure. The capitals will be composite, exceedingly handsome, and will be made of darker granite than the main structure.*
>
> *The doors will be of standard solid bronze and will cost $800. These will open into a rotunda eleven feet square, and on the right and left will*

The Scott mausoleum, photographed several years following its construction. *The Cranch Collection.*

be arranged the catacombs with a mortuary capacity of 24. At the west side there will be an apsis of colored designs, and through these a soft light will stream. The light will also be admitted from, the dome; this was Mr. Scott's idea and it affords means for ventilation. The rotunda will have capacity enough for holding private funeral ceremonies inside. The floor will be laid in marble, cut in geometrical patterns. The finish of the interior will be of Tennessee, Florentine, French and African marbles, and the wainscotting will also be of marble. The interior will be a study for artists and a veritable palace for the future inhabitants.

The foundation for the tomb was laid the following week, with speculation as to whom would be interred inside. In 1890, Scott moved forward with demolishing the old Eliot Mansion on the corner of West Sixth and Peach Streets, constructing a new home in its place. When the mausoleum was completed in the fall of 1891, Scott traveled to the Erie Cemetery, accompanied by Edward Pelton. After a thorough examination, Pelton anticipated Scott's remarks.

"I wonder if the damned thing leaks?" Scott said, eyeing the structure.

Suffering from an acute gastrointestinal illness, Scott traveled to Newport, Rhode Island, for treatment and relaxation. While there, on September 19, 1891, William L. Scott passed away at the age of sixty-three from heart failure.

Scott's death stunned the country. He was hailed by the *New York Times* as one of the greatest industrialists in America, and his estate was assessed around $15 million—others estimated his holdings around $30 million. Scott's body returned to Erie with masses of intricate floral pieces. His casket, furnished in Florida red cedar, was "decorated with 76 pounds of solid silver, 30 pounds of silk, 40 yards of broadcloth, and 10 pounds of eiderdown."[3] Eulogies from all over the country deluged the city, praising Scott's industrial and political influences. Distinguished guests paid tribute, including former president Grover Cleveland, who served as a pallbearer.

Ten thousand witnessed Scott's funeral procession to Erie Cemetery, and Mayor Charles Clarke issued a proclamation that "all necessary business be suspended in this city from three to six o'clock on Thursday, Sept. 24, the day of the funeral." Interred with Scott were the remains of his infant granddaughter Anna Townsend.

With the estate split between Scott's daughters, Annie inherited the mansion, still under construction, at the corner of Peach and West Sixth Streets. Scott's prized breeding horses were sold in accordance with his

The road to Massassauga Point, known as "The Head." *From* Erie, Pennsylvania: An Industrial and Summer Resort City.

will, and by 1902 the Algeria stud farm had been abandoned. Brutally contested by a score of disgruntled family members who disagreed with its conditions, Scott's will was finally settled when the terms of the will were exhausted in 1950.

Scott's estate also quarreled with those in Erie over fifteen acres of land near the Massassauga Point Hotel, a resort and dance hall, in an attempt to prevent public access to the peninsula. The public admonished the estate's actions, which eventually contributed to the creation of Waldameer Park in 1896.

Annie's inheritance included her father's yacht, *Mystic*. Rumored to have once belonged to William "Boss" Tweed of infamous Tammany Hall lore, the steam yacht was lavishly constructed of teak and mahogany. Although Annie relished the yacht, the slightest ripple on the bay caused a cancellation of planned excursions out of fear of seasickness. Such cancellations were welcomed by Captain Patrick McMahon and his crew, who often dined on the Strongs' rich foods, including a midsummer favorite of cracked ice in a cup, a pint of imported champagne and imported Rhine wine.

Because Annie did not have the same passion for sailing, in time the yacht remained idle in the West Slip. After the death of Captain McMahon in 1905, the yacht's fate was sealed. Following the removal of its engines

Above: William Scott's yacht, the *Mystic*. *Erie County Historical Society at the Hagen History Center*.

Left: Annie Strong relaxing on the bow of the *Mystic*. *Erie County Historical Society at the Hagen History Center*.

Above: Matilda "Thora" Strong, accompanied by her chauffeur, leads a group of automobile enthusiasts around Erie. *Erie County Historical Society at the Hagen History Center.*

Opposite, top: Another view, looking east, of Strong's cabin on the Somewhere Estate. *Erie County Historical Society at the Hagen History Center.*

Opposite, bottom: Looking west, Charles H. Strong and an unidentified man pose on the road leading to his log cabin on the Somewhere Estate. *Erie County Historical Society at the Hagen History Center.*

and appliances—overseen by two trusted individuals in Erie's marine community—and under the cover of darkness, the *Mystic* was towed to an undisclosed location and sunk.

Annie and Charles Strong continued to exert their influence with Charles's purchase of the Dispatch Publishing Company and *Erie Dispatch* in 1902. Annie Strong continued oversight of management for the *Erie Evening Herald* in an age when women were afforded few freedoms, as her opulent parties and social events filled the gossip columns of local newspapers.

When not entertaining at their mansion, the Strongs hosted acquaintances and family at Charles Strong's estate, Somewhere. Encompassing one hundred acres, the secluded estate was perched on bluffs overlooking Presque Isle Bay, peppered with luscious woodlots, an apple orchard, bountiful gardens and buildings to house caretakers and other employees. Roads and pathways, lined with three-and-a-half-foot-tall walls of well-maintained rock and boulders, allowed private access to the bay with a small pier and boathouse.

The roadways, the first decorated with electric-powered streetlamps in Erie, curved throughout the property to Charles Strong's log cabin, constructed with boulders and log-framed siding accentuated by elaborate usage of tree trunks, both interior and exterior. The cabin, like Strong's lifestyle, was manifested with wealth and character illustrative of the family's fortune.

Coined "Erie's Most Magnificent Wedding," Matilda "Thora" Scott-Strong and Reginald "Reggie" Ronalds, a Yale University graduate and member of the First United States Volunteer Cavalry, Theodore Roosevelt's "Rough Riders," were married on February 24, 1906.

Similar to her parents, the wedding was held at the Episcopal cathedral of Saint Paul, with guests arriving throughout the week. The *Erie Daily Times* wrote, "Throngs of onlookers in the vicinity of the church where

Annie Strong entertains guests at the Scott Mansion. *Erie County Historical Society at the Hagen History Center.*

the marriage ceremony was performed, completely filled the street, many hundreds being in the vast crowd."

In the lobby of the five-story Reed House hotel on the corner of North Park Row and French Street, parlors were filled to the brim with members of high society. New York City photographer Alfred Pach was seen alongside assistants as he prepared to document the wedding. Hairdressers, manicurists and tonsorial artists guaranteed guests were dressed in their best in "hurried preparations for the nuptial event."[4]

On December 23, 1908, Annie Strong held a Christmas party for the needy children of Erie in honor of her granddaughter Thora, with Erie's "Grand Old Lady," Sarah Reed, known for her charitable works, as the guest of honor. Annie's love of children and philanthropic donations to local charities earned her widespread praise. To children, she was known as the "lady of the castle."

At the turn of the twentieth century, an escalation of vile threats against the Strong family gave rise to additional security placed about the mausoleum, with watchmen guarding the tomb day and night. The mausoleum was one of the few private properties equipped with a police call box in 1892 and two electric lights on its exterior, connected to the residence of the cemetery superintendent. Construction of a watchman's house near the north fence of the cemetery, within walking distance, was also planned.

Following the passing of William Scott, several others were interred in the mausoleum:

John Van McCollum, Annie's uncle, died in Philadelphia on January 19, 1898.

Her mother, Mary Matilda Scott, followed several months later on May 19, 1898, in Atlantic City, New Jersey.

On November 27, 1902, Annie's brother-in-law Richard Townsend succumbed to injuries after being thrown from his horse in Washington, D.C., and was interred in the mausoleum alongside his infant daughter, Anna.

Annie's aunt Anna McCollum passed away on December 20, 1904, in Philadelphia and was interred in the mausoleum.

In her last visit to the mausoleum, on December 24, 1910, Annie Strong noticed nothing out of place, and when questioned by detectives, she was certain the mausoleum's interior was not damaged.

—m—

That night at the cemetery, Chief Wagner held a brief conference with Detective Sergeant Welsh and Patrolman Robinson, agreeing to remain in the cemetery and strategically secrete themselves within view of the tomb in the possibility those who damaged the mausoleum would return.

As a numbing breeze meandered through the tombstones during the early hours of February 9, Robinson and Welsh noticed a pair of men approaching. Welsh clutched his revolver, locking eyes with Robinson as the men inched closer, their feet thudding against the frozen ground.

Suddenly, Welsh and Robinson hurtled to their feet, guns drawn, and commanded the men to halt.

To the officers' surprise, the men were reporters for the *Erie Daily Times*, and after a brief chat, the reporters left, with the lawmen retreating to their frozen refuge. As daylight breached the horizon, searches of the adjoining neighborhoods yielded no tangible clues. Detective Sergeant Libel and his officers, who searched numerous depots, stations and various roadways, came up emptyhanded in their search for the missing corpse of Anna McCollum.

As the citizens of Erie awakened, they were introduced to the most inexplicable crime in the city's history, and the world was also watching.

2

TYRANNICAL, UNLAWFUL AND EXACTING PRACTICES

As Patrolmen Jacob Zimmer and George Warfel guarded the Scott mausoleum on the frigid morning of February 9, 1911, throngs of curious onlookers clamored around the Erie cemetery, eager to glimpse the mausoleum. Around 7:00 a.m., a reporter from the *Erie Daily Times*, joined by a staff photographer, found the mausoleum crawling with plainclothes detectives, uniformed officers and a special watchman hired by the Strong family.

The *Times* photographer managed to photograph the crypt, being warned by a patrolman not to step closer under threat of arrest. From there, the photographer and reporter walked to the cemetery office, where they were told by Superintendent Emma Hay that no photographs were to be taken of the mausoleum without written permission from Annie Strong.

That morning, the *Times* carried the sensational details in bold print:

GHOULS DESECRATE SCOTT TOMB; STEAL WOMAN'S BODY

Providing up-to-date gossip as it evolved, the *Times* revealed extra details about the mausoleum, including the inoperable exterior spotlights and the absence of watchmen, which could have prevented the desecration. Those in Erie waited with great excitement for the arrival of detectives from the Perkins Union Detective Agency, expected before nightfall.

A fatigued Jack Welsh sifted through clues on the cemetery grounds, the most important being footprints traced to a cemetery gate on Cherry

Front page of the *Erie Daily Times* on February 9, 1911. *Author's collection.*

Street. Believing this to be crucial, Welsh recorded the measurements before Chief Wagner held a brief conference with members of the police department. Some detectives believed Anna McCollum's corpse was concealed while the ghouls awaited a ransom from the Strongs. Others had different theories but refused to speculate further.

Acquaintances of the Strong family were infuriated by reports from the *Erie Daily Times*, insisting all bodies were accounted for, claiming Anna McCollum and her husband were secretly interred in the nearby lot of the Tracy family. Newspaper articles from the *Erie Dispatch* and *Erie Evening Herald* also paled in comparison to the *Times*'s minimal reporting on the desecration.

That afternoon, under clear blue skies, *Times* reporters were in the cemetery when Annie Strong arrived at the cemetery office. As she stepped out from her automobile, she was greeted by Superintendent Hay, who directed her attention to the growing mass of reporters, photographers and onlookers. Annie then withdrew to the seclusion of her automobile, ignoring the yawping and queries from the public.

That afternoon, a $1,000 reward was offered by the Erie Cemetery for information leading to "the detection, arrest and conviction of the person or persons violating the Scott Mausoleum in the Erie Cemetery."

As an evening twilight gripped the city, Harry Perkins arrived at the Union Depot. At thirty-six years of age, dapper in appearance, with chiseled features and careful eyes, Perkins waited as his luggage was loaded into an idling automobile before he was driven to the Reed House. After checking in, Perkins returned to the Strongs' automobile and proceeded to the Strong home.

After speaking to Annie Strong, Perkins was brought up to speed on the case and then conveyed to the cemetery, where he was placed in charge of the investigation—including oversight of the police department—before executing a brief examination of the mausoleum's interior.

Benjamin Ling, of the *Cleveland Leader*, was one of the first correspondents to arrive in Erie, assisted by staff photographer Clarence Strieglietz. That evening, he scored an exclusive interview with Charles Strong at his home, and in front of a crackling fireplace, Ling asked Strong about numerous theories suggesting the desecration was done out of revenge.[5]

"There is but one motive that I can ascribe for the fiendish act and that is hope of ransom," Strong said, eyeing the flames.

I can conceive of no other reason for this horrible crime. It is absurd to insinuate that it was revenge. There could be no enemy so revengeful that he could possibly go to this extreme. I wish to deny emphatically that I have any faith in any theory of that sort.

I have taken many blows in my day and I am still able to take many more, but this act has touched me more than anything else. The horror of it is appalling. If it is not ransom that was desired, why, I have thought perhaps the fiends sought to sell the cadavers. But that would be absurd at this late day.

Asked about the possibility of a ransom, Strong said:

Still, if it is ransom, why, have I not heard something? Why has some demand for money not been made on me? As yet I have heard nothing. But, if the most skilled detectives in this country can ferret out this mystery, I shall have them. I have already made attempts to reach the man I want. This case presents a problem for the best of detectives. A veritable Sherlock Holmes will be necessary. If I had heard of this thing first, I should have returned and waited at the mausoleum for the return of those who committed this outrage. From the appearance of the interior of the tomb, it seems that the men intended to return. Had I caught them, I can assure you that a bullet would have been their portion.

Ling asked about the identity of the missing corpse. "I am uncertain as to which body was taken," Charles Strong exhaled from his cigar.

Downtown Erie, looking north, as it would have appeared around 1911. *Library of Congress.*

Charles Strong. *Erie County Historical Society at the Hagen History Center.*

My wife is of the opinion it was that of Mrs. McCollom [sic]. But I do not know. It may have been any of the bodies. The coffins were torn out of their metallic, copper-riveted casings and the name plates removed. The body which was stolen was lifted right out of the coffin, which had been cemented in a metallic casket. The sight that met my eyes and those of my daughter, as we entered the tomb, I shall never forget. We had hurried there in an automobile immediately when we heard about the breaking into the crypt early in the evening. One of the bodies was lying half out of the coffin, where it had been dragged and left by the vandals. It was all so horrible and gruesome. I have, as yet, given no thought as to offering a reward. I cannot say what I shall do about that until I have discussed the situation with my wife again.

That night, a brutal wind thrashed Erie as officers remained on guard at the cemetery. Thousands slumbered as both local telegraph offices were reinforced after nearly being overburdened with transmitting news reports from the city. Telephones remained in constant use as details were disseminated to Cleveland, Pittsburgh, New York City, Chicago, Los Angeles and other cities, with dozens of correspondents burning the midnight oil to report the news for their ravenous readers.

Every train slithering into Erie brought a constant flow of additional correspondents throughout the night, including Edwin Jerome Moore for the *New York Herald* and the *New York Telegraph*, F.H. Bloomer for the *Buffalo Evening News* and R.L. Cannon with the *Cleveland Press* and Scripps McRae league of newspapers, including the *United Press*. By midnight, all hotels were filled to capacity, and the streets outside the cemetery continued to attract the morbidly curious and excitable.

Newspaper correspondents from New York City claimed the *Erie Daily Times* reporters "were playing the story big."

The Associated Press devoted nearly four thousand words to the mausoleum case as it maintained constant communication with correspondents in Erie. Wires for the National News Association "tingled with the facts of the robbery from early until late," and even the Hearst wires were "kept hot" with developments. The *Erie Dispatch* and *Erie Evening Herald* still remained silent and, according to the *Times*, printed only news "not objectionable to its owners."

It was no secret that Charles and Annie Strong went to great lengths to maintain a shroud of privacy. This secrecy, claimed the *Times*, resulted in a minimization of facts about the case, forcing readers to learn new developments from other newspapers. The Strongs' secrecy and their control of the *Dispatch* and *Herald* generated further scandal, with newspapers professing the body of William Scott was stolen. These rumors, however, had little credence, as Scott's casket weighed two thousand pounds and was impossible to move without the aid of ropes and tackle and likely was not able to be removed without the use of explosives severe enough to destroy the mausoleum itself.

The *Erie Daily Times* spilled the tea when it published a scathing editorial about the *Herald* and the *Dispatch*: "The newspaper of the family are as silent as the tomb which has been robbed. They are not willing to even tell an interested public whether or not it is the remains of the late William L. Scott that are missing."[6]

Addressing the rumors spreading like a weed, the *Times* continued:

> As a result of the attempted secrecy all sorts of rumors are afloat and they will only increase in number and size as the days go by unless the public is given the facts. The family newspapers were in a position to give the facts and no one can be blamed but themselves for the extravagant and unreasonable rumors that are afloat. That they are not newspapers in any true sense of the word has been proved plainly enough.

Frederick Phelps, managing editor for the *Times*, wrote, "Trained newspaper representatives are all asking if Erie is a 'one-family city'" and added that when Pennsylvania railroad officials appealed to the police department for services to guard the railroad trestle after it was dynamited, the police purportedly said they were not paid to guard property. "There did not seem to be any hesitancy to use the police department for service at the cemetery and some good citizens are wondering at such inconsistency," Phelps noted. "Evidently some people have a pull and some others have not."

Reverend Father Joseph Brock stirred during the early morning of February 10, 1911, to begin preparations for morning mass at St. John's Roman Catholic Church. When he entered the sacristy, he discerned something was amiss. When he turned on the lights, Brock found the cupboards and drawers containing the priests' vestments open, their contents strewn all over the floor. Nearby, one of the windows was propped open. As the wind howled outside, Brock approached the altar where six chalices, three Ciboriums and a Monstrance, all containing silver and gold mountings, had vanished. A rear section of the altar was also destroyed.

Brock notified Reverend Monsignor Michael Decker, who phoned the police and requested a detective. Detective Sergeant Lambertine Pinney, working the mausoleum case, was detailed by Chief Wagner to lead the

St. John's Roman Catholic Church as it would have appeared in 1911. *Erie County Historical Society at the Hagen History Center.*

investigation. After inspecting the sacristy, Pinney observed the lock of the open window was intact and the frame itself open only five inches. Nuns confirmed the windows and doors were locked the evening before after a final inspection was performed around 5:00 p.m. Pinney felt the vandals worked stealthily and escaped through the window, closing it slightly to not draw attention. Outside, any footprints that might have been left had become completely obscured due to fresh snowdrift from the night before.

Interviewed by police, Reverend Brock recited the previous night's events, which consisted of the preparation for several hundred men to be enrolled as members of the Holy Name Society, acknowledging members of the choir were inside the church until 9:30 p.m. It was possible, Brock suggested, that those responsible entered the church discreetly and remained hidden. All the vestments and articles tossed from the drawers and cupboards were accounted for, Brock told Pinney. Curiously, Pinney noted several valuable candlesticks and the poor box, filled with voluntary contributions, were undisturbed.

After leaving the church, Detective Sergeant Pinney visited pawn shops where brass and silver could be purchased, but no attempts to trade or sell such items were discovered. The detective believed the theft was unrelated to a prior incident when Father Decker was robbed years before. Pinney also felt the stolen items could not garner a value greater than $50, yet their replacement cost was significantly higher, around $400 or $500.

That morning, a distraught Annie Strong collapsed in her home. A local physician established her condition was not serious but advocated she rest, and she was later tended to by her servants.

Expecting the arrival of his father, Harry Perkins met with Chief Wagner inside his office at City Hall and afterward granted an interview with the *Erie Daily Times*. Asked when the break-in at the mausoleum occurred, Perkins was unable to confirm an exact date but believed the deed occurred over several weeks earlier. When pressed if the body stolen was actually William Scott, suggesting the Strong family concealed this from the public, Perkins reacted with a sly smile.

"I don't care to discuss that matter, but I don't want to throw any mystery about that portion of the case and would not say anything to lead you to believe that the remains were those of any one but the woman you have printed."

Erie City Hall. *Erie County Historical Society at the Hagen History Center.*

"Is the family certain as to whose body was taken?"

"Why yes, of course."

"Your agency has no doubt as to the identity of the body?"

"None whatever," Perkins countered.

Asked if the body could have been carried away in a sack, Perkins whistled as he gazed out the window, ignoring the question, only to add that he expected to bring an embalming expert to Erie to examine the bodies in the crypt. Savoring his role in temporarily leading the investigation, the young Perkins dispelled growing accusations of friction between his father's agency and the police, claiming both were "on the most friendly terms."

After his interview, Harry met his father, Gilbert Perkins, at the Union Depot Station around 10:00 a.m. Also present was Charles Franklin, manager of the Philadelphia branch of the Perkins Agency, and operatives

John Drew, Charles McLaughlin, Charles Sproull, John Ross and George Henderson, known as "the General," assisted by a pair of bloodhounds.

The men were whisked away to a nearby dawdling automobile and driven to the Erie Cemetery.

At the cemetery, Gilbert Perkins ordered Henderson to work the bloodhounds. Dropping their snouts to the earth, the dogs charged through the snow, with operatives trailing behind as they frolicked west toward Cherry Street, where the scent vanished.

As Gilbert Perkins commanded the dogs to be worked again, he performed a search of the mausoleum's interior, locating a pickaxe, a broken jackknife, an instrument resembling a can opener, a dark coat, a piece of cloth, a handkerchief, cigarette butts and a broken glass piece from a whiskey flask. Perkins's son Harry removed the evidence and later delivered it to his room at the Reed House.

Outside the mausoleum, Detective Sergeant Welsh spoke to Detective Sergeant Richard Crotty while eyeing the Perkins detectives. Welsh, with an uneasy feeling in the pit of his stomach, told Crotty he felt the mausoleum appeared elaborately staged.

With the evidence removed, Harry Perkins endeavored to move Anna McCollum's empty casket but was unable to dislodge it before his father asked him to try the dogs again. As Gilbert Perkins leaned against the bronze door of the mausoleum, he glanced down at the grisly sight of Mary Matilda Scott's remains gawking back at him.

3

RIVALRIES RENEWED

Gilbert Boyd Perkins was born on September 7, 1842, in Venango Township, Pennsylvania, to William Walter Perkins, a butcher, and Cyrena Hopkins. Perkins grew up in Crawford County and, following the outbreak of the American Civil War, enlisted in the Union army on August 29, 1862, in Harrisburg, Pennsylvania. In September of that year, he joined the 150th Pennsylvania Infantry Regiment as a second lieutenant with Company C. After the Battle of Chancellorsville, Perkins was promoted to the rank of first lieutenant on May 31, 1863.

On July 1, 1863, the regiment arrived as part of the I Corps west of the town of Gettysburg following a clash between Confederate forces and Union cavalry. Engaged in battle alongside the famed Iron Brigade, the 150th Pennsylvania, along with both the 143rd and 149th, defended the landscape around McPherson Farm, experiencing heavy rifle and artillery fire that left substantial casualties, including First Lieutenant Gilbert Perkins, who was wounded in the thigh as the men retreated through the streets of Gettysburg.

With many of his men captured, Lieutenant Perkins and those who remained with the 150th reorganized that evening on Cemetery Hill, east of Gettysburg. Out of roughly 400 enlisted men and 17 officers, 40 were killed, 138 wounded and 69 taken prisoner. Nearly all officers, including Perkins, sustained injuries.

That fall, Perkins was promoted to captain and fought in the Bristoe and Mine Run Campaigns and the Overland Campaign, in which the 150th Pennsylvania again suffered devastating casualties during the Battles of the Wilderness and Spotsylvania Courthouse in May 1864. On June 28, 1864, Perkins was discharged and returned home, marrying Sarah Evaline Hall the following year and residing, briefly, in the village of Cooperstown, New York.

Gilbert and Sarah Perkins's marriage produced six children: Herbert, Gertrude, Claude, Harry, Edward and Walter. By 1870, the family had relocated to the borough of Waterford in Erie County, Pennsylvania, where Gilbert was employed with the post office branch of the U.S. Secret Service. By 1874, he had been promoted to detective. Gilbert had an honorable reputation throughout the northeastern United States and was involved in several sensational arrests, including that of the infamous Oswego gang of counterfeiters in 1880. He later operated out of the Secret Service's office in Pittsburg, relocating his family to the smoky city nestled at the junction of the Allegheny and Monongahela Rivers.

In 1889, Perkins formed the Perkins Union Detective Agency in Pittsburg, eventually employing his sons Harry and Walter in the family business as private detectives. Around the turn of the century, Perkins's prospects continued to climb in Pittsburg, with the agency's escapades and thrilling arrests reported as far as Rhode Island.

When charges of conspiracy were brought against Augustus Hartje, a wealthy paper manufacturer in Pittsburg, during his scandalous divorce, one of Perkins's detectives, Bernard F. McElroy, was accused of forging letters in the case. Other Perkins operatives over the years were charged with various criminal acts, leading some to believe Perkins's agency was crooked.

In the Pittsburg and Tube affair of 1906, company president Charles S. Cameron and councilman William A. Martin were charged with conspiracy to bribe. Gilbert Perkins himself came under scrutiny when he accepted a payment of $10,000 from Cameron, insisting actions were legal, with the payment's purpose being to secure a franchise.

The shady practices of Perkins and his detectives were not unusual, especially in a time when warring agencies, like those of the Pinkertons or the William J. Burns Detective Agency, engaged in shrewd,

Gilbert B. Perkins Sr. *From the Pittsburgh Press.*

sometimes criminal acts, likely viewed in today's society as unprofessional, heinous and likely unconstitutional. Like the other agencies, Perkins took advantage of loose interpretations of the laws and depleted police departments as his men continued to gain employment in sensational cases.

One such case occurred on the morning of March 18, 1909, in Sharon, Pennsylvania, when eight-year-old Billy Whitla, son of prominent local attorney James Whitla, was kidnapped. Hours later, a ransom note demanding $10,000 for Billy's release was delivered. Perkins and his detectives were engaged in the case, and several days later Billy Whitla was freed in Cleveland, Ohio, after the ransom was paid, with James and Helen Boyle later arrested and convicted of the malicious crime.

Following her conviction, Helen Boyle wrote about Perkins:

> *The old man (Gilbert Perkins) is a human vulture, feeding on carcasses of frail humanity, digging into the weaknesses of men and women—preying upon them. The time will come, however, when he will stand before a judge to give an account of his misdeeds, and then he will ask for the mercy he has refused to extend to others.*[7]

After the Whitla case, Perkins visited Erie and was hired by Charles Strong after Strong received threatening letters signed from the "Black Hand." Tasked with finding those responsible, Perkins's investigation was overshadowed by the City of Erie Police Department when three men were arrested and charged.

As the public congratulated the police, a humiliated Gilbert Perkins quietly returned to Pittsburg.

As Harry Perkins worked the bloodhounds again, Charles Franklin spoke to Gilbert Perkins, requesting a search of Erie's "Little Italy" neighborhood to the north. With his familiarity with the area, Franklin felt another sedulous search could yield additional clues. Joined by operative John Ross, Franklin ventured past the cluttered porches and façades of the leery Italian community. Moderate in height, Franklin sauntered along, his sly, mischievous eyes resting over a prominent nose and secreted behind a pair of glasses, his lips crooked to the side as a cigar protruded from his mouth.

Franklin's arrival recalled memories of a former councilman and disgraced private detective who ushered scandal into the Gem City.

Born in Washington, D.C., on June 5, 1866, to Joseph Franklin and Anna Wilson, Charles Franklin's early life remains an enigma. A heavily romanticized article from the *Erie Daily Times* claimed that as a youth, Franklin, sick of life at home, ran away and enlisted in the U.S. Navy as a marine.[8] Franklin's enlistment, confirmed through military records, records a date of August 20, 1888, as a private aboard USS *Michigan*, the U.S. Navy's first iron-hulled warship. City directories for Erie indicate that in 1891 Franklin resided at East Ninth Street. Two years later, he married twenty-three-year-old Mary Elizabeth Grine, daughter of Peter Grine and Carolina Brewer, in Erie, with the marriage producing a daughter, Lillian. Following his discharge from the military, Franklin operated a flour and feed store at the corner of East Eighteenth and State Streets.

Just before three o'clock on the morning of July 17, 1895, the City of Erie Fire Department was informed of a barn on fire on the corner of Eighteenth and State Streets. Noticing smoke from the flames, Patrolmen Fred Hartlein and William Detzel arrived and spotted a man acting suspiciously. Witnesses also informed officers the man had been loitering

USS *Michigan. Erie County Historical Society at the Hagen History Center.*

Charles Franklin.

A younger Charles Franklin. *From the* Pittsburgh-Post Gazette.

in the vicinity fifteen minutes before the fire was reported. These details, along with the strong aroma of kerosene, led officers to place the man under arrest.

The barn was completely engulfed by the time the fire department arrived, with firefighters struggling to prevent the blaze from spreading to Charles Franklin's feed store. The doors of the barn were also thrown open in an attempt to save the horses inside; however, only two escaped before the structure collapsed.

Dr. George Bell, a veterinarian, determined one of the rescued horses was severely burned about the throat and unlikely to recover, and the horses found in the wreckage were determined to have died from severe burns. Property inside the barn, consisting of five tons of hay, several harnesses and feed, totaled $1,000.

The suspected firebug, identified as Edward Lee of South Bend, Indiana, insisted he was innocent and had arrived in Erie with three companions in search of work and claimed he could produce letters of recommendation from previous employers in Erie as well as his companions, still believed to be in the city.

Chief Albert White collected evidence and spoke to witnesses, leading him to a shocking conclusion: the arsonist was none other than Charles Franklin. It was Franklin, White learned, who was seen loitering and entering his barn with a lit pipe before the fire. There were also recent documents showing an increase in Franklin's insurance policy. That afternoon, Franklin arrived at Chief White's office to be questioned, and he made several contradictory statements about the events. When pressed about inaccuracies within his statement, Franklin refused to talk further.

After he was placed under arrest, Franklin was allowed to send for his attorney, A.A. Freeman, who asked for the warrant charging Franklin. Chief White told Freeman a warrant had yet to be sworn, and soon a heated argument could be heard outside Chief White's office. Eventually, Franklin and his attorney agreed to wait until Chief White returned with a signed warrant, which was completed hours later, with Franklin removed from White's office by Patrolman James Higgins for his preliminary hearing, where he bailed out. After presenting a satisfactory account of himself at the time of the fire, Edward Lee was released.

Chief White affirmed his belief Franklin was responsible. This did little to aid Franklin's reputation; he had already accumulated many adversaries in Erie and was privately condemned for his involvement in a rumored badger game, an attempt to extort Erie's wealthiest citizens. The arson case against Franklin, however, hinged on flimsy circumstantial evidence, with A.A. Freeman arguing Franklin's stock of hay and accessories possessed minimal coverage despite the increase in Franklin's insurance, which did not suggest criminal intent.

The case fell apart, and on July 20, 1895, Franklin was released and the charges dropped.

Franklin continued his flour and feed business until he created the Franklin Coal Company, which proved prosperous as he cemented connections to Erie's local fishing businesses. He also became a city councilman for the Sixth Ward. In 1905, Franklin assisted in the search for the murderer of Detective Sergeant James Higgins, one of the officers who arrested him in 1895.

Franklin soon left the coal business and created a detective agency in which he was granted a license to engage as a private detective and operate in Erie on November 13, 1905, operating out of the office of Alderman Frank J.

Patrolmen William Detzel, Fred Hardline and James Higgins, involved in the arrest of Charles Franklin in 1895. *From* The Men Who Made Erie.

Bassett at 822 State Street. Within several weeks, Franklin had unearthed an opium smoking den, arrested those responsible for stealing from the Erie Silk Mill and pursued those of Erie's criminal underworld.

"Franklin," wrote the *Erie Dispatch*, "has stirred up more in the criminal line than the police department in the city of Erie."

On February 20, 1906, Franklin arrested and charged Emmanuel Costa, a laborer with the Campbell Brass Works, with stealing brass from his employer. A search of Costa's home resulted in the discovery of several pieces of brass—which Costa readily admitted came from his employer—but he claimed they were given to him by co-workers in exchange for tobacco. However, when asked to reveal the names, Costa refused.

Appearing before Alderman Frank Bassett, Costa requested the presence of his attorney, Clinton Higby. Higby later arrived and informed Costa that if the case required his presence to call on him again. Afterward, Costa, joined by his employer, Joseph B. Campbell,[9] and Franklin, retired to a private room, where Costa was told if all costs were paid for the case the charges would be dropped. A sympathetic Campbell, not wanting to place further hardship on Costa's family, agreed to the arrangement.

When Franklin presented his fee of $25, including docket costs of $8.50, Campbell considered the sum exorbitant, firmly saying he would pay only on conclusion of the lawsuit. Pressuring Costa, Franklin suggested a junk dealer Costa previously implicated could be responsible for half of the settlement costs. Costa's wife, Mary, gathered $33.50, scraped from neighbors and her minimal savings, and paid Franklin, who considered the case settled.

When Mary Costa later contacted Clinton Higby and told him of the settlement, Higby was alarmed and summoned Franklin to his office for an explanation. Reciting details of the settlement, Higby told Franklin he could not collect more than $1.12 for services under the present law, let alone effect a settlement. Because of the settlement, the Costas could not demand restitution, as this would render them amenable to the same offense as was charged against Franklin, and Franklin could not propose restitution without admitting connivance and participating in such grievous allegations.

Legal scholars recommended the prosecution of Costa proceed and suggested Franklin be arraigned on charges of extortion and compounding a felony. On March 17, 1906, the *Erie Dispatch* wrote:

> *Although the allegations therein made were of serious character, there has been no denial, no request for denial. Seven days have passed and nothing doing. There seems to be a lull on the part of somebody for the purpose of*

giving someone an opportunity to settle the case in some unknown manner, but the difficulty in that direction is that any such settlement simply means again compounding felony.

That day, Charles Franklin filed suit against the *Dispatch* for libel. The *Erie Daily Times* declined to "take sides either for or against the *Dispatch*" in the dispute between Franklin and its adversarial newspaper, opting to maintain a conservative position, yet stopped short of blaming the *Dispatch*, writing:

> *The point* The Times *wishes to emphasize is that if the* Dispatch *took up its criticism as a newspaper and for the one and only object of performing a public service, it is to be commended. It is just possible that Detective Franklin has been doing some things he ought not to have done, and it is also possible that he has done some things that are wrong, but not intentionally. If so, the newspaper does well in settling all such facts before the public.*

On March 19, 1906, Attorney Clinton Higby presented a petition before Judge Emory Walling on behalf of Mary Costa, requesting the revocation of Charles Franklin's detective license. Franklin, through attorney M. Levant Davis, filed his answer to the petition on March 25, defending his actions as unintentional.

Testimony against Charles Franklin began on April 2, 1906, before Judge Walling. Reporting by the *Erie Dispatch* opened the floodgates, with many witnesses testifying Franklin's actions bordered on extortion. Before the trial concluded, Franklin took the stand and defended his actions.

As the public waited for Judge Walling's opinion, the *Erie Daily Times* changed course and criticized the *Dispatch*:

> *Perhaps the morning newspaper has reasons for being afraid of Franklin;* The Times *certainly has not. So far as we are concerned, Franklin, the* Dispatch *and everyone else so disposed can do their worst:* The Times *is going to say just what it thinks it ought to say, regardless of any and everyone, and it is in a position to do just that very thing.* The Times *is in a position to treat Mr. Franklin fairly as well as the* Dispatch *and everyone else, and it is going to remain so.*

On Monday, April 23, 1906, Judge Walling ordered the revocation of Charles Franklin's private detective license. "It may not be as contended that

Mr. Franklin got no more compensation than his services were reasonably worth, but he got such compensation from the wrong parties. The defendants owed him nothing," Walling wrote in his opinion. "A prosecutor cannot employ an attorney or a detective and compel the defendant to pay for his services. And what a prosecutor has no legal claim for, certainly his agent cannot be permitted to receive as consideration for discontinuing a prosecution for a felony."

Franklin's actions, according to Judge Walling, exposed him to further potential criminal action, to be determined by the district attorney's office, which later declined to file additional charges.

The *Dispatch* praised Judge Walling's ruling:

> *The persecution of a man, no matter how bad, is one of the most unpleasant tasks for a newspaper of an individual. Newspapers of the "muck-rake" variety take pleasure in such work merely for sensational purposes. In the case at hand the* Dispatch *carefully investigated the Costa case, and then some others, and felt justified in assuming responsibility and liability by exposing the system. The case was not tried in the newspapers. It was taken before the court in a proper and legal manner and the decision just rendered by Judge Walling is ample proof of justification.*

Charles Franklin later found employment with the Lake Shore Railroad as a detective and relocated to Cleveland in July 1906. He returned to Erie the following year, assisting in several high-profile arrests before joining the Perkins Union Detective agency as an operative in Pittsburg sometime in 1909, later becoming the manager of the agency's branch in Philadelphia, Pennsylvania.

As Charles Franklin meandered through frozen streets and alleys in search of clues, he remained oblivious to ghosts from his past that would soon resurface.

Trudging through the snow after another failed attempt with the bloodhounds, Harry Perkins enlisted the assistance of Annie Strong's chauffeur, Charles Tyson, to help remove the empty casket from Anna McCollum's crypt. Wrenching back on the casket, Perkins suddenly saw a pair of decomposed feet. With renewed vigor, the men heaved again on the casket until it was halfway exposed.

Tyson braced his hand against Perkins's shoulder.

"The body is there!" Tyson cried out. "Look at the hands!"

Believing the body to be Anna McCollum's, Perkins bolted from the mausoleum, with Charles Tyson in tow. They jumped into the Strongs' automobile, with its tires kicking up slush and snow as it sped away, bound for the Strong home. There, Perkins informed Annie Strong of the discovery, and within minutes they departed for the cemetery.

Entering the mausoleum, Annie approached the casket. Bringing a handkerchief to her mouth and wiping tears from her eyes, she confirmed the body was her aunt. Within minutes, she departed for the office of the *Erie Evening Herald*, announcing the discovery to her employees with strict dictation on how the story should be reported. Before going to print, Annie ordered the proofs sent to her in order to censor any "unnecessary details." As she waited, Annie phoned her aunt's relatives in Philadelphia, apprising them of the news.

Around noon, detectives from the William J. Burns Detective Agency arrived and were driven to the Erie Cemetery. There, F. Bourgeois, manager of the Pittsburg branch of the agency, and two detectives performed their own assessment of the mausoleum, insisting they were the first to find Anna McCollum's corpse. They theorized McCollum was interred above the empty space, and after the coffin had been removed by the ghouls, they were unable to return it and resorted to removing the marble slab underneath and discarding the coffin, and her body, inside.

"There is no indication of how recently the mausoleum was entered," Bourgeois speculated to the *Times*. "I think robbery was the motive."

Chief Edward Wagner was asked by the *Times* why operatives from the Perkins Agency, not the police, recovered evidence from the mausoleum.

"We were not permitted to search the tomb. Mrs. Strong gave orders that nothing was to be touched, as she had some prominent detectives coming to the city," Wagner said.

As confirmation spread of the recovery of Anna McCollum's body, a staff correspondent for the *Erie Daily Times* phoned the Strong home, asking to speak to Thora Ronalds.

"Who is this?" Thora Ronalds answered curtly.

"A representative of the *Times*," the reporter declared.

"Well, what do you want?"

"Is there any truth in the rumor that the body of Mrs. McCollum has been found in one of the supposedly empty crypts in the mausoleum?"

"That is for you to find out. I am not at liberty to speak to you at all."

Thora Ronalds immediately hung up the phone.

That afternoon, Gilbert Perkins entered the lobby of the Reed House, which had been transformed into the "'nerve center" for his detective agency. Perkins's presence immediately attracted a swarm of reporters clamoring for comment about Anna McCollum's body. Perkins, beaming with pride, announced he would release a statement, adding he was waiting for his son Harry. Yet only minutes before he had told a reporter for the *Erie Daily Times* they were expecting McCollum's body to be recovered soon.

At 4:00 p.m., Gilbert Perkins confirmed Anna McCollum's remains had been recovered.

After the sun vanished, however, Perkins and his men were still no closer to making an arrest. A clue had been provided to police that an African American laborer named Dan Mathews made a statement weeks before that "something was going to happen" at the cemetery that would "startle the public."

This clue, however, turned out to be another dead end.

Activity inside the Reed House that night thrived as Gilbert Perkins found it impossible to convince newspaper correspondents that all bodies within the mausoleum were accounted for. The consensus of newspaper reporters, and the public, was that a body was still missing, with some accusing Perkins of masterminding a faux story to draw out the guilty parties. Perkins facetiously denounced these theories as ridiculous.

The Reed House. *Erie County Historical Society at the Hagen History Center.*

Frank Crane of the *Erie Daily Times*, skeptical of Perkins's announcement, discussed the case that night with Charles Franklin in the lobby of the Reed House.

"Charles, would it prejudice your case if we put a story on the wire saying that the story given out by the Perkins people that Mrs. McCollom's [*sic*] body being found is a fake and that it was never missing, but that Mrs. William L. Scott's body was stolen from the mausoleum?" Crane asked.

"Don't do that, Frank," Franklin said, removing his cigar. "You will get in wrong. I wouldn't lie to you about this, you know I hate these people and have good reason to hate them."

When Gilbert and Harry Perkins offered to produce affidavits confirming all bodies were in the mausoleum, *Cleveland Press* correspondent Robert McCannon requested permission to reproduce the affidavit. Gilbert Perkins recanted his offer, insisting such a move would jeopardize arrests, expected at any minute, declaring the crime was well planned by two men whom they refused to publicly name.

Asked for a motive, Perkins countered: "I have given up motives. I want the men who did it."

The heated rivalry between the Burns and Perkins Agencies boiled over at the Reed House into the early morning hours, with both sides engaged in heated debates about who had the right to claim the recovery of Anna McCollum's body.

"I am still at a loss to surmise any motive for the terrible deed," Charles Strong said to the *Cleveland Leader*. "I could not believe I had any enemies who would do such an act. Consequently, I cannot think that revenge or vengeance can be the reason."

Far away from downtown Erie, Detective Sergeant Jack Welsh returned to the cemetery to assist the patrolmen on guard, and during the early morning hours, he observed three men standing on the corner of West Nineteenth and Cherry Streets acting in a suspicious manner, although the men later dispersed.

On the morning of February 11, 1911, Detective Sergeant Welsh conversed with reporters before he was pulled to the side by Chief Wagner and told he was being removed from the case. Welsh's removal, the *Erie Daily Times* speculated, was because of Welsh's past as a newspaperman and fear of the Strongs and Perkinses that Welsh would leak details to the public.

Outside the mausoleum, a notable crowd, including members of the Perkins Agency and City of Erie Police Department, continued to swell,

Front page of the *Erie Daily Times* on February 10, 1911. *Author's collection.*

including the presence of Thomas Cochran, an attorney from Mercer County, invited by Harry Perkins. At her home, Annie Strong spoke to detectives from the Burns Agency, confiding her fear that her father's body was missing and insisting detectives confirm his body was still in the crypt before the tomb was repaired and closed.

When Annie Strong arrived at the cemetery, the situation grew tense when she saw a photographer from the *Erie Daily Times*. Annie Strong called out to Detective Sergeant Richard Crotty: "Mr. Crotty, can't you protect me from having my picture taken? If they take my picture they will have to suffer the consequences."

Minutes later, Alured Burton arrived with his wagon, transporting a new casket for Annie Strong's mother. Burton, aided by several assistants, carried the new casket inside the mausoleum. Those nearby watched as pieces of Mary Matilda Scott's damaged casket were gradually removed in buckets and dumped into the wagon.

By the afternoon, all remaining debris had been cleared from the mausoleum.

Responding to the growing rumors and theories in the case, the *Erie Evening Herald* defended its reporting, insisting that because detectives possessed all evidence available, "the necessity for not making public the facts in the case no longer exists." That evening, Annie Strong released her statement through the *Herald*.

"There have been so many misstatements in regard to the horrible desecration done to my father's mausoleum that I am today for the first time free to give out a full statement of the facts in the case which I wish to make known to the public," Annie Strong declared. "All bodies that have been placed in the mausoleum are there at present."

Annie Strong summarized events surrounding the case and presented facts she believed supported her family's refusal to comment further.

"Recognizing the importance of not disturbing anything, to give the detectives every advantage possible, nothing further was done, and everyone kept out of the mausoleum." Strong's statement continued before laying the groundwork for how her aunt's body was "discovered" by her chauffeur and Harry Perkins. In response to rumors her father's body had been stolen, Annie said, "The crypt containing the body of my father was not disturbed in any manner whatsoever."

Annie Strong asserted the police department and Chief Wagner were "co-operating in every way in lending every assistance possible."

The interview only reinforced the public's opinion the Strong family was complicit in keeping the case muted. Such accusations were reinforced when the *Erie Daily Times* interviewed Amelia Hertwig, who asserted she was told by Annie Strong not to speak to the press.

"Prospect of an arrest for the plundering of the mausoleum of William L. Scott in the Erie cemetery grows more remote with each day," wrote *Cleveland Leader* correspondent Benjamin Ling. "From indications tonight, private detectives employed by Mrs. Charles H. Strong, are working to prevent newspaper reporters from unearthing too many clues or to disclose evidence that 'men higher up' are implicated."

Ling described the sizeable crowds at the Erie Cemetery but excoriated the actions of Annie and Charles Strong:

> *From the city administration, Charles H. Strong, it is declared, can have whatever he wishes. As president of the Erie Electric Light and Power company and the controlling power in two newspapers, Strong's dominance in local affairs is almost absolute. His wife is also a millionaire. Mayor Liebel, city officials and the police are all eager to accommodate the Strongs in almost anything. The strength of the family here enables it to keep secret almost as much as it desires in connection with the despoilation of the tomb.*

The *Cleveland Plain Dealer* believed the vandals would never be apprehended:

> *Tonight's announcement is that the investigations in Erie will be continued indefinitely, the family being determined not to abandon the mystery as long as any possibility of its solution remains. No solution is now in sight. Every present probability is that it will never be solved, and that the motive for the violation of all time a matter of speculation.*

Newspapers also compared the case to that of the 1878 theft of the body of Alexander Turney Stewart, an American entrepreneur, stolen from his tomb in New York City and held for a ransom of $20,000. The ransom was later paid and the remains returned, although never verified.

—⁂—

On the afternoon of February 11, 1911, three miles east of Erie, twelve-year-old Arthur Richter, eleven-year-old William Ott and fifteen-year-old Clarence Cantor were busy positioning muskrat traps in the dense woods near the old pesthouse on Fagan Road, within view of the General Electric plant.

The Boys Who Found St. John's Church Articles

Clarence Cantor, William Ott and Arthur Richter. *From the* Erie Daily Times.

Jostling a pile of brush, Ott noticed something shiny. The boys inched closer and found several items wrapped in a dirt-covered priest's hassock. Unwrapping the cloth, the boys discovered gold and silver chalices.

William Ott suggested the other boys stay and guard the items while he went to the home of his neighbor, police captain William Detzel. As the boys plotted their next move, a package express on East Twelfth Street stopped and later transported the boys to Captain Detzel's residence.

Greeted by the three excitable boys who recited their discovery, Captain Detzel called Chief Wagner before phoning Reverend Brock. Detzel and the boys then departed for St. John's Church and delivered the recovered items. All of the items, except for one chalice, were in pristine condition. Impressed, Reverend Brock handed each of the boys a five-dollar bill.

Detectives believed the ornaments were stashed in the woods beyond the city limits until the "excitement" ceased, while others believed a connection existed to the Scott mausoleum desecration, with the thievery done by "local talent"—although this was never publicly explained or expanded upon.

4

A PITCHED BATTLE

On the morning of February 11, 1911, Gilbert Perkins entered the office of Postmaster Isador Sobel at 11 West Eighth Street. After exchanging pleasantries, Perkins informed Sobel he was working on the mausoleum case and asked Sobel if he cared to share any theories about the case. Sobel shrugged, admitting he did not entertain any theories; however, he was curious about Perkins's theories.

Perkins believed only a few pieces of copper were taken from the mausoleum and that it was vandalized by disgruntled former employees of the Erie Cemetery not financially compensated by Annie Strong. Sobel, finding Perkins's approach and theories otherworldly, nodded as he listened. The Strongs would receive two letters, Perkins forewarned, asking if arrangements could be made to locate the letters. He asked Sobel if mail carriers could examine every postal box. A hesitant Sobel told Perkins such a request was nearly impossible; however, he offered to have the post office monitored.

A satisfied Perkins said goodbye and departed Sobel's office.

Sometime during the early morning hours of February 12, a watchman on duty at the Erie County Electric Company on the corner of East Twelfth and French Streets heard the deafening bark of a bullet rippling through the air. Investigating the premises, the watchman examined Charles Strong's office, where he saw a bullet hole in the window. Inspecting the cavity in the glass, the watchman observed that the projectile passed over Strong's desk and was either a .32- or .38-caliber bullet.

On the morning of February 12, Gilbert Perkins stood inside Charles Strong's office, shadowed by his secretary. An intense search of the premises failed to yield additional clues leading to the person responsible. While documenting the powdered glass sprayed all over Strong's office chair, Perkins told Stephen Walker he felt the incident directly related to the mausoleum desecration, carried out to intimidate the Strongs.

As his father took over the case, Harry Perkins returned to Pittsburg, claiming his departure was unrelated to business and he expected to return to Erie on the fourteenth. Harry Perkins's departure was joined by an exodus of operatives from the Perkins Agency, despite assurances from the agency they were not abandoning the case.

Postmaster Isador Sobel. *From* The Men Who Made Erie.

The *Erie Daily Times* remained pessimistic, feeling justice would never be served.

The Erie County Electric Company building at the corner of East Twelfth and French Streets. *History of Erie County Electric Company.*

Those within the City of Erie Police Department assisting with the case continued their diligent search for the missing copper lid from Anna McCollum's casket. Almost comically, the exploration of clues gave way to newspaper correspondents being shadowed by private detectives, keeping a close eye on the reporters to prevent any further information being leaked to the public.

Questioned about rumors she had asked the private detectives in her employ to cease their work, Annie Strong responded in disgust.

"I most certainly have not asked the detectives to quit their work," Annie Strong said. "Do you suppose I would stop now? I will not rest content until those who committed this horrible outrage are behind bars."

Operatives from the William J. Burns Agency retired to New York, continuing their search there for a man "higher up" they felt employed the "ghouls" responsible. The *Cleveland Plain Dealer* claimed a pool of suspects was narrowed down to an individual with connections to Erie. With only a few operatives from the Perkins Agency remaining in Erie, others believed the Strongs were waiting for the exhilaration to die down before engaging in negotiations with the criminals. A renewed inspection of evidence from the mausoleum failed to also materialize, with operatives concluding the pickaxe, absent of identifying markers, had been brought to the cemetery by the vandals.

By the morning of February 13, 1911, the city had slowly slipped back to normalcy as the intrusion of out-of-town reporters and amateur detectives declined. That morning, an envelope addressed to Charles Strong arrived at the post office in downtown Erie, postmarked at 7:00 a.m. Several hours later, the letter arrived at Strong's office in the Erie County Electric Company building.

Skimming through the mail before noon, Strong eyed the envelope before slicing the edge with a penknife. The letter inside was roughly torn on one side. The words, scrawled in pencil, caused him to pause.

The letter read:

P.S. or your house will be blown up.
Mr. Strong
Leave $50,000
at 31'st and
Pennsylvania
Ave
on night of Feb.

21 at 12 P.M. or you will have
your mosoleum
blown up and
if you bring any
police on 29th of Feb.
my men will shoot th
them.
   Black Hand.

Alerted about the letter, Gilbert Perkins set off for the Strong home. As Perkins inspected the letter, Annie Strong informed him she did not want Charles Franklin working on the case. Perkins lightly jested that Franklin was responsible for his Philadelphia office and could vouch for his character.

"I don't care. He is not the kind of man I want on this case," Annie protested. "It appears to the Perkins detective that they must be going on the theory that it takes a thief to catch a thief."

Perkins acknowledged her concerns before securing the letter in the breast pocket of his coat. When he descended the front steps of the Strong home, the press were oblivious of the receipt of the threatening letter.

That evening, Charles Franklin departed Erie for Philadelphia.

When he entered Postmaster Sobel's office, Gilbert Perkins was approached by Samuel Brainerd, the newly promoted assistant postmaster. Perkins triumphantly handed the letter to Brainerd, explaining the threatening contents as Brainerd studied the envelope and postmark. Perkins suspected a "colored" employee of the Strongs wrote the letter.

Was it possible to ascertain, Perkins asked, if the letter was mailed from the vicinity of Twenty-Sixth and Peach Streets? The paper, added Perkins, was sold by a dozen stores within that neighborhood. Brainerd removed the letter, keeping his attention on the postmark on the envelope, asserting the time on the postmark ruled out the possibility of it being mailed from Twenty-Sixth and Peach Streets, suggesting it could have been mailed from the Reed House.

As Sobel exited his office, Perkins announced the arrival of a letter. Sobel took the envelope and letter, observing the "peculiar texture" of the paper as he scanned the missive before passing it back to Perkins.

The "Black Hand" letter mailed to the *Erie Daily Times* on January 20, 1911. *Author's collection.*

"No 'Black Hand' person ever wrote that," Sobel scoffed. "They have spelled 'Pennsylvania' correctly."

The letter's orthography, Sobel continued, was too "proper and educated" to have been written by an illiterate criminal. Perkins, ignoring Sobel's comments, asked why the letter was torn. Sobel shrugged, suggesting it was fabricated to present "the worst letter ever produced." A disappointed Perkins triumphantly declared that when the guilty party was found, the torn pieces of paper would be in their possession.

Threats from the Black Hand were not foreign to those in Erie. One example occurred on January 23, 1911, when the *Erie Daily Times* received a letter from the Black Hand threatening to blow up the *Times*'s building if $15,000 was not paid.

Instead, the *Times* mocked the threat, with cartoonist Walter Kiedaisch incorporating it into his daily cartoon, accompanied by a creation he called "The Crow."

On February 14, Charles Strong received an anonymous letter from Cleveland, Ohio.

The letter, dated February 13, 1911, read:

Mr. Strong, Dear Sir:

I see by the Cleveland papers that one, Charles Franklin, is there to look up your troubles. Mr. Strong, I think it would be a good thing to watch Franklin. If the late Chief Sam Woods were alive, Franklin would be giving Erie a wide berth. He was arrested in Erie in connection with barn burning. At the time, Mr. Woods brought out his black-mailing record. He married a street woman. She was a good looking woman. She also had a younger sister and Franklin used to send them out to meet certain wealthy men. He would have them picked out. Then after the wife or girl came home and told him what had happened, he would write the man a letter, demanding his presence at his house on the corner of Seventeenth and French street, on a certain date.

Then when the man came, he would bring in whatever woman it was and make them get down on their knees and confess what they had done. It was seldom, but what the man gave a good sum of money, as the girl was under age.

Franklin, at that time, had a tin star and said he belonged to a detective agency in Chicago. Franklin used to say he would come to Erie, a millionaire, some day and that these big stiffs owed him a living. You were one of the marked ones, but you did not take to the bait. I am sending you this, thinking it may do you some good.

"The general opinion is that an effort is being made to have the entire affair die down and hush up all facts in connection with it as quickly as possible," wrote the *Erie Daily Times*, believing the investigation had ceased. Other papers, such as the *Cleveland Leader*, noted the particular absence of the Strongs' granddaughter, Thora,[10] whom the *Leader* believed was being held as a prisoner inside the Strong mansion.

"This case has just begun," Gilbert Perkins informed the *Cleveland Leader* when pressed about the lack of an arrest in the case. "No matter who are the guilty parties, we shall arrest them. All we want is enough evidence to get a conviction. But I tell you this is a 'cheap job.' The reason for it will surprise everyone when it is discovered."[11]

Perkins operative John Drew was spotted loitering around the corridors of the Reed House.[12] Later he was granted permission by Postmaster Sobel to case the lobby of the post office in downtown Erie in an attempt to locate the letter writer. With resources scarce, Perkins also placed an operative near the mailbox on the corner of Twenty-Sixth and Peach Streets. Letter carriers, under orders from Postmaster Isador Sobel, were instructed to be on the lookout for suspicious letters addressed to the Strong family and commanded to deliver such items to Sobel immediately.

On the morning of February 15, another letter arrived at Charles Strong's office:

> *C. Strong*
> *You leave $50,000*
> *at 11 P.M. Feb. 28, 1911*
> *at 31 st ant Pennsilvanea*
> *Avenue or you will have*
> *   your branes*
> *blowed out. Either you*
> *or your wife. If you*
> *brung any police along*
> *hey will be shot and*
> *my men will take a*
> *strong battle.*
> *(You*
> *(Son-of-a-bitch)*
> *   Black Hand*
> *deth*

Between "Black Hand" and "deth" was a crudely drawn face and crossbones. The left side of the paper was roughly torn, similar to the first letter. Gilbert Perkins inspected the second letter at the Strong residence. "These people," Perkins said. "They certainly are desperate."

Perkins paused, looking over to Annie Strong.

"I'm very anxious about you, Mrs. Strong," Perkins said. "I think I shall go to the Reed House and fetch Mr. McKean to come over and protect you."

"I don't want any more protectors," Annie Strong said.

The sly smirk on Perkins's face receded as he nodded in acknowledgement. As he started for the front doors, a butler handed him his hat. Turning, he looked at Annie, now joined by her husband.

"I should warn you to be very careful of your little grandchild."

Perkins again visited Postmaster Sobel's office, dramatically emphasizing the arrival of another threatening letter, just as he had predicted. Sobel exhaled a deep sigh as Perkins dropped the letter on Sobel's desk. Perkins then moved about Sobel's private room nervously as Sobel read the letter.

Sobel shook his head, certain the letter was written by the same hand, except now that individual decided to litter the letter with "a rage of spelling errors," including the word Pennsylvania. Sobel, a former attorney, openly disputed the immature nature of the letter.

On February 17, the Scott mausoleum was retrofitted with an electric burglar alarm, wired directly to the Strong home. A pair of headlights, according to the *Times*, were installed, intending to "burn during all the hours of darkness hereafter."

Perkins, questioned at the Reed House by a reporter for the *Times*, acknowledged he was quietly working on the case and confirmed no recent developments.

"It is generally accepted now that the possibility of any arrest being made is extremely remote," admitted the *Times*.

Charles Strong, concerned with his wife's mental state, felt she had taken too much of the burden of the investigation upon herself. Annie later called attorney John Sterling in New York City, and the next day Charles Strong informed Gilbert Perkins through the telephone that the assistance of his agency was no longer needed. Strong ordered all documents, including the letters, be handed over to Henry Fish, a local attorney.

Perkins complied with Strong's wishes and quickly left for Pittsburg.

On the morning of February 22, 1911, a man departed a railroad coach car, stepping into the crowd of men, women and children as they dashed about the platform of the Union Depot train station. As he was nearly obscured by whirling smoke from the hissing passing locomotives, few paid attention to him. He was tall, exceedingly lanky, with a neatly trimmed moustache and vigilant pair of eyes perched atop a thin nose. At forty-four years old, Postal Inspector John Oldfield was one of the most powerful law enforcement officers in America.

Born on January 2, 1867, in Ellicott City, Maryland, John Frank Oldfield, known as "Frank" to friends and family, was recognized in his youth as "one of the most notorious troublemakers"[13] in his hometown. Oldfield came from a wealthy family and worked alongside his four brothers at the Hamilton Oldfield Iron and Pump Works as well as a neighboring sawmill where his father was a partner.

Meticulous in both appearance and hygiene, Oldfield "dressed as if he worked on Wall Street, with the finest handmade suits from a Baltimore

Postal inspector John Frank Oldfield, photographed in December 1910. *The Oldfield Collection.*

haberdashery."[14] After holding positions in the local Republican Party, where "political rallies often were indistinguishable from street gang clashes,"[15] Oldfield later served as the sheriff of Howard County, Maryland.

Oldfield was sworn in as a postal inspector on March 7, 1899. Within a short time, however, Oldfield had difficulty settling into the role as he encountered numerous expectations and procedures he was not particularly fond of. In August 1899, Oldfield assisted his brother Clarence Oldfield's campaign for the Howard County Central Committee and supported candidates approved by his family. Because postal inspectors were forbidden to engage in politics, Oldfield was recalled to his post in Chattanooga, Tennessee, and dismissed from the U.S. Postal Inspection Service.

With his wife, Margaret Galena, pregnant with their third child, Oldfield, through the help of his father's political connections, was reinstated on February 15, 1901. Following his reinstatement, Oldfield was assigned to the Cincinnati Post Office and later relocated with his wife and children to Athens, Ohio. Soon, Oldfield was instrumental in such cases as the arrest and conviction of Edmund Driggs, a congressman from Brooklyn, New York, involved in a bribery scandal with the Brandt-Dent American Cashier Company via postal stamp dispensing machines. He also hunted down postal employees pilfering money from post office registers and those who used the U.S. Mail for the purpose of gambling and pornography.

Oldfield's most famous case occurred in 1909, when he dismantled the "Society of the Banana," a syndicate of the Black Hand responsible for extortion and murder in both Ohio and Pennsylvania, leading to the conviction of America's first organized crime ring. Oldfield had set out for Erie when he was informed by his superiors that the Strongs had received threatening letters and sought his expertise.

After getting settled, Oldfield was briefed about the case by Stephen Walker at the County Electric Company building and provided a small batch of case-related documents. Afterward, Oldfield was introduced to the Strongs; visited the office of Henry Fish, where he gained custody of the threatening letters; and then familiarized himself with the city, including the Scott mausoleum.

On February 23, 1911, Chief Wagner received a letter. Recognizing the handwriting on the envelope, he swiftly opened the envelope and read the contents:

Cheef of Police.
Dont you dare
to send any police
to 31 at Pennsylvania
Ave on night of Feb. 28
at 11 P.M.
as your men
and mie men will
have a pitched batt
battle.
We demanded $50,000
from Strongs
    Black Hand
    deth

Chief Wagner strolled to the Strong home and spoke with Annie Strong before turning the letter over. Annie read the letter and turned it over to Inspector Oldfield. Days later, detectives from the Pinkerton Detective Agency arrived to assist with the investigation.

On the night of February 28, 1911, a bag with marked currency was deposited in a large field near East Thirty-First Street and Pennsylvania Avenue. Joining Pinkerton detectives were Chief Wagner; Roundsman William Brown; Patrolmen August Heisler, George Warfel and Jacob Zimmer; and Inspector Oldfield. As daylight broke over the crest of the horizon the following morning, a blanket of fog rolled through the field

Present-day view of Pennsylvania Avenue looking south, location of the "stump field" where police kept surveillance after the arrival of the "Black Hand" letters. *Author's collection.*

75

littered with stumps and overgrown shrubbery, leaving those concealed in darkness emptyhanded when the letter writer failed to appear.

Another unsuccessful attempt was made the following night, leaving the men to walk away fatigued and frustrated.

On March 2, 1911, Chief Wagner failed to appear at headquarters for the second day in a row. His absence attracted the attention of a reporter from the *Times* who learned Wagner was secretly venturing to a rural area on the outskirts of the city at night, conferring with strange men.

When the police department refused to comment, reporters for the *Times* dug deeper and discovered Wagner's change of daily habits was related to threatening letters sent to Charles Strong.

"BLACK HAND LETTERS SENT TO MRS. CHAS. H. STRONG SAID TO BE THE CAUSE OF PINKERTONS HERE" was the headline on the front page of the *Erie Daily Times* on March 3, 1911. That afternoon, a reporter from the *Times* questioned Chief Wagner in his office. When the reporter sprang information on him about the Black Hand letters mailed to the Strongs, Wagner began to pace before turning to the reporter.

"I don't know anything about the 'Black Hand' letter."

"Do you think the same people sent the letter that desecrated the Scott mausoleum?"

"I don't know anything about it."

"No hard feelings if we use the story is there, chief?"

"None whatever," Wagner said, waving his hand. "I have nothing to say."

"Shall we say you are not talking?"

"Say I don't know anything about the matter."

The reporter continued, informing Wagner the Pinkerton detectives were in the city.

"Let them stay here," Wagner responded, unfazed.

"But is your department working in conjunction with them, chief?"

"We are attending to our own business."

The *Erie Daily Times*, in connecting the threatening letters to the mausoleum case, strangely remarked Gilbert Perkins and his sleuths were not asked to assist with the case.

In the state capital of Harrisburg, the "Black Hand" bill, aimed to prevent crimes involving threatening letters, was introduced by C.M.C. Campbell of Allegheny County and referred to the committee on judiciary general, overseen by Milton W. Shreve, a former lawyer and district attorney from Erie. Similar to another recently proposed bill, which determined the desecration of a mausoleum a felony, punishable by imprisonment, the "Black Hand" bill gained bipartisan support, making such crimes punishable by up to three years imprisonment and a fine of $1,000.[16]

The beginning of March saw unusual activity reported around the mausoleum as workmen finished performing repairs to the interior of the mausoleum. In addition to wiring the premises with a burglar alarm, several well-known electricians and workmen were seen working under the supervision of Thomas O'Dea of the Edison Electric Light Plant.[17]

For those in the sleepy borough of Girard, Pennsylvania, Erie seemed almost a world away. Such pretenses changed on the morning of March 10, 1911, around 4:30 a.m. when a tremendous explosion erupted from the R.S. Battles Bank, pulsating through Main Street, rattling the windows and doors of storefronts and homes as far as a mile away. Sam Mackey, who lived next door to the bank with his wife,[18] said, "The explosion felt like the earth underneath had ruptured." Mackey sprang from his bed and ran to the window, observing five men in the street outside the bank. Lifting the windowpane, he jutted his head out.

"What are you doing here?" Mackey yelled.

The men fled, disappearing around the corner of Olin Avenue. Postmaster Will Murray, aroused by the explosion, peeked out his window and saw the five men before they ran away. W.B. Hicks, a conductor for the Cleveland & Erie line, also witnessed the suspicious men following the explosion.

Onlookers scampered to the bank from all directions. Its brick façade was visible through the plumes of dark billowing smoke. Within an hour, the crowd outside grew to over one hundred.

Charles Webster, a cashier, along with Will Kibler and his two sons were the first to enter the bank. Nearly all the windows were blown out, the electric lights were destroyed and the floor was littered with discarded books, stationery and other smoldering debris among a sea of shattered glass. A quick inventory of the bank found nothing missing except for a concealed revolver. Above the fireplace, a painting of the bank's founder, Rush Battles, remained untouched.

C. Lloyd departed for Erie in search of glass to repair the broken windows and the services of an expert locksmith to secure the vault. The First National Bank arranged to assist in operating with sufficient funds until the vault door at the Battles bank could be opened, with additional assistance from the National Bank of Girard.

Above: The R.S. Battles Bank in Girard, Pennsylvania. *Erie County Historical Society at the Hagen History Center.*

Left: Photograph showing damage to the vault door inside the R.S. Battles Bank. *From the* Erie Daily Times.

Although the bank's interior sustained extensive damage, important clues still remained. Window casings on the west end of the building showed the signs of attempts to gain entry with a chisel. After a failure to gain access through the front doors and windows, those responsible entered by smashing a window in the directors' room on the western border of the vault. A trail of burnt matches led directly to the vault door, the handle of the combination lock having been blown through the ceiling from the shock of the blast.

The blast, caused from poorly placed dynamite tied to the handle of the outer door of the vault (three inches thick and constructed with two one-half-inch-thick plates of steel), blew outwards, leaving a hole in the ground nearly one foot in diameter. The bank ledger, placed between the two doors of the vault the day before, was reduced to shreds.

It was believed that after the fuse was lit, one of the thieves ventured to the park west of the bank, while the others secluded themselves in the rear alley as they waited for the explosion.

News and rumor quickly spread throughout the countryside; however, none of the clues led to an immediate arrest. Frank Fischer, living in the village of Avonia, witnessed five men, described as "foreigners," walking in a hurried manner on East Lake Road toward Erie after 5:00 a.m. Constable Thomas Atwood of Girard, joined by Chief of Police D.W. Zeigler and William Reimer, a shoe merchant, left Girard on the 10:30 a.m. trolley for Fairview, where they exited and continued by carriage to East Lake Road.

Reimer, who had observed a suspicious man the night before "loafing around" the corner of Main Street and Olin Avenue, described him as five feet, nine inches in height, about 150 pounds and wearing a soft black hat and short black overcoat. The man's features remained obscured in the dark as he appeared to watch the bank. Reimer's description was corroborated by others, including a woman who, when passing the same man, observed him turning his head toward a telegraph pole to conceal himself. Two other suspicious men, tough looking in appearance, were spotted the day before selling scissors for twenty-five cents a pair.

That afternoon, a locksmith with the National Safe & Lock Company of Cleveland gained access to the vault with plans to reopen for business the following morning.

By 6:00 p.m., Atwood, Zeigler and Reimer reached an area between the mouth of the churning Walnut Creek and the beaches below Waldameer Park. As the sun was swallowed by the horizon, the men stood bewildered on the sandy beach, the trail having grown cold. A sharp breeze rolled off the battering waves of Lake Erie.

The lagoon and beaches north of Waldameer. *Erie County Historical Society at the Hagen History Center.*

In Girard, suspicious persons were arrested and questioned as Chief Zeigler endeavored to secure a pair of bloodhounds, and Frank H. Watson, the shrewd county detective, was dispatched to Girard to assist in the investigation.

That night, at police headquarters in Erie, Captain Detzel was informed four suspicious men were spotted boarding the 9:00 p.m. trolley at Waldameer. Officers were dispatched and secured descriptions of the men from the conductor, with those working patrol that night given descriptions of the four men. Also joining the investigation were detectives from the Pinkerton Detective Agency. The evidence, according to the "Pinks," indicated the work was carried out by amateurs and shared similarities to the Scott mausoleum desecration and recent burglaries of churches throughout Erie County.

As one of the strongest banks in northwestern Pennsylvania, the R.S. Battles Bank was believed to encase large amounts of currency, with scuttlebutt of dollar bills piled like cordwood inside the vault. Although the bank had been robbed twice, in 1863 and 1894, a night watchman was never employed, and the bank never installed an electric alarm system.

As the dragnet approached Erie, it was believed the men responsible were secluded in the woods outside the city limits, near Waldameer. A search led by Pinkerton agents reached settling basins near the peninsula where twenty-six Romanian immigrants were employed by the T.A. Gillespie Company and housed in encampments. With the encampment under surveillance day and night, agents ferried witnesses from Girard to the camp in an attempt to confirm the identities of those seen in Girard before the blast. Superintendent E.S. Williamson, of the T.A. Gillespie Company, was hounded relentlessly by Pinkerton detectives about the immigrants under his employ and their activities. Four Romanians working for the company, arrested previously in Erie, came under renewed scrutiny; however, the identities of any prime suspects were never disclosed by anyone outside of the department.

In mid-April, a pair of summer cottages near Waldameer beach were found broken into, with Pinkertons determining a bar was used on the doors and windows. The damage matched the window casings of the Battles Bank. Soon, the Pinkertons concluded that the men, on their way to Erie, stopped to rest in the woods near Waldameer, where they entered the cottages and stayed put until things cooled down.[19]

The property owners decided to protect their property in the future by barricading the windows and doors.

5

CRAWFISHING

O n March 13, 1911, a man named Edward Prendergast shuffled past a garbage dump on the corner of East Fifth and German Streets. There he found, among the heaping piles of trash, several chalices and holy vessels belonging to a church. There was also something else—the discarded silver trimmings from a casket.

Aiming to keep the disclosure quiet, Chief Wagner denied silver trimmings from a casket were found but confirmed the recovery of chalices and religious items stolen from local churches. Despite Wagner's refutation to the press, Prendergast was adamant the police were involved in a cover-up.

As the weeks progressed, Inspector Oldfield managed to cloak his investigation in secrecy, and it wouldn't be until mid-April that newspapers learned the fabled postal inspector was hot on the case. Assisting Oldfield were other postal inspectors, including Edward Hutches of Urbana, Ohio, who previously worked with Oldfield in the Society of the Banana investigation. James Cortelyou, postal inspector in charge of the Philadelphia office and all post offices in the commonwealth, was assigned on March 20. From the beginning, Oldfield

Postal inspector Edward Hutches. *The Oldfield Collection.*

interviewed detectives, police officers, reporters, attorneys, those in the Strongs' employment and others.

Oldfield's attention was attracted to the unusual behavior of Gilbert Perkins, particularly his prophecies envisaging the arrival of the threatening torn letters.

Soon, Oldfield was in possession of evidence leading him directly to those responsible for sending the threatening letters to Charles Strong with culpability in the mausoleum case.

The trail led straight to the Perkins Union Detective Agency.

INSPECTOR HUTCHES WAS ORDERED by Oldfield to travel to Indianapolis in preparation for arrests in the Black Hand letter case. He arrived on April 7, where he met local Postal Inspector William C. Ela, who had been in contact with Oldfield prior to Hutches's arrival. Ela informed Hutches that he was asked by Oldfield to present charges against Gilbert Perkins before a U.S. commissioner and to obtain a warrant for Perkins's office.

James M. Walsh, a postal inspector from Parkersburg, West Virginia, traveled to Indianapolis, arriving there on April 12 to assist the investigation; met with Hutches and Ela; and was introduced to the Black Hand case. Soon, the men were joined by Inspectors William Cleary of Indianapolis and Walter Cookson of Columbus, Ohio.

Oldfield telegraphed the inspectors in Indianapolis, asking when an arrest could be made. Acting on advice from a U.S. attorney, the inspectors agreed to carry out the warrants the next morning at ten o'clock, with U.S Marshals Merrill D. Wilson and D.C. Rankin of Indianapolis given the civil search warrant and Indianapolis City Police detectives Keller DeRossette and Harry Ullery assisting the

Harry Ullery (*top*) and Detective Keller DeRossette (*bottom*) of the Indianapolis City Police Department. *The Indianapolis Public Library.*

inspectors. The search warrants directed the men to search for torn pieces of paper matching the Black Hand letters and a roll of copper from the Scott mausoleum.

At precisely 10:00 a.m. on April 13, 1911, postal inspectors, assisted by local law enforcement, entered the lobby of the State Life Building in downtown Indianapolis. They severed the telegraph wires and police and telegraph call boxes before climbing the stairs to the Perkins office. Upon entering the office, they were met by branch manager John Ross and Walter Perkins, with Perkins immediately being placed under arrest as the charges were read to him. Gilbert Perkins and operative George Henderson arrived minutes later, and Deputy Marshal Rankin placed the elder Perkins under arrest, requesting all documents from the Perkinses in their possession.

Gilbert Perkins handed over several papers and an envelope to Inspector Woltz, who secured the items into a larger envelope. As both men were escorted from the office by U.S. marshals, Gilbert Perkins told the inspectors

The State Life Building in downtown Indianapolis, where the Perkins Union Detective Agency office was located. *Library of Congress.*

the envelope he surrendered contained private papers and requested its return, which was denied.

As Inspector Cleary requested all files related to the mausoleum case, George Henderson turned for the door but was stopped by Detective DeRossette. Henderson, raising his hands in the air, told the men that if Perkins was wrong he "didn't want to be mixed up in it."

Entering Gilbert Perkins's private office, John Ross stopped the inspectors and refused to turn over the documents requested until presented with a search warrant. After the warrant was shown, Ross reluctantly retrieved the documents, which were passed over to Inspector Hutches.

After departing the agency's office, inspectors engaged in a brief search of Perkins's Indianapolis home at 2004 Alabama Street but failed to locate any additional evidence. On the lawmen's return to the government building, they were greeted by Gilbert Perkins and his son, again asking for the return of his private papers.

Inspector Hutches again refused, telling Perkins the men did not have the opportunity to review the documents.

"Perkins," Inspector Woltz later recalled, "appeared very anxious and wrought up over the fact that we would not give him the envelope."

"You need to get these papers out of Indiana immediately," Inspector Cleary warned Hutches after the inspectors were informed Perkins had started legal preparations to regain possession of the documents he turned over.

Fearing the courts in Indiana would order the documents returned before an examination was made, all papers were placed in a suitcase under Inspector Ela's supervision, with the key given to another inspector to ensure its integrity. Dashing around the office in preparation to leave, the men set off for the railroad station to board the last train to Columbus, Ohio, in a race against time.

—※—

In Philadelphia, Pennsylvania, around the same time Gilbert Perkins and his son were arrested in Indianapolis, Postal Inspector Arthur Furner telephoned Charles Franklin in his office, asking if Inspector James Cortelyou could visit, as he wished to speak with him. Franklin agreed. After Cortelyou was told Franklin was in his office and agreed to talk, Furner and Cortelyou, assisted by Inspector W.S. Ryan and Deputy Marshal Meyer, left for the Perkins Agency office in the Pennsylvania building.

After exchanging pleasantries, Cortelyou requested Franklin's presence at his office in the federal building to discuss important matters. Franklin agreed, notifying his clerk he would return within two hours. Once at Cortelyou's office, the inspector requested a stenographer, telling Franklin he had questions he wanted to ask, with his clerk recording a transcript.

Franklin obliged without hesitation, and both men conversed for almost three hours as Franklin recited his employment with the Perkins Agency and previous work as a detective in Erie, acknowledging his license had been revoked because of an article published in Charles Strong's newspaper, the *Erie Dispatch*. Discussing the mausoleum case, Franklin received a telephone call from Harry Perkins telling him to start for Erie at once and to bring an operative. Franklin also provided extensive details of the investigation and confirmed he left for Philadelphia on February 13, only later learning of the agency's dismissal from the case.

Cortelyou asked Franklin to write on four pieces of paper as he dictated from two letters, with two in pencil and two in pen.

"I will write as many as you like," Franklin said contentedly.

After Franklin completed the dictations, the federal officers treated him to lunch. Returning to Cortelyou's office, as the men passed the Philadelphia Record building, Franklin asked Cortelyou if the paper he held was the original letter mailed to the Strongs.

"Which paper?" Cortelyou asked.

"The one with the irregular edges," Franklin said, motioning his hand, tracing the contours of the torn edge.

Cortelyou said the letter was a tracing. What alarmed him the most, however, was that Franklin had denied any cognizance of the letters during his questioning. Franklin's statements to Cortelyou indicated direct knowledge of the letters and their contents.

When Cortelyou concluded his questioning, Franklin stood up to leave but was told he was under arrest. After the charges were read, Franklin, who

Above: Downtown Pittsburgh. *Library of Congress*.

Opposite: Postal inspector James T. Cortelyou. *From the* Philadelphia Inquirer.

appeared stunned, briefly telephoned his attorney before being shepherded to an arraignment before a U.S. commissioner.

That night, Inspectors Ela, Woltz, Hutches and Cookson arrived in Columbus, Ohio, and immediately set off for Inspector Cookson's office in the federal building. There, Woltz and Hutches unlocked the suitcase, inspecting the large envelope that contained the papers from Gilbert Perkins. Opening the envelope, Hutches also spotted the small envelope that held a return card from the Reed House in Erie. Woltz told Hutches he better examine the contents, and as Hutches opened the envelope, two pieces of paper fell onto the floor.

Woltz pointed at the papers triumphantly.

"Ed, Ed!" Woltz cried out. "I guess we have got our connection, get your letter!"

Hutches grabbed one of the Black Hand letters, laying it out onto the table before matching the torn edge with the pieces of paper. They both fit perfectly. Just as Gilbert Perkins had predicted, when the person responsible for writing the letters was found, on them would be the torn pieces of papers from the Black Hand letters.

The inspectors, alive with excitement, telegraphed Inspector Oldfield in Pittsburg of their discovery.

Oldfield ordered the inspectors to leave at once for Pittsburg.

In smog-filled downtown Pittsburg, something strange was going on at the federal courthouse, where it looked "as if government agents were being massed for a big effort."[20] A dozen agents were inside the office of Postal Inspector George Craighead and joined by Captain John Washer of the U.S. Secret Service. As the men entered and exited the building, they declined to comment to a growing crowd of reporters.

Then came the news, first as whispers, among the reporters—an arrest in the Black Hand investigation involving the Strong family in Erie.

With lightning speed, the news traveled north to the shores of Lake Erie. When he learned of the arrest, Chief Wagner was not surprised. Later asked about the involvement of the department in connection to the arrests, Wagner's reply was minimal: "The end is not yet."

A staff correspondent from the *Erie Daily Times* picked up news about the arrest of the Perkinses in Indianapolis and phoned authorities there and in Pittsburg, confirming the reports. Just before 9:00 p.m., as crowds poured out of the Colonial theater, they came upon a group of barefoot newspaper boys shrieking with excitement and "staggering under the weight of large bundles of extra editions of The Times."[21]

"Extra-Extra, Times Extra!" the boys gamboled under the blazing theater marquee. "All about the arrest of Perkins detectives for an attempt to blackmail the Strongs!"

Crowds swarmed the newsboys, amassing so large that the street in front of the theater was blocked to vehicle traffic. Within minutes, all papers sold out, with "knots of people"[22] clustered around every newsboy and those with newspapers, devouring every detail.

Those who purchased papers gave nice bonuses to the youngsters.

"Gee, I never made so much coin in my life before!" one boy shrieked with a toothy grin.

On State Street, a similar scene played out with crowds bunched around every streetlamp and illuminated storefront. Another edition was announced forty-five minutes later and carried an updated story of the sensational arrests. Among the crowd were the rich and poor, prominent attorneys, businessmen and local officials. As the excitement reached its zenith, one of the Strongs' automobiles stopped against the curb at State and Eighth Streets; someone jumped out and purchased several copies of the *Times*.

In a strange twist, the Strongs learned of the arrests through the *Erie Daily Times*, which had again outscooped their own papers.

A cool breeze dawdled about the city as the crowds outside the *Times*'s building on East Tenth Street lingered into the early morning hours.

"People were on the street, they wanted to know about the Indianapolis arrests." The *Times* chuffed, "It was the Daily Times that gave them the news. It was a record-breaker in point of sales."

Regarding the arrests, the *Times* wrote:

> *If one-half is true, that is alleged against the Perkins detective agency, the Strongs are certainly playing in the hardest kind of luck. If the story that is going proves to be true, it is to be hoped the Strongs will have courage enough to put such an alleged traitorous agency out of business forever.*

On the morning of April 14, 1911, a dense blanket of fog clung to the Monongahela valley as the squad of postal inspectors arrived in Pittsburg, later meeting with Inspectors Craighead and Oldfield in the office of Secret Service captain Washer, joined by another inspector, George Tate, from Youngstown, Ohio.

Oldfield laid out all the Black Hand letters before the inspectors on a large table, carefully matching the letters with corresponding torn pieces of paper.

Pittsburgh, Pennsylvania. *Library of Congress.*

All other documents from Indianapolis were turned over to Oldfield and remained in his possession. At the same time, in Erie, Secret Service agents descended on the city, triggering the assumption more arrests would occur in that city.

Approached by a *Times* reporter about Gilbert Perkins's arrest, a prominent attorney in Erie admitted he was dumbstruck by the events: "I cannot understand why Gilbert Perkins would undertake a thing of that kind. I know for a fact that he has done a large business and has many profitable clients." The attorney added, "I know fully well that he had trouble with the government authorities years ago, but he was the last person I would have suspected of attempting to blackmail Mr. Strong. But then the secret service people don't make very many mistakes."

That afternoon, arriving at his office in the Fitzsimmons building in downtown Pittsburg, Gilbert Perkins emphatically denied the charges. News of the arrest of Charles Franklin was also just starting to spread in that city and Erie.

"I never wrote an anonymous letter in my life," Perkins said. "It will be found that the government agents have proceeded on information received from rival detective agencies. You know what happened almost 1,900 years ago on this good Friday? Well, this is persecution, too."

In Erie, Postal Inspector Craighead exited a lengthy conference with Oldfield and his squad of inspectors, exhibiting confidence when questioned by reporters.

"We worked up our own evidence. Post office inspectors obtained search warrants, and at the same hour yesterday visited the branch agency of the Perkins bureau in Indianapolis and Philadelphia, and examined the premises." Craighead added, "The officers took no chance of collusion. The moment they entered the offices they severed the telephone wires and cut out the 'buzzers' and police and telegraph call boxes."

Asked about Perkins and Franklin proclaiming their innocence, Craighead issued a more "sinister" response: "I bet $1,000 I will make them look sick."

On the afternoon of the fifteenth, Charles Franklin returned to his office in Philadelphia, besieged by reporters.

"I was not arrested," Franklin yelled. "Put me down as saying that I will neither confirm nor deny the arrest. You had better see the government about it. You see how we are placed. I can't talk about this matter."

Franklin's denial, according to the *Erie Daily Times*, was because of the various branches of the Perkins Agency and the continuing risk that other operatives would be arrested in the future.

Franklin teased a bigger surprise in the coming days; however, when pressed for details, he refused to concede any information.

"It is a funny thing the government kept this arrest secret," Franklin smirked. "Do they always do that in Philadelphia?"

In the absence of Inspector Cortelyou, J. Whitaker Thomson, a U.S. district attorney, refused to comment on Franklin's arrest or additional arrests, with every inspector in the Philadelphia office instructed to keep quiet on the matter. In Pittsburg, U.S. District Attorney John H. Jordan was more than happy to discuss the next steps he intended to take before presenting the case before a grand jury.

"We know who wrote the letters and know where they were written," Jordan said. "The quality of paper used in writing the 'Black Hand' letters was an important clue to the government. We have traced this paper and also know where it was purchased."

Jordan confirmed eight postal inspectors were working nonstop to secure further evidence. When asked about the possibility of further arrests, Jordan declined to comment.

"Any in Erie?" a reporter prodded.

"Erie is playing an important part in this entire investigation and it may be that the developments from that city will cause further surprises. More, many more, were implicated in this matter than the public have any idea," Jordan said. "When the whole matter is made public, the people of Erie will

United States District Attorney John H. Jordan, photographed in his office in Pittsburgh. *From the* Pittsburgh Post.

have more than one sensation. More than that cannot be published with safety now."

Not far from Jordan's office, Gilbert Perkins and his son Harry were engaged in deep consultations about their defense in the case. Gilbert Perkins later released a statement: "We have thought over this matter last evening and this morning. We are innocent of the charge brought against us as we are of the opinion now that when the case is fought by us and the jury has heard the evidence we will be honorably acquitted. We are of the opinion the Federal authorities have made a mistake. That is all."

The arrests in the Black Hand letter case created further undue excitement in Erie, with the *Erie Daily Times* revealing the arrival of three U.S. Secret Service agents to work alongside Postmaster Isador Sobel to secure further evidence. Other sources, with "excellent authority," claimed warrants already issued to other unnamed persons, and a mysterious woman in Erie, long sought after by federal agents for her involvement, was unable to be located.

As the yellow journalism spiraled out of control, Franklin spoke freely to an *Erie Daily Times* correspondent in Philadelphia:

> I am mystified and at a loss as to what these charges mean. I know that I have not done anything out of the way, and I have the greatest confidence in my superiors. Why the crime committed against the Strong tomb affected me almost as strongly as it did any of the members of that family. I went up there and worked on the case back to this city to attend matters here. I would willingly now devote my life to finding out who committed that crime. When I learned by reading of it in the newspapers of the sending of that note to Mrs. Strong I felt that it was a particularly dastardly joke, if it was a joke. Then to have this come on top of it makes me feel might bad. I can tell you. I know members of the Strong family, and I want their respect.

Asked if it was true all bodies from the mausoleum were accounted for, Franklin deflected, only commenting that he supported Annie Strong's statement released in the *Herald* about the discovery of Anna McCollum's body. Those in Erie were primed with excitement for the trial that was to follow. Inspector Oldfield, relentless in his search for more evidence, traveled to Cleveland, Pittsburg, Philadelphia and other cities in an attempt to tie up loose ends.

—⁕—

On April 25, 1911, a typewritten postcard addressed to Charles Strong arrived at the office of the *Erie Dispatch*. The postcard read:

> *Dear Sir: - I note by your dirty sheet of this morning you are crawfishing. Criticizing an act and making a fool of yourself and the Morning Dispatch are two different things. Now be a man and stand by your assertions made from time to time. The Dispatch has been a frost ever since it was started by its bad management and I don't believe you will improve the condition of the same. I believe in roasting poor shows and give credit to good ones, but you have not done so.*
> *A FRIEND OF THE PUBLIC.*

Made aware of the postcard's existence by his secretary, Strong arrived and viewed the postcard, deciding to notify Inspector Oldfield. Later that day, following a meeting in Strong's office, Oldfield took possession of the postcard and sought out the assistance of Assistant Postmaster Brainerd, who confirmed the postcard was picked up by a postal carrier from a south Erie mailbox before it was processed through the South Erie Post Office.

By early May, Oldfield's investigation revealed a suspect: Achatious Harry "Hutze" Knoll, an Erie native and well-known cornetist and musician. Growing up, Knoll belonged to the Knoll family of gifted musicians and was a member of the Knolls Band in the 1870s. A concert virtuoso and renowned composer who entertained all over the world, Knoll was a local celebrity and fervent supporter of Erie's music community.

On Tuesday, May 2, 1911, Oldfield and Brainerd lumbered down the tree-lined sidewalk until they reached 314 West Tenth Street, the handsome, two-story brick residence of Hutze Knoll. After knocking at the front door, both men were graciously welcomed inside, with Oldfield introducing himself, asking Knoll if he had recently sent any postcards to Charles Strong.

Knoll denied mailing any postcards, particularly to Charles Strong.

Pacing around Knoll's sitting room, admiring music memorabilia and photographs that adorned the walls, Oldfield asked Knoll if he owned a typewriter. Knoll confirmed he did, and after Oldfield asked if he could view the typewriter, Knoll led both men to his second-floor office where a typewriter sat on a wood desk.

Oldfield entered, scanning the room, his gaze focusing on the drawers of the desk. He turned to Knoll, motioning to the typewriter, and asked if he had any postal cards. Knoll said there were none in the house; however, Oldfield replied quickly that a small card or piece of paper would suffice. Brushing past Oldfield, Knoll tugged on one of the drawers, revealing a bundle of blank postcards fastened together with a rubber band.

"What luck," Oldfield said with a sly smile to Brainerd, stepping aside. "Those will do."

Oldfield asked Knoll to take a seat in front of the typewriter as he dictated a message.

"Charles H. Strong, Esq.," Oldfield rambled, as Knoll's fingers thumped against the keys. "President the Morning Dispatch."

Knoll paused, refusing to type anything further. Oldfield reached over Knoll's shoulder, yanking the postcard from the typewriter cylinder. Brainerd and Oldfield instantly pointed out defects in the letters, matching the postcard received on April 25. Oldfield told Knoll he was confiscating the typewriter and hours later presented a complaint against Knoll before U.S. Commissioner Frank Grant, who issued a warrant for Knoll's arrest.

Knoll was arrested at his home later that day by Deputy Marshal Robert Firman.

Oldfield again managed to fly under the radar, and the *Erie Daily Times* became aware of Knoll's arrest eleven days later when reporters learned he was scheduled for a preliminary hearing on May 16 at the U.S. Federal Courthouse in Erie. At his preliminary hearing on the afternoon of May 16, 1911, Knoll was bound over to a grand jury in July and released on his own bond.

On the afternoon of April 28, 1911, Charles Franklin was arraigned in Philadelphia with Uriah P. Rossiter of Erie and Horace Paulderman of Philadelphia as counsel. For reporters, the preliminary hearing revealed the evidence against Franklin and the Perkinses.

The government testified the Black Hand letters were written on paper from the Perkins Agency office, and the defendants involved—Gilbert Perkins, his son Walter and Charles Franklin—conspired to obtain employment from the Strongs in writing the threatening letters.

Charles Strong testified that afternoon about his discussions with Gilbert Perkins, who assured him an arrest would be made, promising that "the torn pieces of these Black Hand letters would be found on the person apprehended."

Inspector James Woltz testified about the raid and papers surrendered by Gilbert Perkins, visibly showing the torn pieces of paper matching against the jagged edges of the Black Hand letters.

Postmaster Sobel testified about discussions with Gilbert Perkins and the letters.

Inspector Cortelyou produced the standard letters written by Charles Franklin, two in pencil and two in ink. Handwriting expert William Pengelly of Columbus, Ohio, testified he believed the writer of the standard letters, Franklin, was also the writer of the Black Hand letters. The torn pieces of paper and Black Hand letters, reported the *Erie Daily Times*, created a "dramatic climax" during the hearing.

After attempts from his attorneys to rattle witnesses for the government stalled, Franklin declined to testify and was ordered held under a heavy bail in the amount of $2,500, with his trial scheduled to be held in Erie in July.

As the month of April drew to a close, attorneys hired by Gilbert Perkins, W.H.S. Thomson and Charles A. O'Brien, solicitor for the City of Pittsburg, aided by Frank Thomson and Thomas Cochran, lobbied members of Congress with a petition to investigate postal inspectors involved in the Black Hand case, attempting to have the trial postponed.

The son of a well-known doctor in Beaver County, Pennsylvania, William Henry Seward Thomson graduated from Washington and Jefferson College and was admitted to the bar in Cabell County, West Virginia, before returning to Beaver County, where he started his own business. After his arrival in Pittsburg in 1894, Thomson became one of the city's most well-respected attorneys.

Charles A. O'Brien, born in the south Pittsburg neighborhood of Carrick, graduated from St. Vincent's College in Wheeling, West Virginia, in 1872. After his graduation, O'Brien was admitted to the Allegheny bar and practiced as an attorney until 1903, when he co-founded the firm O'Brien and Ashley with attorney Charles W.

Defense attorney W.H.S. Thomson. *From the* Pittsburgh Daily Post.

Ashley. The partnership continued until 1909, when O'Brien was appointed city solicitor for Pittsburg.

The petition, signed by Gilbert B. Perkins, Walter W. Perkins, Charles Franklin, Annette Thomas and John Drew, claimed the Perkins Agency had operated for thirty-three years and never violated laws within the United States and declared postal inspectors fraudulently, and falsely, brought charges against operatives of the agency. The petitioners labeled the arrest of Gilbert Perkins, his son and Charles Franklin as illegal and an invasion of their rights as citizens, suggesting Franklin had been subjected to the "third degree" and accusing the William J. Burns Detective Agency of assisting government agents in a "cover up" against the detective agency.

Defense attorney Charles A. O'Brien. *From the* Pittsburgh Press.

Perkins's petition, however, was widely dismissed by those in Congress and the House of Representatives.

Further details about the case continued to leak to the public as the trial in July steadily approached, revealed through the *Erie Daily Times*. "BULLET HOLE THROUGH WINDOW AT EDISON PLANT," expatiated the *Times* on May 3, 1911, laying out the evidence against the Perkinses and Franklin, supporting the government's belief the Perkins Agency was motivated in seeking additional work for money.

Sometime during the first week of May, Horace N. Thayer, owner of H.N. Thayer Carriage Works, received a threatening letter from the "Black Hand" demanding sixty-five dollars in unmarked bills be deposited in a location where "no policeman or detective would be tolerated." The letter also instructed Thayer to place an envelope bearing a cross at the entrance where the money was to be placed and write the letters "O.K."

Failure to comply with the writer's demand, the missive insisted, would result in Thayer's home being blown to pieces. Thayer's first instinct was to pay the ransom because of the small amount. When he later presented the issue before postal inspectors and police, he was told not to pay because additional demands would likely follow.

A second letter, similar to the first, arrived a week later. Thayer then met with Chief Wagner, who assured him he would look into the matter. On the day of the reported handoff, Thayer phoned Chief Wagner to discuss what plans were in place to capture those responsible. Thayer's concerns were met with annoyed indignation from Wagner, resolute in his promises that the matter was under control.

Unsatisfied, Thayer solicited assistance from others who discovered that not only had the blackmailers' demands not been met, but also Wagner instead placed a relative, Roundsman Andrew Wagner, in a nearby building as a lookout, instructing him not to follow through with the letters' instructions.

"The detective work that followed was about the rankest ever witnessed and as a result the writer of the two letters is still at liberty," attacked the *Times*, adding that Wagner's policy "has been to say little and put forth every effort to hold tight to his job."

Post office officials and police, especially Chief Wagner, refused to comment.

Editorial cartoon showing Gilbert Perkins, Harry Perkins and Charles Strong. Drawn by cartoonist Walter Kiedaisch of the *Erie Daily Times*. *Author's collection.*

"It is however true that the case when finally given to the public in its details will not vary much from what is here given in this evening's *Times*," predicted the *Times*.

On the morning of May 25, 1911, George Reid Yaple, editor for the *Times*, was approached by Chief Wagner, who engaged in a brutal verbal assault, telling Yaple he was "sick and tired of being criticised by the *Times*," and that if the criticism didn't cease, he and Yaple would "come together." Yaple told Wagner the *Times*'s reporting was based on information from a reliable source.

The *Times*, Yaple continued, "would continue to be conducted fearlessly, regardless of threats of personal violence by officials or others."

Later that day, the *Times* tore into Wagner in an expansive editorial:

> *For a chief of police who knows there are gambling dens running in open violation of the law, wide open on every hand; who has been unable to land a single grave-desecrator, or murderer, or Black-Hand writer, numerous as have been the offenses, to take exception to any kind of a criticism, shows the extreme littleness of the man holding such a big job.*

Wagner was also criticized in effigy by *Times* cartoonist Walter Kiedaisch.

Inspector Oldfield, assigned to the case despite the minimal demand of sixty-five dollars, vowed to "put forth as much effort" in the case as was done with the "Black Hand" case involving the Strongs.

With the trial nearly a month away, Harry Perkins issued a statement on the morning of June 15, 1911, in another attempt to galvanize support in opening an investigation against the Postal Inspection Service and Captain John Washer of the U.S. Secret Service:

> *Our petition is now in the hands of a Congressional committee and we feel certain that a very rigid investigation will be made as the Democrats who are now in charge of house affairs would deem it a great pleasure to expose loose methods in the post office department which has practically been under the control of the Republicans for some time.*

During one of his returns to Erie, Inspector Oldfield provided a rare interview to reporters, praising the work of postal inspectors who "acted within their legal rights" and confirmed no move was made until the evidence warranting it was properly secured. The government, Oldfield continued, was ready for trial and predicted the evidence produced would be the "best

The Chief—"I'm not to be criticised. See !"

Cartoon criticizing the Chief of Police Edward Wagner during the "Black Hand" case involving Horace Thayer. Drawn by cartoonist Walter Kiedaisch of the *Erie Daily Times*. *Author's collection.*

guarantee that the postal department had sufficient grounds on which to base their contentions."

When asked about Franklin and Perkins, who claimed their rights were violated, Oldfield smiled. "It is a farce," he retorted.

Charles Franklin, also in Erie, engaged on his own journey to gather evidence for the upcoming trial and prepared for the return of his attorney, Uriah P. Rossiter, who was in Philadelphia, to help iron out Franklin's defense.

On June 28, 1911, Chairman William A. Ashbrook, of the house committee on expenditures in the post office department, responded to Perkins's petition, confirming the matter against the Postal Inspection Service would be investigated after the courts in Erie disposed of the case against the Perkins agency.

Gilbert Perkins and his attorneys, however, had another trick up their sleeves.

—m—

At 10:00 p.m. on July 1, 1911, Detective Sergeant Richard Crotty of the City of Erie Police Department arrived at the Reed House and arrested private detective Thomas J. Dempsey. When Dempsey inquired about the warrant, Crotty informed the charges claimed he used the U.S. mails for improper purposes in sending threatening letters to General Charles Miller, president of the Galena Oil Company in Franklin, Pennsylvania.

✦✦✦✦✦✦✦✦✦✦✦✦✦✦✦✦✦
✦   ✦
✦ **DETECTIVE ON**   ✦
✦   **WHOM PERKINS**   ✦
✦   **PUTS THE BLAME**   ✦
✦   ✦
✦✦✦✦✦✦✦✦✦✦✦✦✦✦✦✦✦

The charges were directed by one of his rivals, Gilbert Perkins.

After Venango County sheriff Frank Williams arrived around 1:00 a.m., Dempsey was swiftly transported to the city of Franklin, arriving there several hours later. When Dempsey appeared before a local alderman that morning with his attorney, Homer R. Blair, he furnished bail and his preliminary hearing was scheduled for Wednesday, July 5, at 10:00 a.m.

Exiting the alderman's office, Dempsey spoke to reporters, denying he was responsible for sending threatening letters in that city.

"I never even saw the letter and know nothing whatever about it," Dempsey protested. "My arrest is nothing but a 'frame-up,' planned and carried through by Gilbert B. Perkins,

Private Detective Thomas J. Dempsey. *From the* Erie Daily Times.

head of the Perkins Detective Agency, of Pittsburg. He and his principal assistant have been charged by the postal authorities with having sent Black Hand letters to the Charles H. Strong family in Erie and they have sought to throw suspicion from themselves upon me by causing my arrest for the Miller letter. None of the local authorities or General Miller has anything to do with this prosecution, and I doubt if any of them believe I had any hand in the letter writing."

The *Erie Daily Times*, reporting on Dempsey's arrest, revealed immediately after the arrest of the Perkinses and Franklin in April that the agency concocted a plan to connect Dempsey with the threatening Black Hand letters in Franklin in an attempt to derail the government's case in Erie.

Dempsey, born in the Irish village of Castleplunket, immigrated to America in 1890 and settled in Pittsburg, working as a contractor before joining the Sixty-Ninth Infantry Regiment, one of twelve national guard units from New York federalized for service during the Spanish-American War. While stationed in Florida, Dempsey contracted malaria, which affected his kidneys and developed into rheumatism. Following several hospitalizations, Dempsey went AWOL, later returning to his regiment, and was court-martialed. He was found guilty and sentenced to hard labor for six months; however, he was only briefly confined before his release from active duty in 1899.

After returning to Pittsburg, Dempsey moved to Venango County and was employed with the railroad before becoming a detective with the Franklin Police Department. He later engaged in work as a private detective in both Franklin and Erie.

For Inspector Oldfield and those involved in the Black Hand investigation, Dempsey's arrest was expected. Since the case in Franklin involved charges not brought by postal inspectors, the government's plans to proceed with the trial in July remained undeterred.

By July 8, 1911, Charles Franklin had returned to Erie to complete arrangements for his trial. Charles A. O'Brien engaged in preparations to appear before the House Committee on Expenditures in the Post Office to again demand an investigation in response to the raiding of the Perkins Agency offices and seizure of documents from those offices, declaring the government had colluded with the Burns Detective Agency.

Speculation reigned among the public, fueled by attorneys for both sides, as plans were drawn for trial. It was certain Thomas Dempsey's arrest would figure prominently in the defense's panic-stricken attempts to deflect blame from the Perkinses and Franklin, altogether proving to

State Street in downtown, Erie, Pennsylvania. This view looks north. Note the towering federal building in the distance. *Erie, Pennsylvania: An Industrial and Summer Resort City.*

be the defense's worst-kept secret, with many witnesses appearing at Dempsey's preliminary hearing in Franklin expected to appear during the Perkins-Franklin trial.

Members of the Perkins Agency were openly giddy with excitement, eagerly telling all who would listen that they intended to "fasten" the Black Hand letters in Erie to Dempsey.

Defense attorneys for the Perkinses expected to have at least twenty witnesses from various parts of the country, with the government expecting just as many, if not more. Newspaper correspondents began gravitating to Erie as witnesses were expected to start arriving in the city on July 14, with a majority expected to arrive up until Sunday, the sixteenth, the day before the government presented the case before the federal grand jury.

Thomas Dempsey, arriving at the Union Depot in Erie on July 10 with his attorney, told waiting reporters his arrest by the Perkinses was "the biggest outrage ever perpetrated by the Perkins Union Detective agency."

"When the time comes, I will show that I am entirely innocent,"[23] Dempsey said, adding he was not charged by federal authorities and expected to be called as a government witness in the Perkins-Franklin trial, almost guaranteeing the Perkinses would allege he wrote the Black Hand letters to Charles Strong.

"There will be something doing if they do; somebody is going to get in wrong." Dempsey smiled, "And you can just lay a little bet that it won't be your Uncle Dempsey."

6

SENSATIONAL AFFAIRS

alfway through the month of June 1911, Erie continued to flourish with feverishness and entertainment. Saloons and businesses filled to capacity, streets were cluttered in all directions and droves of men, women and children congregated on the sidewalks—all mashed together against the bustle of the downtown trolley line and public sentience, with scorching temperatures at nightfall causing inhabitants to forage for a much-needed crisp reprieve.

On the night of June 30, 1911, Philadelphia & Erie Train No. 41, while rounding Five Mile curve on the outskirts of the city, was boarded by armed bandits who soon engaged in a furious gun battle with members of the crew, resulting in only a few minor injuries.

The cadaverous heat wave continued to pound the northeastern United States, with hospitals in Pittsburg filled to capacity with heat-stricken patients and other cities reporting deaths from high temperatures. By the morning of July 3, 1911, temperatures in Erie were stagnant at eighty-seven degrees, considerably cooler than the one hundred degrees in Pittsburg.

Faring better than most cities in the country, in part because of the winds drifting off Lake Erie, Erie remained pragmatic. At the corner of East Tenth and Peach Streets, the cornerstone of the YMCA building was laid before a large crowd, with the scorching heat forcing speakers for the ceremony to stand in a sheltered automobile across from the building.

On July 4, 1911, temperatures reached a record-high ninety-five degrees. The Erie Fire Department called every man within its ranks, nearly one hundred, to duty in preparation for Fourth of July festivities. Pleasure seekers cluttered the beaches below Waldameer Park and grazed throughout its spacious tree groves. Trolley cars rattled through the city, loaded to capacity. The sweltering heat and lure of fireworks failed to deter roughly three thousand sightseers, "fanning desperately to keep the heated air in motion," from cramming inside the "Tabernacle," straining "their ears to catch the magic words" of evangelist Billy Sunday. Sunday delivered his sermon on "the unpardonable sin,"[24] although relief from the lingering heat wave, promised by the weather bureau in Washington, D.C., would not arrive for some time.

"Erie is not half as bad as she is painted," Billy Sunday declared before departing on July 10. "Let anything bad happen and the world is told about it in glaring headlines in the papers."

When Sunday's campaign ended, a record 8,000 men and women had packed the Tabernacle. During his six-week stay in the city, an audience of 350,000 ventured to listen to Sunday's passionate sermons.

By the afternoon of July 14, 1911, brothers Charles and George Martz were arrested at the Perkins Union Detective Agency office in Pittsburg and charged with conspiracy on charges presented by Gilbert Perkins. Both brothers later went before a local alderman, were found in default of $5,000 bail and committed to the Allegheny County Jail to await a preliminary hearing.

Perkins defended his actions, insisting Charles Martz, a former operative and railroad detective, confessed he was the chief witness for the government

The Tabernacle, constructed at the corner of West Twelfth and Myrtle Streets, where Billy Sunday preached, with a capacity to hold seven thousand persons with standing room for an additional three thousand. *From the* Erie Daily Times.

during his upcoming trial and propositioned that for $500 his brother, George, "might forget a portion of the testimony" against the defendants. Because of this, Perkins explained, he had no other choice than to charge the brothers with conspiracy.

Hearing about the Martz brothers' arrests, District Attorney Jordan sent Department of Justice agent Harry O'Bleness to visit the brothers in the Allegheny County Jail. George Martz, O'Bleness reported to Jordan, maintained his innocence, adamant he was lured to Perkins's office on July 13 and questioned about evidence and his brother's rumored testimony for the government. When the brothers were asked to return the next day, they were arrested.

"This move will avail the Perkins people naught," Jordan said. "Neither will it prevent Charles B. Martz from giving his testimony, which is of a very important character, when the Perkins and Franklin cases are called for trial in the Federal Court at Erie on Next Monday."

District Attorney Jordan appeared before Judge James Young of the U.S. Court in Pittsburg on the morning of July 15, presenting a release on a writ of habeas corpus, which, although granted, did not include Martz's release from the Allegheny County Jail. Plans were made for Martz to be transported to Erie on the morning of Monday, July 17, and housed in the Erie County Jail during his stay there.

Learning the petition for habeas corpus had been granted, Perkins was unmoved but pleased Martz was not released from the conspiracy charge, all while insisting he acted on advice from attorneys who confirmed he had "very good grounds for charging conspiracy."

On July 16, 1911, Gilbert Perkins was interviewed by the *Erie Daily Times*. Perkins, the reporter wrote, appeared pale, drawn and extremely nervous, having "aged considerably since visiting Erie that past February." A reporter for the *Erie Evening Herald*, who later ambled about the lengthy corridors of the Reed House with Perkins, wrote: "The faces of the Perkins' look careworn and give evidence of the worry and strain under which they have been for several months past."

Despite declining heath, the senior Perkins remained optimistic, telling the *Herald*: "Not only will we prove our own innocence, but we will show who is guilty of writing the Black Hand letters to Strong. The post office people know we did not write the letters and in my opinion they know who the guilty party is, but still they are prosecuting us." Perkins also spoke of "skeletons" in the Strongs' closet, threatening, if necessary, they would be "taken from the closet" and displayed during the trial.

Operatives from the Perkins Agency established their headquarters at the Reed House and New Commercial Hotel. At the Reed House, they were joined by government officials, including those from the U.S. Secret Service, with the "two contending forces swarmed about the lobby of the hotel and rumors of all sorts were afloat."[25]

As the sun that night was drenched in an explosive orange hue, government officials were closely shadowed by Perkins operatives and vice versa, in eager anticipation for the terrific legal fight to follow.

"No stone has been left unturned," wrote the *Erie Evening Herald*. "All manner of sensations are promised for the coming week during the trial."

The case against Gilbert Perkins and Charles Franklin was scheduled at the federal courthouse in downtown Erie at 2:00 p.m. on Monday, July 17, 1911, with a trial beginning immediately should an indictment be returned. U.S. District Attorney John Jordan announced charges against

The U.S. Federal Courthouse in downtown Erie. *Erie County Historical Society at the Hagen History Center.*

Walter Perkins and Annette Thomas, the Perkinses' stenographer, would not be presented, but that did not rule out the government calling on them on cross-examination as witnesses.

Judges James Young and Charles Orr arrived from Pittsburg around noon and engaged in a luncheon before traveling to the federal courthouse. Detectives from the Burns Detective Agency also arrived that morning. Gilbert Perkins, weeks before, had served members of the agency with subpoenas to appear for the defense; however, Burns operatives were later told their presence was not necessary, leading to continued speculation that if they testified, it would be on behalf of the government. Also arriving were postal inspectors, newspaper correspondents and staff photographers, and throngs of onlookers staked out the crowded platforms of the Union Depot hoping to catch a glimpse of the arrival of Charles Martz that afternoon.

Outside the federal courthouse, crowds congested the entrance, extending across the street to Central Park as they waited. The *Erie Daily Times*, in its morning edition, regurgitated a lengthy summary of the mausoleum case with photographs and sensational details.

Judges Who Are Presiding In U. S. Court Here This Week.

Judges Charles Orr (*left*) and James S. Young, photographed inside the Federal Building. *From the* Erie Daily Times.

Grand jurors drawn for the afternoon session were notified to report at 2:00 p.m. Because two courts would be operating simultaneously, the circuit courtroom would be used for the other trials. With the courthouse's small rooms, attendants were advised to take extensive measures to prevent overcrowding. By the time the afternoon session began, the courtroom was filled to capacity, spilling out into the corridors, with those unable to gain admittance pushed out as the courtroom doors slammed shut. The court crier announced the arrival of Judges Young and Orr as they took their seats on the bench.

Clerk William T. Lindsey and U.S. Commissioner Grant announced the names of the twenty-four jurors, who took their places inside the jury box when called. The first juror, J.E. Abbott, a jury commissioner from Southport, would have been foreman, but being a double amputee, he was excused. W.H. Simmons, a prominent merchant from Clarks Mills, was appointed foreman of the grand jury.

After being administered the oath of office by Clerk Lindsey, the jurors listened as Judge Young presented his charge, proclaiming a lengthy explanation was gratuitous because the oath was self-explanatory. Young reminded the men of their duties, emphasizing the dignity and importance of being drawn as a U.S. juror.

"Liberty is such a precious thing," Judge Young boomed, "that no man can be tried for an offense against the United States until a United States grand jury has passed upon his offense and therefore the duties are very important."

Then Judge Young announced the government would present the case before the grand jury and would regulate their hours of meeting, with all jurors considering all cases promptly.

At 2:30 p.m., the grand jurors were removed from the courtroom by Tipstaff George Marvin to allow petit jurors for the other civil and criminal cases to be called. Arriving at the courtroom on the fourth floor, District Attorney Jordan presented a brief opening statement before calling Charles Strong as the first witness. Several prominent witnesses followed, including postal inspectors. In total, the grand jury listened to twelve witnesses before they decided to retire and report their findings. The court waited until 4:00 p.m. before excusing all jurors for the day.

Outside, the crowd that remained, quick to devour the latest updates, learned they would have to wait for a possible indictment. The following morning, members of the grand jury were polled, but only thirteen were present when called on. Because the law required sixteen jurors, with twelve necessary to agree on a true bill, a brief recess was called to search for the

ATTENDING SESSION OF COURT

Left to right: Warden Lewis of the Allegheny County jail; Captain John Washer of the Secret Service; and W.H. Simmons, foreman of the grand jury. *From the* Erie Daily Times.

missing jurors, who were later found on the fourth floor, waiting for the others so they could "arrive in the court as one body."[26]

After a second roll call, twenty grand jurors were present.

Asked by Clerk Lindsey if the grand jury had any presentment, Foreman Simmons handed four typewritten pages to Lindsey, who then handed the documents to Judges Young and Orr. A true bill[27] was announced against Gilbert Perkins and Charles Franklin, each charged with five counts:

First—That the defendants devised a scheme to defraud Charles H. Strong and his wife to obtain money under false pretense.

Second—That they used the United States post office as a means to effect the scheme to defraud. In this count is included a copy of the second letter received by Mr. Strong, which reached him on February 15.

Third—That the defendants on February 13 actually mailed in Erie a Black Hand letter addressed to Mr. Strong demanding $50,000.

Fourth—That on February 15 the defendants mailed in Erie a second Black Hand letter addressed to Chas. H. Strong.

Fifth—That the defendants conspired to defraud Mr. and Mrs. Strong in writing and mailing the two letters.

Language within the indictment also revealed evidence suggesting Perkins and Franklin were plotting to kidnap the Strongs' granddaughter, Thora Ronalds.

Charles A. O'Brien declared the defense did not have an opportunity to examine the Black Hand letters and asked for a delay until the letters could be properly perused, defending his request as material and important, believing it would take several hours. O'Brien claimed he requested permission to view the letters two weeks before but was informed by District Attorney Jordan such requests were not considered a practice in the U.S. Court, insinuating the government was withholding evidence until an indictment was returned.

District Attorney Jordan forcibly objected to the letters being allowed out of his possession, but was inclined to allow the defense an examination of the letters as long as they were in the custody of a representative of the United States District Attorney's Office, which was soon agreed upon.

In an attempt to secure as much time as possible to review the evidence, Charles O'Brien requested the jury be drawn but not sworn in until the afternoon session. Jordan argued against this, suggesting from the time

From left to right: Joseph Cashbaugh, George Oricson, Horace G. Dorsie, W. A. Frye, Wm. H. Graham, Thomas Boyle, Chas. A. Grimes, N. L. White, J. S. Mitchell, J. P. Russell, Chas. Graham, H. L. Crotty. —Photo by Times Staff Photographer.

Jurors for the Perkins-Franklin trial, photographed in front of the Federal Building in downtown Erie. *From the* Erie Daily Times.

jurors were sworn in until discharged, they would not be allowed to mingle indiscriminately within the crowds, tainting its credibility.

Judges Young and Orr announced a recess until 2:00 p.m., with District Attorney Jordan and one of his assistants retiring to the consultation room with defense attorneys to examine the letters. The jury list was then reviewed, with nearly all those drawn responding and expected to return that afternoon. It was learned during the recess that Charles O'Brien and W.H.S. Thomson would lead the defense with attorneys Rossiter and Thompson acting as consultants.

This conflicted with other reports indicating Rossiter and Cochran withdrew from the cases after a "split had occurred" the night before, despite Rossiter previously telling the *Erie Evening Herald* that attorneys for both defendants planned to work together.

During the recess, experts for the defense, assisted by Attorney O'Brien, conferred in the postal inspector's office, examining two of the letters in view of District Attorney Jordan and Inspector Arthur Furner, a process that lasted for more than two hours with the frequent usage of a microscope.

When court convened promptly at 2:00 p.m., Judge Young took up proceedings in the smaller courtroom, presiding over cases of counterfeiting, post office robbery, bankruptcy violation and national bank larceny with Judge Orr presiding over the Black Hand trial.

Despite the temporary setback, both sides announced they were prepared to move forward, with the defense primed to debate numerous technicalities and fight every point raised by the government as allowed. The jurors, who had been whittled down to twelve after review by the government and defense attorneys, were sworn in and took their place inside the jury box: George Arrison, Thomas Boyle, W.L. White, J.F. Russell, W.G. Fry, H.L. Crotty, W.H. Graham, Charles A. Grimes, Charles Graham, Horace G. Dorsie, Joseph Cashabaugh and J.S. Mitchell.

The trial of *United States v. Gilbert B. Perkins and Charles Franklin* had begun.

7

A DESECRATION REVISITED

T hick, stifling air permeated the congested courtroom as the sun gleamed through the windows. Seated at the government's table were U.S. District Attorney Jordan; his assistants, Robert M. Gibson and Harry S. Leydeck; Chief Postal Inspector James Cortelyou; and Inspector John Oldfield. In addition to the defendants, attorneys W.H.S. Thomson and Charles A. O'Brien, assisted by J.S. Wilson, an ex-judge from Beaver County, and Judge Wallace of Lawrence County populated the defense table.

Displayed in clear view were the infamous Black Hand letters and envelopes, enclosed in special glass cases.

"We will hew to the line," Judge Orr warned as he addressed the courtroom, "keeping out, in all the cases, extraneous testimony and unnecessary witnesses. This is not a circus, but one of the most serious courts in this country."

District Attorney Jordan announced the government was ready.

Before Judge Orr could respond, Charles A. O'Brien presented a motion to quash[28] the third count of the indictment, which was

Judge Charles P. Orr. *From the Pittsburgh Press.*

loudly objected to by Jordan. Judge Orr agreed to hear the defense's argument only for O'Brien to reverse course, with the motion overruled. Ralph Sterrett and Charles Brevillier of Erie were sworn in as official stenographers, and shortly before 3:00 p.m., District Attorney Jordan commenced his opening statement, approaching the jury: "Gentlemen, you are sworn to try, what is in my opinion an important case. It has come to the attention of the government authorities that certain things have been done through the United States mail, in violation of the laws regulating the post office."

Jordan described the discovery of the desecration of the Scott mausoleum on February 8, 1911, raising the four-page indictment before the jurors. "All of the defendants named in this indictment are detectives and are connected with the Perkins Union Detective agency that has its main office in the city of Pittsburg."

In meticulous and dramatic fashion, District Attorney Jordan spoke of the desperation of the Strongs in seeking an agency to assist in the investigation, hiring the Perkins Union Detective Agency from Pittsburg. With the arrival of Harry Perkins on February 9 and the defendants, Gilbert Perkins and Charles Franklin, on the following day, the Perkins detectives, Jordan continued, were unable to accomplish much and were aware their services would not be required much longer. "Then Gilbert Perkins had a talk with Mrs. Strong and told her she would receive threatening letters, demanding money," Jordan boomed, pointing to Perkins. "He told the same thing to Postmaster Sobel."

Parading each letter and its corresponding envelope, Jordan described the arrival of the first letter on February 13, reciting the contents loudly before the court. He promised, through the testimony of Postmaster Isador Sobel, that Perkins predicted the arrival of another letter, which came on February 15. Another conversation with Perkins, Jordan said, presented inconsistencies, strewn with spelling errors.

The paper, used in writing these letters was torn in a peculiar way as you will see and Mr. Perkins said that he thought the guilty party would be apprehended and when they were, this would be found in their possession. Gilbert Perkins left this city on or about February 18th. When he was arrested by United States marshals and post office inspectors at Indianapolis he was asked to show the contents of his pockets and in a large envelope was found a bank book, a codicil to his will and a sealed envelope bearing in the corner, the words "Reed House, Erie, Pa." In this were pieces of paper that fitted into the ragged edges of these letters.

"We will show this paper to you gentlemen and allow you to put it with the letters to see how well the ragged edges of this paper fit the ragged edges of the letter," Jordan continued. "We will show you by witnesses that Charles Franklin was in this city at the time of the mausoleum mystery and that he knew of the letters being received by Mr. Strong. We will show you that a large sized man purchased paper and envelopes at an Erie drug store that corresponds to the paper and envelopes used in writing the letters to Mr. Strong."

At 3:15 p.m., Conrad Klein, proprietor of the Reed House, was the first witness called. Klein confirmed the dates Gilbert Perkins and Charles Franklin registered at his hotel, with Franklin departing on February 13 and Perkins on the eighteenth, corresponding with the arrival of the first two supposed Black Hand letters.

Spectators vied for a look at Charles Strong when he was called and approached the stand. His wife, Annie, was seated in a corner of the courtroom, fanning herself while conversing with a friend and her daughter. Annie, a reporter wrote, was "deeply interested" in the trial and often lifted her lorgnette during her husband's testimony.

Following a brief introduction, Charles Strong recited the events of the evening of February 8. "We were sitting at dinner. It was about 7:30 o'clock, I believe, when someone telephoned to Mrs. Strong that the doors of the mausoleum had been broken open."

"Did you go to the mausoleum?" Jordan asked.

"Yes," Strong said. "When we got there the doors were open. We entered under the light of a lamp and found the place wrecked. One crypt was badly damaged and two others had been broken open and tools and levers thrown into the lid of the casket it contained. The debris was scattered all about the place. One coffin had been removed from a crypt and had been placed near the door. That coffin contained the body of my wife's mother."

The courtroom was riveted by Strong's testimony, teetering on the edge of their seats.

"Then what did you do?"

"Why, at first I was stunned. Then we went home, leaving a policeman on guard at the mausoleum. Arriving at home we discussed what should be done to catch the vandals. Mrs. Strong called up Mr. Stewart in New York. He is her legal adviser."

"What happened next?"

"After some discussion they agreed that it would be well to employ the Perkins Detective Agency. Mrs. Strong then called up Perkins at Pittsburg and she was told they would send a man immediately."

"Who came?"

"Harry Perkins."

"When?"

"The next day."

"How long did he remain?"

"I think Harry Perkins remained in Erie until the following Monday."

"When did Gilbert Perkins appear on the scene?"

"I think he appeared on Thursday, the 10th."

"What did he do when he first came?"

"I am not able to answer that because I didn't happen to be there."

"Did he have his interviews with you or your wife?"

"With my wife."

District Attorney Jordan showed Charles Strong the first Black Hand letter and envelope, asking Strong if he recognized it. Strong nodded, indicating it was the letter received on February 13.

"Did Mr. Perkins say anything to you about receiving a threatening letter before you received this?"

"Not to my recollection."

"What did you do with the letter?"

"I gave it to my wife to give to Perkins."

District Attorney Jordan displayed the letter from the fifteenth. Strong confirmed it was the letter given to his secretary, who was instructed to turn it over to Gilbert Perkins. Jordan completed his questions and sat down as Charles O'Brien stood up and began his cross-examination, immediately affirming Charles Strong never spoke to Gilbert Perkins about the potential of receiving threatening letters.

Strong confirmed this was true.

"You have already said you employed Perkins?"

"Yes."

"You have known Mr. Perkins a number of years?"

"I had known him. Yes, I had met Mr. Perkins."

"You had employed him before?"

"I object," Jordan interrupted. "The question is not material."

"Objection sustained," Judge Orr responded.

O'Brien asked Strong about the arrival of the Black Hand letters and the events that followed. Strong reaffirmed his prior testimony, confirming the letters were given to Perkins. Asked if he could remember the physical condition of the letters and their edges, Strong could provide only a general recollection. When shown the edges by O'Brien, Strong confirmed, to the best of his memory, the jagged edges were the same when the letters arrived.

"More I cannot say," Strong said, "as I took no scientific measurements."

Before Strong departed the witness stand, District Attorney Jordan engaged in a brief recross-examination about local attorney Henry Fish, with Strong confirming Fish was in charge of delivering the results of the mausoleum investigation and that his wife, Annie, oversaw the management of the case.

"Mr. Strong, would you have had time to change the appearance of these letters?" Jordan asked.

"I would not."

"Did you ever change these letters in any way?"

"No," Strong replied defiantly.

Attorney Henry Fish identified a receipt listing articles received from Perkins on February 18 but had difficulty in remembering when Perkins turned over the documents related to the case and simply could not recall giving the Black Hand letters to Inspector Oldfield, although he acknowledged some documents were in the custody of Charles Strong's secretary. Asked for clarification by Jordan, Fish said he felt the letters were among the property turned over to Oldfield, confirming his law partner, Albert Chapin, was present when Oldfield took charge of the documents.

With the hour growing late, Judge Orr adjourned court for the afternoon.

"Be very careful not to listen to any conversation regarding the case," Judge Orr warned jurors. "If anyone tries to talk with you about it report it to the court in the morning. "

Continuing his testimony the next morning, Fish confirmed the Black Hand letters remained in his office about three or four days before they were delivered to Inspector Oldfield and, through a brief cross-examination by the defense, confirmed the letters were never altered in their appearance.

Albert Chapin testified the two Black Hand letters were in the possession of Henry Fish, and he saw the letters turned over to Inspector Oldfield, describing the law firm was solely acting as trustee for the Scott Estate. After Chapin stepped down, Annie Strong was called as the next witness.

Heads pivoted from all directions as Annie, "looking pretty" and "fashionably attired,"[29] approached the stand, and through a brief introduction, she confirmed she was the daughter of William L. Scott and was married to Charles Strong. When asked to describe the mausoleum desecration, Annie took a deep breath and testified she was told about the break-in and later viewed the "work of the vandals for herself."[30] The conditions of the mausoleum, Annie continued, were "terrible with the outer door broken open and the caskets inside disturbed."[31]

After arrangements were made with police to guard the mausoleum, Annie said she returned home and phoned attorney Sterling, one of the trustees for her father's estate, requesting the best detectives be sent but was informed it would be impossible for the Burns Detective Agency to arrive until Friday, the tenth. Being of an urgent nature, Annie admitted she suggested Perkins Union Detective Agency, as her husband had used their services before.

Harry Perkins, Annie continued, responded by wire that he would come to Erie the following day. The next day, Gilbert Perkins telephoned from Indianapolis, announcing he was bringing a pair of bloodhounds and "heard of her troubles there." Gilbert Perkins, Annie said, arrived on the tenth along with the bloodhounds; however, they were used sparingly and sent away the same day. Detectives from the Burns Agency arrived on February 10 from New York, sent by attorney Sterling and Annie's sister in Philadelphia. After his son, Harry, left for Pittsburg, Gilbert Perkins told Annie he suspected two men were responsible for the desecration, one named Gilmore, alias Pat Collins, and the second known as "Mahaffey." However, Perkins told her he was at a crossroads as to how to proceed with their arrests.

"What did you make of that?" Jordan asked.

"The whole matter was in his hands."

Perkins, testified Annie, asked if she obtained the services of a medium or received threatening letters, only remarking to her it was strange when Annie said no threatening letters had been received.

On February 13, the first Black Hand letter arrived and was handed over to Gilbert Perkins, who remained in her home throughout the morning. When he returned that afternoon, he suggested a man named Corey, one of her employees, might be implicated in the affair. Annie testified that when Perkins saw the letter, he believed it was sent by those who committed the "mausoleum outrage," telling her she had enemies who were "desperate men."

This contradicted Perkins's initial theory when he arrived in Erie that the desecration was committed by drunken men. Questioned by District Attorney Jordan if she suggested more men be put on the job, Annie denied doing so, saying Perkins suggested she pay attention to the torn edges of the letter, predicting another would arrive. "He told me the letter would be written on the other part of the paper to show that the people who wrote it meant business. He asked if I would object to arrests being made and I told him no."

After Perkins refrained from arresting the suspects, he suggested Annie speak to Thomas Cochran, a personal friend and attorney, who came to her home and informed her that because Perkins was acting as an agent on her behalf she would be responsible for any arrests and Perkins did not want her implicated in the affair. The conversation ended with Perkins asking Annie if he arrested the men if she would allow Cochran to prosecute the case.

On the morning of February 14, Annie continued, Thomas Cochran told her Perkins's operatives could not work alongside the Burns Agency, asking if the rival detectives could be withdrawn. Annie told him this was not possible, as the mausoleum case was connected to her father's estate.

District Attorney Jordan asked when she learned Charles Franklin was working on the case. Annie recalled first meeting Franklin outside the mausoleum on the tenth and admitted she told the Perkinses she objected to Franklin's presence on account of his reputation.

Jordan displayed the second Black Hand letter. Annie confirmed it arrived on February 15 and was turned over to Gilbert Perkins. Annie reiterated to District Attorney Jordan she told the Perkinses she objected to Franklin's involvement in the investigation because of his past.

Attorney Thomson objected, implying she could relate the conversation but must not give her reason.

After a brief pause, Annie continued, claiming Franklin left the Sunday or Monday night following his arrival and confirmed the Perkinses were asked to withdraw on February 18, denying involvement in their dismissal, insisting the direction came from attorney Sterling in New York City. Referring to several papers in her hand, Annie confirmed the Perkins Agency was paid $1,170.64 for services rendered and attorney Cochran $100.

District Attorney Jordan asked Charles Franklin to stand, asking Annie if she recognized him.

Annie lifted her field glasses, glaring at Franklin. "That is the gentleman who spoke to me at the mausoleum."

Beginning his cross-examination, Charles O'Brien inquired about the hiring of the Perkins Agency. Annie testified she hired the Perkinses after her husband used them in 1909, reiterating her testimony about meeting Charles Franklin and her involvement with the Burns Agency.

Annie said Gilbert Perkins suggested "they had better quit" due to the friction with operatives from the Burns Agency.

"Didn't Harry tell you two or three times before you received any letter that they would quit?" O'Brien asked.

"After the trouble with the Burns men, Harry Perkins said that he was sorry they had not withdrawn."

Referring to Franklin, Annie had taken a dislike to him based on his reputation. Pressed about what she knew of his reputation, attorney Thomson interjected the question was too broad and it was withdrawn. Annie Strong, told by Judge Orr she was not required to respond, declined to answer.

O'Brien quizzed Annie about a letter she received denouncing the Perkins Agency.

"Who wrote the letter?" O'Brien asked.

"I don't know," Strong replied, insisting the letter played no role in the agency's discharge, repeating the discharge was initiated by trustees of her father's estate.

O'Brien approached Annie, handing her a letter.

"Is that your letter?"

"It is a letter I dictated, but not my writing."

A smile "encircled" the defense table, suggesting a precursor of the "surprises" promised by defense attorneys. O'Brien then read aloud the names of eight operatives of the Burns Agency, asking Annie if she knew if they were in Erie. Annie could recall the names of only four of the men. District Attorney Jordan followed with an objection, stating that it was not proper cross-examination.

O'Brien ignored Jordan's objection, asking Annie if she ever suspected Gilbert Perkins was responsible for the letters.

Before she could respond, Judge Orr sustained the objection.

After Annie Strong concluded her testimony, District Attorney Jordan offered the anonymous "Cleveland letter" into evidence. For the first time, the public learned of Charles Franklin's "reputation" as Jordan recited the letter before the court.

Outside the federal courthouse, a photographer for the *Erie Daily Times* took photos of Annie Strong exiting the building, shielded by bodyguards as she climbed into her automobile.

Isador Sobel testified he was an attorney and served as postmaster for fourteen years, acknowledging he knew Gilbert Perkins and remembered their first meeting occurring on February 11, 1911. "He told me he was here on the mausoleum case and asked me what theory I had. I told him I didn't have any, and asked him what his theory was. He said they had made a complete examination and nothing had been taken away but a little copper. He said there was a possibility that Mrs. Strong had tipped some of the men

Star Witness Dodges Newspaper Photographers.

Annie Strong leaves the Federal Building in downtown Erie, surrounded by bodyguards. *From the* Erie Daily Times.

at the cemetery more than others, and those who did not get as much as the others did it for spite."

Sobel added, "He said there would be two Black Hand letters in this case and we should make some arrangements to locate them. He wanted me to have carriers examine all boxes for letters to the Strong family, but I told him I could not do that, but would make arrangements to have it watched in the office, and he went away apparently satisfied."

"What happened next?"

"Two or three days after that he came into my office on Eighth Street and said, 'Here is one of the letters, just as I told you.' He handed me this letter, I looked at the envelope and after examining the envelope I took out the letter and I suppose I read it over half a dozen times before I spoke. Then I said, 'No Black Hand person ever wrote that. They have spelled mausoleum and Pennsylvania correctly.[32] Why, I would have to look in the dictionary myself to be sure about mausoleum.' Perkins told me the man who wrote the letter tore it ragged on purpose, and when he caught the man he would find the paper on him. He then said another letter would come and when it does it will be torn, just like this one. Before leaving my office, Perkins cautioned me that another letter would come, and there in a few days Perkins came to my office and he had another letter. He said, 'Well, here is the second letter.'"

Jordan asked Sobel if he knew a man named Dan Mathews. The name, Sobel said, sounded familiar, but he could not confirm where he heard it.

Stephen Walker, Charles Strong's secretary, testified about the arrival of the second Black Hand letter and delivering it to the Strong home. Walker also testified about the bullet fired through the window of Charles Strong's office window at the Erie County Electric Company building. Walker testified that when Perkins learned of the incident, he remarked it was a strong circumstance connected to the mausoleum case.

After Walker's testimony, court recessed for lunch until 2:00 p.m.

Assistant Postmaster Samuel Brainerd, the first witness called for the afternoon session, confirmed that before his current role he was superintendent of mails at the Erie Post Office. Brainerd testified about Gilbert Perkins meeting with Isador Sobel on February 13 and his examination of the postmark on the envelope. Perkins, Brainerd said, suspected a "colored" man and asked if the letter had been mailed at Twenty-Sixth and Peach Streets. Brainerd confirmed the time on the postmark implied the letter was mailed from the Reed House.

Brainerd testified that an operative from the Perkins Agency was stationed at the post office and mailbox at Twenty-Sixth and Peach Streets. Identifying the second Black Hand letter, shown by District Attorney Jordan, Brainerd confirmed it was delivered to the Erie Post Office by Gilbert Perkins.

When asked if it was possible the second letter had been mailed at the post office without being noticed, Brainerd said this was possible, or it could have been discreetly mailed from the Reed House.

Brainerd stepped down without being cross-examined.

Postal Inspector James Woltz, the final witness called that afternoon, spoke in "a well modulated voice, yet audible throughout the room."[33]

Jordan asked Woltz about the arrest of Gilbert and Walter Perkins in Indianapolis: "After the information had been made and the search warrant had been secured, we placed these instruments in the hands of United States deputy marshals and two city detectives of Indianapolis, and went to the building in which Perkins had his office. The inspectors remained in a corridor, while the city detectives and the deputy marshals went up the elevator to the offices. Soon we followed them."

Woltz continued, "When we entered the office we discovered that Walter Perkins had been placed under arrest, but G.B. Perkins was not there. Walter

Perkins told us his father had gone to the bank, but would be back soon. A few minutes later G.B. Perkins came in, accompanied by one of his operatives by the name of Henderson. Perkins was told that he was under arrest. He walked toward his son, but a deputy marshal stepped in between them. A deputy marshal said to Perkins: 'Mr. Perkins, we want all the papers and things you have upon your person.' Perkins had a bank book in his hand and he handed it to the deputy marshal. Then he reached into his pocket and took out a long envelope, which he also handed over to the deputy. A letter on the envelope of which was printed 'G.B. Searl & Co.' was also handed over by Perkins."

"Who was present while this went on?"

"Inspectors Ela, Hutches, Cookson and myself, Deputy United States Marshals D.C. Rankin and Merrill Wilson and City Detectives Henry Ullery and Keller De Rossette."

"What did Mr. Perkins say?"

"He said: 'You can have anything on my person.' But after he handed the long envelope to one of the deputy marshals, [he] said: 'I beg your pardon, but I would like to have that envelope back again. It contains nothing but the codicil of my will and is purely a personal matter.'

"I told Mr. Perkins the envelope would be returned to him after we had had sufficient time to examine its contents. I turned the envelope over to Inspector Hutches, who sealed it up in a large envelope which he had been instructed to bring along with him. Perkins' name was written on the back of this envelope so that it could be properly identified. Perkins and his son were then taken to the Federal building by Rank and Wilson and, after they left, we locked the door of the office and began a search for certain things which we expected to find."

"Who was there with you?"

"The post office inspectors and Henderson, the Perkins operative, and a young fellow named Ross, who was a stenographer for Perkins and who stayed behind to take charge of the office. After a thorough search of the two rooms constituting the Perkins office we went to rooms on the second floor above at the urgent request of Henderson, who said that if Perkins was wrong he didn't want to be mixed up in it. But there we found nothing. The rooms were empty. In Perkins' office we asked Ross if there were any papers bearing upon the Strong case and he admitted there was, but refused to tell where they were located. When he was shown the search warrant and we demanded the papers he produced them from a filing case. While Inspector Cookson and I were going through the papers there came a knock at the door. It was Perkins and his son. Perkins demanded the return of the long envelope which had been taken from him. We refused to turn it over. He seemed to be very anxious and wrought up over the fact that we would not give him the envelope."

"Then what occurred?"

"Well, we were told by some persons that Perkins was very anxious to secure that envelope and we might be attacked."

"I object!" howled W.H.S. Thomson. "Let this man stick to direct testimony. We want no conclusions!"

"That is correct," said Judge Orr. "Sustained."

Woltz continued: "We packed the papers we had secured from Perkins in a suitcase belonging to Inspector Ela and boarded a train for Columbus, Ohio, where Hutches, Ela, Cookson and myself went to Cookson's office."

"Then what did you do?"

"We opened the large envelope containing the stuff secured from Perkins."

"What came out of it?"

"An envelope containing some correspondence of Walter Perkins and the envelope containing the codicil of Mr. Perkins' will."

"Then what?"

"Well, we emptied the envelope containing the codicil upon a table."

"What came out of it?"

"A paper containing a list of operatives of the Perkins agency, their telephone numbers and a list of applicants."

"What else?"

"An envelope, unaddressed, containing the return card of the Reed House, Erie, Pa. This envelope was sealed."

"Was that letter in the envelope given you by Perkins?"

"It was."

"Was it sealed?"

"It was."

"Who was present?"

"Inspectors Ela, Hutches, Cookson and myself."

"What did you do with it?"

"We passed it around and examined it carefully. Then I said to Hutches: 'Ed, I guess you had better get your knife out and open it.' Hutches opened the letter and turned it upside down and shook it."

"What came out of it?"

"Two torn pieces of paper. When we saw them we danced about the table," Woltz responded, holding up the two torn pieces of paper for jurors. "I cried out: 'Ed, Ed, I guess we have got our connection, get your letter.'"

"Then what did you do?"

"We fitted one of the pieces of torn paper into the torn part of one of the 'Black Hand' letters received by Mr. Strong."

"Which letter did you have?"

"It was the one written upon manila or scrap paper. I am not very familiar with them."

Jordan displayed one of the letters.

"Is that the letter?" Jordan asked.

"Yes."

Jordan approached Inspector Woltz.

"Now, I want you to show the jury how this torn piece of paper fits into this letter."

Positioning a large book on his knees, Woltz turned to the jurors as he pieced the torn piece of paper against the edges of the letter, with Jordan displaying the "completed letter," ensuring each juror had an opportunity to view it.

As Attorney Thomson stood to view the letter, Perkins grabbed Thomson by the shoulder before he walked away. "Get over there quick," Perkins whispered.

District Attorney Jordan handed the letter to Judge Orr, who examined it briefly before returning it with an "affirmative shake" of his head. Returning the letter to the government table, Jordan again turned his attention to Woltz.

"Then what did you do?"

"We notified Inspector Oldfield, who was in Pittsburg, of our find. He was in charge of the entire case. He told us to come to Pittsburg, which we did, arriving in the city shortly after five o'clock in the morning. We went to the Federal building, but there was no one there. I guess it was too early for them to be around. Then we went across the street and had breakfast. Then we went back to the Federal building where we found Inspector Oldfield. To Inspector Oldfield we explained the finding of the torn pieces of paper and how one of them fitted the letter received by Strong. Inspector Oldfield had the other letter and the second piece of paper fitted in it perfectly."

Woltz reenacted the same method of joining the torn piece of paper and the second Black Hand letter.

The fastening of the letters and torn pieces of paper, the *Erie Daily Times* said, was "the most dramatic incident of the trial up to that time."

Leaping to his feet, quick to begin his cross-examination, Charles O'Brien rounded the defense table.

"What was the conference about which you held in Ela's office in Indianapolis?"

"Oh, methods of procedure to secure evidence."

"Evidence for what?"

"The 'Black Hand' letters received by Strong."

"After the consultation you decided to make the raid upon Mr. Perkins' office?"

"Yes."

"What did you expect to find?"

"We expected to find the torn pieces of paper and pieces of copper plating from one of these coffins in the mausoleum."

O'Brien dramatically paused.

"Do you accuse the Perkinses of breaking into the tomb?" O'Brien cried loudly.

"We charge them with sending the 'Black Hand' letters."

"Then you worked up on the theory that Gilbert Perkins was connected with the desecration of the mausoleum?"

"I did."

"You expected to find pieces of copper taken from a coffin in the mausoleum?"

"Yes."

Pressed further, Inspector Woltz affirmed this was the belief among all the other inspectors. Asked if by "other inspectors" he meant Inspector Oldfield, Woltz maintained he did not mean Oldfield in particular.

"Well, you didn't find them."

"No, but we found something else equally as good."

"Did Mr. Perkins wear an overcoat when he came in to the office that day?"

"To the best of my recollection he did not."

"Did you hear any member of your party say: 'Don't remove your overcoat, Mr. Perkins, you are to come with us'?"

"I did not."

"Did you demand Perkins' belongings?"

"I did not."

"Well," O'Brien said, looking to the jury. "Somebody did."

"Yes."

"Who?"

"A deputy United States marshal."

"Well, it was at your direction?"

"It was not. I have no authority over deputy United States marshals."

"When these articles were taken from Mr. Perkins—"

"They were not taken from Mr. Perkins. He handed them over."

"Well, when Mr. Perkins handed over his personal effects upon demand were they laid down any place?"

"No, they were placed in an envelope which was sealed up, and which, I believe, is exhibit O."

"When the envelope was sealed up you didn't know what was in it?"

"No."

"Then you searched the office, pulled out drawers and threw everything all over the floor?"

"The only thing placed on the floor was some advertisements and things removed from a cedar chest and some empty whisky bottles found in a hat rack box."

"Did you cut the telephone wires?"

"Yes."

"Did you kick the telephone box from the desk?"

"I did not."

"Who searched the desk?"

"I don't know. I was out of the room."

"There is nothing whatever bearing upon the case except what you say was found in that envelope?"

"Yes, there was some papers—reports which Ross had taken from the Strong case."

"What did you mean by saying, a while ago, about getting out of Indiana as quickly as possible?"

"We didn't want Gilbert Perkins to recover his stuff until we had looked into it thoroughly."

"You skipped out right away?"

"We certainly did."

Before Inspector Woltz could be questioned further, court was adjourned until the next morning.

That night at the Reed House, a reporter from the *Cleveland Plain Dealer* asked Charles Franklin why the defense did not object to the anonymous "Cleveland letter" being placed into evidence. Franklin said he wanted the letter presented before the jurors and insisted he knew the identity of the letter writer, assuring the man's identity would be revealed before the trial concluded.

8

COPPER PLATES AND DIMINISHED ODDS

ERKINS FACING ORDEAL," screamed the *Pittsburgh Post*. "PERKINS SLEUTH IS ATTACKED," scribed reporter J.K. Burnett for the *Pittsburg Press*. "TELLS ABOUT RAID IN TOMB SLEUTHS," divulged the *Cleveland Plain Dealer*. "COPPER PLATE FROM MAUSOLEUM ENTERS INTO THE PERKINS CASE" headlined page 3 of the morning edition of the *Erie Evening Herald*.

Shocking accusations from the trial were transposed again to the front pages of newspapers around the country as the government built their case against Gilbert Perkins and Charles Franklin, with newspapers praising Inspector Woltz as a "good witness" for the government. His thrilling minute-by-minute account of the raid of the Perkins Agency's Indianapolis office appeared in dozens of newspapers.

"Woltz proved to be the star witness of the case so far and very seldom has a witness acquitted himself so creditably and without confusion under a heavy cross fire as he did," said the *Erie Evening Herald*.

The most astonishing accusation, however, was the belief Perkins and his operatives were responsible for the desecration of the Scott mausoleum.

On the morning of July 20, 1911, as defense attorneys entered the courtroom, in an attempt to deflect damaging testimony from government witnesses, the lawyers predicted they would reveal the identity of the guilty party and exonerate Gilbert Perkins and Charles Franklin—supplemented with rumors of arrest warrants for government witnesses implicated of perjury.

Wallace Buchanan, superintendent of mails for the Indianapolis Post Office, confirmed the post office box for the Perkins Agency there was

Gilbert Perkins (*left*) and Charles Franklin (*right*) outside the federal courthouse in downtown Erie. *From the* Erie Daily Times.

numbered 467. Postal Inspector Edward Hutches was called next and testified he was an inspector for territories in Ohio and Kentucky, selected to assist in the case, and traveled to Indianapolis on April 7, where he linked up with the other inspectors.

Hutches testified that prior to his arrival in Indianapolis, he was not familiar with much of the case and swore to the information within the warrant before a U.S. commissioner, which was turned over to Deputy Rankin of the U.S. Marshals, and the other search warrant was turned over to Indianapolis city detectives. Hutches's testimony about the raid of the Perkins office and arrests mirrored that of Inspector Woltz, confirming evidence presented by the government was the same handed over by Gilbert Perkins.

When inspectors arrived in Columbus on April 14, Hutches said the documents from Perkins were removed from Inspector Cookson's office and the envelope opened by Inspector Woltz, confirming the torn pieces of paper on the government's table were those that came out of the Reed House return envelope. Before departing for Pittsburg, Hutches testified the documents were placed in Inspector Ela's custody.

Through cross-examination, Attorney O'Brien seized on the investigation into the Perkins Agency. Hutches defended the investigation against the Perkinses based on evidence received from the other inspectors. Hutches's answer did little to satisfy O'Brien, who hammered Woltz for a more exhaustive answer until Judge Orr refused to permit an argument with the witness, followed by an objection from District Attorney Jordan in relation to O'Brien's questioning.

Despite Judge Orr sustaining the objection, an exasperated Charles O'Brien argued the search of Gilbert Perkins's person and his Indianapolis office was illegal. The Supreme Court had decreed no office or house may be searched by federal officers except in the pursuit of counterfeit coins or contraband goods.

"Suppose it was an illegal act, what has it to do in this court?" Judge Orr asked, adding the legality of the search was not the regularity of the search warrant but whether or not the defendants were guilty of the offenses they stood charged of.

O'Brien countered with his desire to test the creditability of the government's witnesses but was again interrupted. "Mr. O'Brien," Judge Orr warned, "the court has sustained the objection of the district attorney. Proceed, please, with your cross-examination."

Inspector Hutches testified he was not aware communication wires to the Perkins office had been cut, believing some wires were being disconnected. During a brief inspection of Perkins's home there, Hutches said the warrant mentioned a copper plate from the Scott mausoleum, confirming a minimal search was made of the Perkins home, with no copper plate located. Asked to elucidate the hurried retreat from Indianapolis, Hutches claimed it was because the train to Columbus was the last one that day and they wanted to ensure they boarded it in time. Asked if the inspectors were aware evidence obtained during the raid was damaging to the Perkinses before their departure, Hutches testified they were not.

"They had not time to examine the papers," Hutches asserted.

O'Brien concluded his cross-examination without any further questions.

Post office inspector William Ela, like the others before, testified to the arrest and search at the Perkins office in Indianapolis, and when cross-examined, he confirmed the main object of the search was a piece of copper plate from the Scott mausoleum.

Conrad Klein, proprietor of the Reed House, was recalled and showed the Reed House return card from Indianapolis, confirming the envelope was the same used when Perkins operatives were in Erie that February.

The next witness called was Keller DeRosette; however, he was not present, and Deputy Marshal D.C. Rankin took the stand, testifying he and Deputy Merrill Wilson served the warrant for the arrest of Gilbert and Walter Perkins. Rankins confirmed Deputy Wilson asked Gilbert Perkins to hand over all papers and that these papers were passed over to Inspector Hutches.

Merrill Wilson, U.S. deputy marshal, was called next, but before he could testify, a recess was announced until the afternoon. During the recess, District Attorney Jordan spoke to reporters, indicating the government hoped to rest their case the following day.

That afternoon, Deputy Marshal Wilson testified he vaguely knew of the Perkins Agency before the arrests, and his testimony was similar to Marshall Rankins, acknowledging he asked Gilbert Perkins and his son to relinquish all papers in their possession. When District Attorney Jordan showed several documents in evidence to Wilson, he confirmed they were the same Gilbert Perkins handed him and completed his testimony without being cross-examined.

Inspector William Cleary testified about the raid and arrests in Indianapolis, confirming a copper plate from the Scott mausoleum was rumored to be in Gilbert Perkins's possession. Through brief cross-examination, O'Brien asked who said the copper plate and trimmings from the coffin lid were in Gilbert Perkins's possession.

"On what grounds was a search warrant issued in Indiana for a property that had been stolen in Pennsylvania?"

"On information and belief, the only grounds on which a search warrant can be issued."

"Where did you receive this information?"

Cleary reluctantly asked for clarification. O'Brien asked what evidence inspectors possessed to issue a search warrant.

"From the evidence that we had."

"On whose testimony did you get the evidence?"

"We don't have to have testimony," Clearly said, explaining the inspectors met before the raid and agreed to search the office based on the evidence presented.

O'Brien's attempt to learn the source of the accusations against Perkins failed to materialize.

Indianapolis City detectives Harry Ullery and Keller DeRossette testified about the raid, confirming they assisted postal inspectors and U.S. marshals.

William Allen, an attorney from Warren, Pennsylvania, testified about a conversation with Gilbert Perkins in that city, claiming Perkins said the desecration of the Scott mausoleum was part of a scheme to extort money from the Strongs, enacted to convince them of the "desperate character of the people and the necessity of compliance with their demands."

Edward Wagner, chief of police, testified that Gilbert Perkins, in a conversation on February 10, felt the desecration was a crude job and imagined threatening letters would follow. Wagner also testified Perkins spoke to Charles Strong about offering a reward, similar to when he received threatening letters in 1909.

District Attorney Jordan asked Wagner about his interactions with Franklin.

"I was in the courthouse one day," Wagner said, "when I turned and saw Mr. Franklin giving me the high sign to come out into the hall. I went out to talk to him. He said that he was working on the mausoleum case and used the words, 'You know what damn little use I have for them.'"

Franklin, incensed by Wagner's testimony, vaulted to his feet, only to be lured back to his seat by Attorney Thomson, who engaged in a silent conference with Franklin.

Wagner recommenced, testifying Harry Perkins told him other detectives engaged on the job wanted to work with the police department and Wagner offered any assistance necessary.

Wagner was briefly cross-examined before Captain John Washer of the U.S. Secret Service was called and testified about the meeting in his office on April 14 with postal inspectors, confirming the Black Hand letters and torn pieces of papers were the same examined that morning. Postal Inspectors George Craighead and George Tate also testified about the meeting in Washer's office, confirming Inspector Oldfield was present, with the letters and evidence brought from Indianapolis.

Postal Inspector James Cortelyou was then called by the court crier, encountered by a "craning of necks and a buzzing in the court room as the big crowd desired to get a glimpse of the investigator." Spectators gawked as Cortelyou, below medium height with a pale face and black hair, sat down. His eyes, continued the *Pittsburgh Post*, were that "of an idealistic Sherlock Holmes."

Cortelyou nodded to District Attorney Jordan and, after an introduction, began his testimony, confirming he was acquainted with Franklin and was assigned to assist Inspector Oldfield in the case on March 20, 1911, holding numerous several conferences with Oldfield, the last taking place on April 12.

District Attorney Jordan asked Cortelyou about Charles Franklin's arrest.

"After receiving instructions to investigate the mailing of the two Black Hand letters to Mr. Charles Strong, I found the Perkins agency in Philadelphia and had several conferences with its manager, Charles Franklin," Cortelyou said. "In all I think I had seven extended conferences and then came the day on which a warrant had been issued for his arrest. On the forenoon of that day I got in touch with him by telephone and, on ascertaining he was in his office, I made an engagement to meet him there. When I reached his office in the Pennsylvania building, I told him I desired him to accompany me to my office in the Federal building, as I had important matters to discuss with him. He asked me to say nothing to a woman clerk in his office and before he left with me, he told her he would be gone probably two hours."

"What happened next?"

"On reaching my office, I told him I would take down his answers and he consented. During the three hours' examination he told me all about his engagement with the Perkins agency, the assignments he had worked in Philadelphia and elsewhere, his being called to Erie after the desecration of the Scott mausoleum, and his absolute ignorance of a motive for such work by the desperate vandals."

The most damning of Cortelyou's testimony was Franklin blaming the revocation of his detective's license on Charles Strong and his newspaper, the *Erie Dispatch*. District Attorney Jordan grabbed Franklin's typed testimony from April 14, intending to enter it into evidence, only to have defense attorneys vigorously object, claiming the transcript, brought in such an indirect way, would not be permissible in direct testimony.

Judge Orr said the testimony had some bearing in the case because Franklin performed detective work in Erie and ruled all voluntary statements must be confined to the case on trial. Jordan argued Franklin's statements, supported by Cortelyou and the transcript, indicated Franklin harbored strong feelings against Charles Strong.

Cortelyou continued: "Towards the end of the examination I asked Franklin if he would write four letters for me. 'I will write as many as you like,' he responded. I then had him write from my dictation the wording of the two black hand letters received by Mr. Strong, addressing two of them to Mr. Wagner and two of them to Mr. Strong. I had him write one set in pencil and one set with pen."

"You have these letters here?"

"I have."

"Will you produce them?"

Cortelyou handed four handwritten letters to Jordan, who entered them into the record.

"What happened after that?"

"Well, as it was lunch time, I asked Franklin and some of the Federal officers to accompany me to luncheon. While we were walking from the Federal building, with Inspector Furness on the outside, and Franklin between us, Franklin asked me if I would answer one question. I replied that I would and the following conversation followed: 'Was that paper, which you read from in your office, the real letter, or a duplicate?' Franklin asked.

'Which paper?' I asked. 'Why, the paper with the ragged edge,' replied Franklin, at the same time waving his index finger downward through the air to designate an irregular curve."

"What was peculiar about Franklin's question?"

"Franklin had told me that he knew nothing of the 'Black Hand' letters except that there had been some sort of letters sent by the Perkins' representatives. I wondered how Franklin knew about the sharp, ragged edges of the letters, before they had been described to him, or to anyone."

Judge Orr interrupted, adjourning court for the afternoon.

As the spectators poured out of the courtroom, Charles Franklin was asked about Cortelyou's testimony. "I am at a loss what to say about it," Franklin said. "I knew nothing about these fragments of papers at the time

Charles Franklin photographed purchasing the *Erie Daily Times* during his trial. *From the* Erie Daily Times.

Cortelyou talks about. He dictated to me from a paper tracing, which was somewhat jagged, and my reference was to that."

A newspaper correspondent claimed defense attorneys fingered a man they felt was responsible for the Black Hand letters and kept the suspect under constant surveillance, although Charles O'Brien deemed the reports false. A defense witness, whose identity remained unknown, told a reporter another man—known in Erie, although currently in Cleveland—would be revealed as the writer of the letters and soon arrested.

Despite an inability to rattle the testimony of government's witnesses, supporters of the defense remained optimistic an acquittal was on the horizon, especially Harry Perkins, who said the defense was preparing to spring a surprise in the courtroom in the coming days.

"There is something coming," Gilbert Perkins hypothesized.

Just as confident was District Attorney John Jordan, who told the *Pittsburgh Gazette Times*, "Our progress is very satisfactory."

That afternoon, Hutze Knoll quietly exited the federal courthouse a free man when charges against him were discharged because of insufficient evidence.

That night, much-needed precipitation throttled the city of Erie as all hotel and rooming houses were jammed to capacity. With the arrival of the Perkins-Franklin trial, Erie continued to succumb to the aggravating obstacle of a lack of lodging. One weary voyager from out of town that night traversed from door-to-door in search of lodgings, crossing paths with a patrolman near West Seventh and Cherry Streets.

"I have telephoned every hotel in the city and I have called on all the rooming houses I could locate," the man pleaded, "and each is filled."

Despite the only other event in Erie being the local horse races, Erie, wrote the *Erie Daily Times*, faced a "problem."

Dozens of newspaper correspondents were forced to find rooms and take meals wherever they could, although most booked their rooms in advance. In southern Erie, some correspondents slept on floors to catch some much-needed sleep. Those who arrived too late settled for lodgings as far as the borough of North East.

When asked how he obtained copies of the Black Hand letters on the morning of July 21, Cortelyou, continuing his testimony, said Inspector Oldfield provided the original letters, with tracings used to dictate to Charles Franklin before his arrest.

"I asked Franklin if he knew about the Black Hand letters, and he replied that he did not, except what he had read in the Erie newspapers,"

Cortelyou said, reciting Franklin's arrest and arraignment. "'Was my testimony relative to your questions about the irregular shape of the paper from which I dictated to you correct?' I asked of Franklin after his second hearing at Philadelphia, and Franklin said it was."

Queried if the original letters and standard letters were submitted to handwriting experts, Cortelyou confirmed they were. District Attorney Jordan furnished the Black Hand letter to Chief Wagner on February 23, asking if he dictated the letter to Franklin.

"No. I had a tracing of this letter and used that in dictating it to Franklin."

Shown the first two Black Hand letters, Cortelyou identified them, adding they were submitted to handwriting experts.

Beginning his cross-examination, Charles O'Brien was told by Cortelyou all information in the case was turned over to Inspector Oldfield. Asked if he could point to Oldfield, Cortelyou motioned to the government's table. Cortelyou told O'Brien the papers were given to him by Oldfield around March 20. Asked about his interview with Charles Franklin, Cortelyou testified he was told to withhold information about the charges on advice from a U.S. district attorney.

"You invited Franklin to come to your office on a very important matter, but did not arrest him, even though warrants were in your possession?"

"Yes," Cortelyou said, confirming Franklin was in his office for three hours before the arrest warrant was served.

O'Brien asked how long Franklin was interviewed before informed he was under charge.

"About two and one-half hours."

"Did Franklin not ask to be allowed to send for his attorney?"

"He did not."

O'Brien continued to cajole Cortelyou into admitting Franklin asked for an attorney before being reprimanded by Judge Orr for his method of cross-examination. O'Brien argued that because Cortelyou was a representative of the government, he had a right to pursue the course of questioning. Asked who submitted the letters to handwriting experts, Cortelyou confirmed that was done by Inspector Oldfield.

Realizing he was unable to shake Cortelyou, O'Brien finished his cross-examination.

Chief Wagner was recalled and identified the letter received on February 23, confirming he turned it over to Annie Strong, who was also recalled and confirmed the letter sent to Chief Wagner was given to her and then surrendered to Inspector Oldfield.

Post office inspector Arthur Furner confirmed he was in Inspector Cortelyou's office when Franklin was arrested, testifying he originally phoned Franklin to confirm he would be available. Franklin, Furner reiterated, voluntarily agreed to go to Cortelyou's office.

"Did you tell Franklin you were both post office inspectors?" Jordan asked.

"We did."

"Did Franklin know that the questions and answers were being taken by a stenographer?"

"He did."

"Did he object in any way?"

"He did not."

Furner testified Franklin never asked for his attorney and discussed Franklin's interview with Inspector Cortelyou, affirming Cortelyou's testimony that Franklin denied all knowledge of the Black Hand letters and his willingness to write the letters upon dictation. Furner confirmed Cortelyou's chief clerk acted as stenographer during the questioning and that the men were joined by Deputy Marshal Myer and Inspector Ryan. Furner's cross-examination was brief before Inspector William J. Ryan spoke about Franklin's interview in Cortelyou's office, adding greater importance to Furner and Cortelyou's testimony.

Abner Okum, Cortelyou's chief clerk, confirmed he acted as a stenographer during Franklin's interview, taking down the questions put to Franklin along with the responses. Okum testified the copy of the transcript presented by District Attorney Jordan was a true and correct copy.

Jordan offered the transcript and notes into evidence but withdrew them after Attorney Thomson argued that they be thrown out.

Frank Crane of the *Times* testified about his interactions with Charles Franklin, reading from several pages of notes corroborating Franklin's distaste for the Strong family. John H. Callaghan, a clerk in Mayor Libel's office, testified about his discussion with Franklin about the case.

Just after 11:00 a.m., Postal Inspector John Frank Oldfield confirmed he was in charge of the investigation, arriving in Erie on February 22. Oldfield denied seeing any of the letters prior to his arrival and learned of the case only after meeting with Charles Strong's secretary. He later secured the Black Hand letters from Henry Fish. Oldfield, when shown the first two Black Hand letters, confirmed he obtained them from Henry Fish and Annie Strong. Oldfield testified he presented one of the letters to Inspector Ela, whom he sent to Indianapolis with a warrant for a search of Perkins's office, using the letter to secure a warrant. Oldfield also testified about the subsequent meeting in Captain Washer's office in Pittsburg on April 14, 1911.

"Did you compare the torn paper produced by Woltz with the letter in your possession?"

"I did."

"What did you find?"

"The two pieces of paper, the letter and the sheet produced by Inspector Woltz, fitted together perfectly."

The remainder of Oldfield's testimony equaled the testimony of the previous inspectors. After Franklin's arrest, Oldfield testified he met with inspectors there under the direction of Inspector Cortelyou. Asked if he knew handwriting experts William Pengelly and David Carvalho, Oldfield acknowledged he did and confirmed showing them the various letters in the investigation.

"No further questions," Jordan concluded.

O'Brien greeted Inspector Oldfield, asking him to repeat his introduction to the case. Oldfield recited his arrival to Erie, his introduction to the case and the events leading up to the arrests in Indianapolis and Philadelphia, claiming the facts in the case were learned after obtaining information from those he interviewed throughout the investigation.

"Any detectives consulted?"

"No."

O'Brien, clutching a piece of paper, read the names of operatives from the Burns Agency.

Oldfield responded with a sharp, incisive "No" after each name was read from the list.

"Did you confer with that man Biederman?" O'Brien thundered, pointing to a man near the judge's bench.

Oldfield glanced over at Biederman, a Burns Agency operative, testifying he met the man, introduced as "Berry," at Henry Fish's office and they barely spoke longer than five minutes, denying the two held any lengthy conference about the case. Oldfield declined Biederman's offer of assistance, as he was a government employee. Following their meeting, Oldfield confirmed he never spoke again to Biederman.

"Did your instructions to the inspectors making the arrest and search at Indianapolis have anything to do with a copper plate?" O'Brien roared after Oldfield acknowledged he ordered inspectors to acquire a warrant for all documents related to the mausoleum case.

"My instructions were to search for a part of the covering of a casket, three copper plates."

It was at this moment a smile stretched across W.H.S. Thomson's face.

Asked about his instructions to Inspector Ela, District Attorney Jordan objected to O'Brien's questioning.

"Overruled," Judge Orr retorted.

"I instructed Mr. Ela to use the Black Hand letter I had turned over to him in securing a search warrant, and I told him to look for copper plates that might be there," Oldfield continued.

"What copper plates did you want to find?"

"The copper plates missing from the caskets in the Scott tomb."

"When did you hear of the Indianapolis arrest?"

"April 13th, at Pittsburg by wire."

"No further questions," O'Brien said.

At 12:30 p.m., District Attorney Jordan offered the various letters and papers into evidence coordinating with the witnesses called by the government. Following this, a recess was ordered until the afternoon, with dozens of newspaper correspondents sprinting to telegraph offices to wire the latest updates to newspapers throughout the country.

As the government inched close to wrapping up the case, the defense's inability to prove government agents conspired with the Burns Detective Agency became even more apparent, and District Attorney Jordan had decided to wrap up the government's case with two of the country's leading handwriting experts.

The first, forty-six-year-old William Pengelly, had the appearance of a banker, which was no coincidence, as he was employed as an auditor for the National City Bank of Columbus and had engaged in the field of examining questioned documents for fifteen years in relation to numerous criminal cases, including several anonymous letter cases for the government.

Sitting on the witness stand that afternoon, Pengelly confirmed he performed an examination of the letters in the case, including the letters written by Charles Franklin, and proceeded to explain the results of his examinations of the letters, explaining "many incongruities and inconsistencies" in the letters not considered "natural writing,"

William Pengelly, handwriting expert for the government. *Author's collection.*

adding similarities in the formation of both the Black Hand and standard letters, written by Franklin.

Pengelly's opinion was that the Black Hand letters did not possess the natural writing of the letter writer. Natural writing, according to Pengelly, was performed without thought. The "unnatural writing" in the letters, Pengelly continued, was more noticeable, whereas the envelopes displayed more natural writing than the letters.

"There were so many similarities in the anonymous letters and standard letters that I came to the conclusion that both were written by the same man. Whoever wrote the chief of police letter also wrote the other anonymous letters," Pengelly said.

"You never saw Charles Franklin write?" Thomson asked, beginning his cross-examination after repeating Pengelly's qualifications.

"No, sir."

"Or never passed upon any of his checks?"

"No, sir."

"Do you base your judgment upon these writings?"

"I have said that I do."

"Wasn't it a fact that you determined that the writer of those letters was a mighty good penman?"

"He was pretty good."

"Isn't it clear to you that the writer of these letters used a free forearm movement in writing?"

"Yes."

Thomson asked if it was true the formation of certain characters within the words of the letters indicated a cramped style of writing.

Pengelly disagreed.

Thomson produced photographs of the Black Hand letters and envelopes.

"Where did you get those?" District Attorney Jordan thundered, slamming his hand on the table. "They stole them!"

"Do you recognize these photographs?" Thomson continued.

"I object!" Jordan boomed. "These photographs have not been proven and it is not proper cross-examination."

Judge Orr sustained the objection as Jordan sat down, visibly fuming. Thomson resumed.

"Mr. Oldfield got you into this case?"

"Mr. Oldfield called upon me, yes."

"Did he give you some of these papers the first time he called?"

"He showed me the Black Hand letters."

"He left them with you?"

"Yes."

"Didn't he explain this case to you?"

"No, he did not."

"Did you ever talk to any person about the work you was [*sic*] doing in this case?"

"No, I did not."

"Didn't you talk to some people in Columbus?"

"I don't think so."

"You talked to Professor Wood about it?"

"Oh yes, I mentioned it to him."

"Didn't you tell Professor Wood about Oldfield explaining the case to you?"

"I don't think so."

Thomson pressured Pengelly into acknowledging the Black Hand letters in Erie were the same as those received in Franklin, all written by the same person, which drew an objection from District Attorney Jordan in reference to Thomson's line of examination.

Again, Judge Orr sustained.

"Your honor," Thomson beseeched. "I will explain why I want to ask these questions of the witness. I have the right to test the creditability and integrity of a witness. I want to show that he told that the Black Hand letters received by various parties which he had under examination had all been written by the same person and now he testifies that the Black Hand letters received by Mr. Strong and the standard letters written by Franklin were written by the same person."

William Pengelly turned to Judge Orr, asking he be permitted to explain what he believed the reason was for Attorney Thomson's argument. Orr allowed Pengelly to proceed.

Pengelly explained that while in possession of the Black Hand letters sent to Charles Strong, he received a letter from Professor George Wood, who was expected to testify as an expert for the defense, asking for assistance in the Black Hand letters from Franklin. Pengelly, after receiving the letters, determined all were written by the same individual. Despite not having finished examining all the letters, Pengelly supplied his opinions to Professor Wood and mentioned assisting the government with the Black Hand letters from Erie.

Following Thomson's cross-examination, both District Attorney Jordan and Judge Orr privately read a letter written by Pengelly to Professor Wood. Unlike the morning session, which included no cross-examination of government witnesses, that afternoon the *Erie Evening Herald* remarked, "The defense paid very careful attention to the testimony of Mr. Pengelly and the experts to be called by the defense took full notes."

David N. Carvalho, the government's final witness, was perhaps the most well-known handwriting expert in America, having served as an expert examiner of handwriting for more than forty-one years, including as handwriting expert of the grand jury in New York City for thirty-five years, during which he examined over 3,500 documents. A prior employee of the U.S. Treasury Department, Carvalho was also involved in disputed election cases, with the Perkins-Franklin trial being the 1,429th time he offered testimony in a disputed handwriting case.

Carvalho testified he made a preliminary examination of the Black Hand letters on April 5, 1911, first examining the letters in dispute for departures from regular standards of handwriting.

Speaking directly to the jury, Carvalho said the standard letters, written by Charles Franklin, indicated a "very definite hand," similar to the "Black Hand" letters, written in pencil in a nervous hand, which Carvalho believed was normal when writing from dictation, with one peculiarity being the letter was small and not capitalized.

David N. Carvalho, handwriting expert for the government. *Library of Congress.*

Explaining the different varieties in writing, Carvalho observed departures from normal handwriting practices and showed members of the jury portions that confirmed departures from normal handwriting and indicated the writer's hand was masculine. The letter, Carvalho continued, started disguised, beginning nicely until something attracted his attention, causing him to "fall into something else."

In the first Black Hand letter, Carvalho found thirteen different angles and slopes, with the uniqueness being the "tipping over" of the letter *e* in the word *leave*. There was also the dollar sign in "$50,000," with the writer writing the sign over the number 5.

Even from a hasty examination, Carvalho concluded it was clear the writing was done to disguise the writer's identity. The Black Hand letters, Carvalho confidently declared, were the same as the standard letters written by Charles Franklin. Before Carvalho could continue, however, court was adjourned until Monday, April 24, 1911, at 10:00 a.m.

That evening, Thomas Dempsey and his attorneys were approached by reporters, with the private detective vowing he was prepared to combat any allegations made by the Perkins Agency. As he departed Erie, Dempsey promised his return to the city when the trial resumed on Monday. One of the biggest surprises entering the weekend, however, was Perkins operative Charles Martz returning to the Allegheny County Jail in Pittsburg. Although puzzling to some, most felt the charges brought against Martz presented a risk to the government, one that District Attorney Jordan did not want a part of.

Throughout the weekend, newspapers indulged in endless speculation about the defense's strategy. It appeared they continued to focus on implicating Thomas Dempsey as being the writer of the Black Hand letters in Erie. There was also the mysterious letter dictated by Annie Strong to Gilbert Perkins, presented during the second day of the trial. The *Erie Daily Times* predicted this could be connected to the defense's strategy. Those connected to the defense continued to guarantee the reveal of "secrets," although newspaper correspondents, and the public, felt these utterances were nothing more than bluster with no supporting evidence.

The case, many felt, could be over within the next week.

On Saturday, July 22, District Attorney Jordan, his assistant Robert Gibson and several postal inspectors were engaged in lengthy conferences. At the Reed House, Gilbert Perkins and Charles Franklin, assisted by their attorneys and Perkins's sons, remained in constant consultation.

A scandal nearly erupted when Mattie Cochrane of Erie accused District Attorney Jordan of engaging in methods using the "third degree," threatening her with punishment if she refused to appear as a witness. Speaking to the *Gazette*, Cochrane said she had been subpoenaed on Wednesday, the nineteenth, and answered the summons at the federal building and later spoke to District Attorney Jordan in the postal inspector's office. Jordan asked if she was prepared to identify handwriting belonging to Charles Franklin. Cochrane claimed she could not identify Franklin's handwriting, and on Friday, July 21, during the trial, she was again approached by Jordan, asking if she was prepared to testify.

When threatening to leave during a recess, Cochrane was soon met by Jordan and a half-dozen postal inspectors, with an annoyed Jordan telling her if she wasn't careful she would get in trouble.

"He said to me: 'Young lady you will be taken before the court and punished,'" Cochrane said. "Just then Inspector Cortelyou stepped in and said something to Mr. Jordan. I think he said: 'This is no way to treat a lady,' and after this the inspectors and Mr. Jordan left the room. As they were leaving Inspector Oldfield turned to me and said: 'I can produce a man who will say that he saw you and Franklin writing together a thousand times,' and I said, 'Well, you produce him.'"

District Attorney Jordan was unable to be located for comment; however, Inspector Cortelyou, speaking to the *Gazette*, affirmed the meeting did occur but disputed portions of Cochrane's story, acknowledging the inspectors may have been "just a little over zealous."

On Sunday, July 23, 1911, over forty witnesses slated to appear for the defense were lodged at the Reed House, with rumors claiming Gilbert Perkins was preparing to charge the Strongs and others with conspiracy. Perkins, later asked about the rumors, would neither confirm nor deny their veracity, and the Strongs declined comment. With Judge Orr visiting neighboring Chautauqua Lake with his family and jurors scattered throughout northwest Pennsylvania, Harry Perkins continued his cavalcade to reporters, announcing the defense planned to dismantle David Carvalho's testimony when court resumed the following day.

Speaking to the *Erie Evening Herald*, Gilbert Perkins said the defense might show the letters were planted on him due to conspiracy. It was the Burns Agency, Gilbert Perkins insisted, that was responsible, claiming they knew where the copper plates from the mausoleum were and arguing they planted them in his office. Conferences between defense attorneys and witnesses continued later into the night, ending a weekend, according to the *Erie*

Evening Herald, that consisted of "many stories of surprises afloat from all sides and some of them have a dime novel climax" as an anxious public waited with anticipation to see if promises of scandal and surprise would bear fruit.

At ten o'clock on the morning of July 24, 1911, David Carvalho continued his testimony. After explaining the similarities between the standard and the Black Hand letters, Carvalho testified it was not particularly strange to find writers with peculiarities between their method and form of writing but remained adamant no two writers would have all peculiarities found in both the Black Hand and standard letters.

"There are certain kinds of marks in the standard writings that denote a very good penman, and we find these same marks in the disputed writings. The writer had unusual ability in making the long letters above the base line and that characteristic prevails in the Black hand letters."

Carvalho approached the jurors, taking considerable time to explain the peculiarities connecting the letters while pointing out the visible "abnormal method of writing" by the letter writer.

"Taking the line, 'you men and my men will have a big battle,' we find the writer started the first line letter 'y' at a certain position under the line above."

After picking up the standard letters written by Charles Franklin, Carvalho backtracked to the jurors.

"Here again we find the marks, but they are slanting. But in all my experience I have noticed marks used like the two in these letters. It was a habit with the writer and the slant was probably an attempt at disguise." Carvalho said, pointing to another section of the letters, "Another peculiarity of the standard letters is that the 'E' in each case is a blind letter. Instead of a loop the pen returns on its own line. Now in the disputed letters we find each letter 'e' made with an abortive loop, evidently an attempt to get away from some habit in making the letter. To be perfectly fair I want to say that in the line at the bottom 'you son of a bitch' the 'o' and the 'd' differentiate. They are not alike. The reasonable opinion is, to the best of my knowledge and belief, that the writer of the Black Hand letters is the same person who wrote the dictated letters." He then returned to the witness stand.

David Carvalho confirmed to W.H.S. Thomson during cross-examination the dates he received the letters for examination as well as additional samples of Charles Franklin's handwriting, from books and letters furnished by Inspector Oldfield.

"Would you say then that your opinion is based entirely upon the letters in this case or partially upon the other furnished you?" Thomson asked.

"I was in doubt, or rather, I was not satisfied until the request writings were given me and I had thrown out the others," Carvalho said.

"You had great difficulty in arriving at your conclusion, doctor?"

"Well, I have spent a great deal of time."

"Was it because it was so hard to decide that you took so long?"

"No sir. Do you want to know the real reason?"

"Why, certainly."

"Well, sir, one of the defendants in the case was a friend of mine. I put it off and hated to form a definite opinion," Carvalho said before stopping. "Are you asking these questions with the knowledge of your associates in this case?"

"I'll be responsible for the question," assured Thomson.

"Well," Carvalho continued. "I waited and waited for this friend, who had come to me and promised to send other writings, to come or send the writings he had promised me, but neither came. I went away to Canada for three weeks, leaving the letters locked up in New York, then I came back and set diligently at work studying the letters."

"You only reached a conclusion about a week ago?"

"About that long ago."

Thomson asked Carvalho if he had photographic reproductions of the letters. Despite an objection from District Attorney Jordan, Carvalho confirmed he possessed photographs of the letters to allow him to continue his examinations in absence of the originals.

"Do you treat the request writings as normal or abnormal?"

"If there was only one writing, I might think that they were not normal but the documents are in ink and pencil duplicates. I would prefer them written under different circumstances."

Qualifications of the writer, Carvalho admitted, were important to determine because the letters indicated the writer possessed skill and a high order of penmanship; but as a whole, Carvalho testified the letters were of only medium skill. Asked if a fluent writer would be best able to disguise his handwriting, Carvalho said, "The poorer the writer the greater his ability to disguise his writing. The better the writer, the harder it is for him to disguise his writing."

After Attorney Thomson concluded, District Attorney Jordan stood up.

"You said in cross-examination that it has been difficult for you to reach a conclusion because one of the defendants is a friend of yours. Who is that friend?"

Taking a gulp of air, Carvalho shifted his gaze to the defense table.

"Mr. Perkins," Carvalho said shakily.

District Attorney Jordan grabbed a bundle of checks and two books, showing them to Carvalho, with the witness confirming these were the other handwriting samples mentioned during cross-examination. Jordan moved to offer the items into evidence.

"Doctor," Attorney Thomson said, "was it June 8th that Perkins called to see you?"

Carvalho pulled a letter from his pocket, reading it carefully.

"June 9th."

District Attorney Jordan asked Judge Orr for permission to read the three Black Hand letters and the Cleveland letter, which was granted.

The courtroom remained deathly silent as Jordan recited each in dramatic fashion.

"Your honor," Jordan concluded, "I think we are through, but the papers in this case are large and I may have overlooked something. May I ask that court adjourn until afternoon?"

Judge Orr granted Jordan's request and announced a recess until 2:00 p.m. Defense attorneys immediately hurried into a private conference as the courtroom emptied.

Following the recess, District Attorney Jordan announced the government would rest.

The battle anticipated by defense attorneys had arrived.

9

THE SCAPEGOAT

A ttorney W.H.S Thomson applauded the jurors for their close attention given to witnesses called by the government, asking they give the same consideration to the defense.

"We ask that you withhold your decision until you hear all of the evidence," Thomson said. "The charge is that Mr. Perkins and Mr. Franklin have conspired to do an unlawful act, to send certain Black Hand letters to Mr. Strong to extort money under threat of destruction of life and property. This is a most serious case for the defendants, involving reputation, and technically their all. Three crimes have been committed. First, some person broke into the Scott mausoleum and laid their unholy hands on the sacred bodies of the dead. Second, some black-hearted coward wrote letters demanding $50,000, or their lives would be taken. Third, an attempt has been made—and I want it fully understood that I am not speaking of the United States district attorney nor the government officials, but two or three men to be named—to fasten the other crimes on this old gentleman, Mr. Perkins, who has engaged in business 40 years."

Charges of conspiracy, Thomson declared, would be defended by counter-conspiracy against the government, and through four experts, the defense would exonerate Charles Franklin of being the writer of the Black Hand letters. Similar to the government's opening statement, Thomson explained the involvement of Gilbert Perkins and Charles Franklin, insisting the Perkins Agency wished to work in harmony with the Burns Agency.

"But the Burns man refused," Thomson said sullenly, claiming Perkins asked three times to be relieved from the case, although he sympathized with the Strongs.

"There is no hostility between Mr. Perkins and Mrs. Strong except as their minds have been poisoned by other persons."

Thomson said Perkins's actions after the arrival of the "Black Mail" letters were not suspicious at all, detailing the additional steps by Perkins until the agency's discharge on February 18. After Charles Franklin had been "distrusted by Mrs. Strong," Thomson continued, Perkins instructed Franklin to return to Philadelphia.

"The man, who will appear in this case, was in Erie at the time that the Black Hand letters were mailed. He was in Erie when the letter denouncing Mr. Franklin was written. He has been an enemy of Mr. Perkins for years. He declared that he would get even if it took him 20 years. We will prove that he is a skillful writer and that he wrote all four letters, by the tests of four handwriting experts who have studied the handwriting of Mr. Dempsey and the handwriting of Mr. Franklin. Keep your eye on him. We will prove to you that this man was in Indianapolis when the raid was made on the Perkins office by calling two men who recognized him. At a certain hearing in Pittsburg, this man was met by another to whom he said that he had not seen him since we raided Perkins. One of these men is a justice of the peace. Those torn pieces of paper were put in the envelope taken from Mr. Perkins.

"They were not in the envelope when taken from his pocket. In it were the parts torn from the letters for the purpose of planting the crime on Mr. Perkins. We will call a gentleman to whom he said, 'You defendants had better look out; they intend to put it on me.'"

The copper plates from the mausoleum, Thomson maintained, were carried "secretly to a place in Erie at night." Referring to the documents handed over by Gilbert Perkins, Thomson said the defense would show Perkins placed the codicil to his will and a list of operatives into the envelope no more than forty minutes before his arrest. Perkins, Thomson's voice rose, never asked for the envelope to be returned, only the codicil for his will.

"The whole scheme was a conspiracy of the men who wrote the letters, for the purpose of driving out of business the Perkins detective agency."

After thirty-five minutes, Harry Perkins was called as the first witness and testified about his credentials, acknowledging he notified Charles Franklin to come to Erie. Perkins testified about helming the investigation until his father arrived and took over, including the details of the discovery of

Anna McCollum's body. Detectives from the Burns Detective Agency were assigned to the case when he told Annie Strong of the discovery.

"Did you find certain articles in the mausoleum?" Thomson asked.

"Yes, we found pieces of cloth, a broken knife blade, a handkerchief, cigarette butts, a broken piece of a whisky flask, and silver hand plates which had been removed from one of the caskets. I assisted in gathering up these things."

"Did you turn them over to your father?"

"I did. I took them to his room in the Reed House."

"What next?"

Perkins testified he interviewed Amelia Hertwig and spoke with detectives from the Burns Detective Agency at the mausoleum before District Attorney Jordan objected to Thomson's questioning. Judge Orr overruled the motion, telling Jordan he could not see the relation of his argument to the line of questioning. Supplementary objections leveled by Jordan in an attempt to keep the Burns Agency from being mentioned were equally unsuccessful.

Attorney Thomson argued that it would be impossible for the defense to continue in this manner and in a disdainful tone said the government would have to admit to the truth. Jordan pointed defiantly at Thomson, accusing him of unprofessional remarks before Judge Orr cracked his gavel in an attempt to restore order.

After several minutes, Harry Perkins continued, explaining he had been approached by a Burns detective questioning him about Dan Mathews, briefly considered a suspect by Perkins. Perkins, who interviewed Mathews in the presence of Charles Franklin and Detective Sergeant Richard Crotty, told the rival operative he did not think Mathews was involved, leading the Burns detective to become enraged and accuse someone of leaking information.

Other details in Perkins's testimony consisted of discussing a reward with Annie Strong, which he advised against, as it would have hindered the investigation and attracted outsiders attempting to claim the reward. Perkins confirmed he left Erie for Pittsburg on February 13, 1911.

Through brief cross-examination, District Attorney Jordan asked Perkins the names of the operatives from the Perkins Agency who assisted with the mausoleum case.

Silence reigned as Charles Franklin ambled to the witness stand. Testifying about his arrival in Erie, Franklin's narrative led up to his arrival at the Erie Cemetery and details of the interior of the mausoleum. Deemed "particularly graphic" by the press, Franklin described how he pried open the broken coffin lid belonging to Mary Matilda Scott with Detective Sergeant Richard Crotty.

Annie Strong, sitting in the corner of the courtroom, buried her head in her hands and openly wept.

Asked who he felt committed the desecration, Franklin thought the work was done by "half drunk ghouls."

Franklin spoke of searching the neighboring streets of Little Italy and speaking to Gilbert Perkins, requesting permission to return to Philadelphia to work on a pressing case there, adding he left Erie on February 13 and did not return until after his arrest.

On February 23, Franklin claimed he was in the cities of Harrisburg and Chambersburg, which could be corroborated by daily reports from the agency office.

Asked about his arrest, Franklin testified he arrived at Inspector Cortelyou's office in the federal building and provided reports as requested in the mausoleum case. When shown the four standard letters, Franklin admitted they were written by him. Franklin, when asked about his first impression of the Black Hand letters, chalked it up to nothing more than "newspaper sensationalism."

"Will you please state whether or not you wrote any of these letters?" Thomson asked, showing the Black Hand letters to Franklin.

"I did not."

"Did you ever have any knowledge of them?"

"Not until the day of my arrest except as I was told."

Asked about the conversation between him and Frank Crane in Erie, Franklin disputed portions of Crane's testimony before District Attorney Jordan rose to begin his cross-examination.

Franklin recited details of his tenure with the Perkins Agency and past employment, including his work as a licensed detective in Erie. When Jordan asked Franklin if he lost his license, Attorney Thomson sternly objected. Judge Orr overruled the objection, and a brief legal skirmish ensued, with Jordan arguing the question was relevant because of Franklin's creditability as a witness.

Orr instructed Jordan to refine his question.

"Did you blame the Strongs for having your license revoked?"

"I most certainly did not."

"Did you tell the chief of police that you blamed the Strongs for this?"

"Most positively not, he is one of the witnesses I want to explain."

"Where were you in Erie just prior to February 10th?"

"I was here on January 22nd and was also here on January 12th and 13th."

"Where did you stop in Erie in January?"

"At the Reed House."

"Did you say that when you wrote these letters Mr. Cortelyou requested you to write 'Black Hand,' and write it large?"

"He did."

"Was it natural?"

"I wrote it," Franklin said. "It must be natural."

At 4:15 p.m., District Attorney Jordan concluded his cross-examination, and court was adjourned until the next morning.

The next morning, Olive Buller, a stenographer and bookkeeper for the Perkins Agency in Philadelphia, confirmed she was custodian of the daily reports and identified a logbook produced by Attorney Thomson, reasserting the dates of Charles Franklin's travel to Erie and his visit to Harrisburg on February 23, 1911. She admitted she was familiar with Franklin's handwriting through additional papers.

Despite a brief objection by District Attorney Jordan, Buller was not cross-examined.

John McCain, John Drew and Charles McLaughlin, operatives from the Perkins Agency, testified about their involvement in the mausoleum case, with McCain's testimony detailing his brief departure to Conneaut in an attempt to locate a man named "Gilmore."

Whispers carried through the courtroom as Gilbert Perkins feebly perched himself on the stand, testifying his attention was first called to the case while in Indianapolis after receiving a telegram from his son. Thomson asked Perkins to describe the mausoleum's condition when he arrived in Erie.

"In the tomb my eyes met a horrible sight," Perkins stammered. "There were the partly demolished coffins with their gruesome contents, copper plates bearing the names of Mr. and Mrs. McCollom [*sic*] and Richard Townsend on the floor. Casket handles and debris were also scattered on the floor of the tomb. I was convinced that it was the job of amateurs. They had chiseled around the marble slabs closing the end of the crypts when they could have broken them easily with a hammer. While some of my men were searching for clues, Franklin and Harry saw something in what appeared to be an empty crypt which excited their curiosity. Further investigation revealed that it was a body. Undertaker A.P. Burton was called and it was learned that no body was missing. I was besieged by newspapermen who demanded to know if it were true that no body was missing, but I would not answer them and I told them to see Mrs. Strong. I gave my theory there and then, and it is the same today."

"Objection," shouted District Attorney Jordan.

Judge Orr sustained, informing Perkins to only testify about what he did and the reasoning for his actions, not theories.

Perkins nodded, testifying about clues leading to a man previously employed with the Erie Cemetery and a "pal" named Connors, from Buffalo. The men, Perkins said, were traced to a boardinghouse in Conneaut, and he later sent some of his men there, but no clues developed that justified an arrest.

When questioned about the Burns Agency, Perkins proclaimed he tried to work with their detectives.

"I asked the Burns agent in charge here why we could not work together, as well as two lawyers could," Perkins claimed, wringing his hands in frustration, "and he said it could not be done."

"I studied deeply to fix upon the probable motive. I worried a great deal and was on my feet day and night. Finally I came to the conclusion that two drunken, desperate men had broken in there and tore things to pieces and that letters would follow. That was my theory then. It's my theory today. I made the statement to others with whom I conferred."

"Why did you say you thought letters would follow?"

"Because I was convinced that whoever did the job did not go to the tomb for gain. They did not expect to find anything there. They did the job to intimidate the Strongs and it was a theory my long experience in criminal affairs suggested. I believed the tomb was broken into to frighten the Strongs so that they would give when a demand was made. I expected the letters to follow."

"You heard Mr. Sobel testify?"

"I did."

"Did you have any conversation with Postmaster Isador Sobel prior to receiving the first Black Hand letter?"

"I did not."

"He said," continued Thomson, reciting Sobel's testimony, "you and he had a discussion regarding the spelling of the word 'Pennsylvania' in the 'Black Hand' letter. Did you?"

"Now, I don't recollect, as I didn't pay much attention to the letter."

"He said that on the first interview after the receipt of the first letter you asked him why did he supposed [*sic*] the letter was torn in that peculiar manner, and then explained that when the man who wrote the letter was captured the torn piece of paper would be found on him. Did you make any such statement?"

"None whatever."

"Did you say to him that the second letter would be torn the same way?"

"I did not."

"Did you predict to him that the torn pieces of paper would be found on the man who wrote the letters?"

"I did not."

Asked about the agency's discharge, Perkins said he was told to call Charles Strong. After phoning Strong in his office, he was told Annie Strong had assumed full charge of the investigation and the agency was no longer required to work on the case.

"Why was Franklin sent back at an earlier date?"

"It appeared that Franklin had some enemies here and Mrs. Strong had received a letter from Cleveland warning her against Franklin. My son said Mrs. Strong did not want Franklin at work on the case, so I relieved him of further duty on the case on February 13th."

Perkins returned to Pittsburg on February 19 and two days later received a special delivery letter from Annie Strong before departing to work on a murder case in Warren, Pennsylvania. While in Warren, Perkins learned of his son-in-law's suicide in Indianapolis and departed by way of Erie.

Thomson then quizzed Perkins about his arrest in Indianapolis.

"I came down to my office that morning with some papers which I had secured from the office of Mr. Adams. I wanted to go to a department store nearby, but before going I took from my pocket several letters, envelopes containing the reports of four or five operatives, and a lot of little booklets. I put all these on my desk. Then I placed in a long envelope a list of the names and addresses of my operatives, and the codicil to my will."

"What kind of an envelope was it?"

"A large envelope which Mr. Ross handed to me."

"Now, I'll ask you. Did you have about you or anywhere near you a Reed House envelope?"

"No, sir, I did not."

"Had you ever seen any of the pieces of paper torn from the letter?"

"I had not."

"Had you any knowledge of them?"

"I had no knowledge whatever."

Perkins, in a loud, dramatic tone, claimed that when he returned to his office he found the postal inspectors, a dozen men in all.

"I was shocked," Perkins said. "As we were about to start one of the men said, 'If you have any papers about you, you had better deliver them now.' We turned over the papers in the confusion that prevailed and walked out with the marshals."

"It was stated by Mr. Woltz," said Thomson, "that you asked for the return of the long envelope. Did you ask for the return of that envelope?"

"I did not."

Perkins became apprised of the charges against him during his preliminary hearing in Indianapolis and when he returned to his office found it had been wrecked during the raid.

Judge Orr interrupted Perkins as Thomson expressed Perkins's description of his offices after the raid was material in connection to the government witnesses. Orr allowed Perkins's testimony to proceed, with Perkins adding the telephone wires were cut and his valuable papers taken.

"I show you the Black Hand letters and ask you if you have any knowledge of the writing or the sending of these letters?" Thomson asked.

"I have not."

District Attorney Jordan declined to cross-examine Perkins, and court then recessed for lunch.

That afternoon, John Drew, an operative with the Perkins Agency, testified about working alongside James McCain in locating the man named Gilmore and James Connors, former employees of the Strongs, as well as a visit to a saloon at Twenty-Sixth and Peach Streets. Drew testified he purchased envelopes at the Erie Drug Company at Twenty-Sixth and Peach Streets and another business in addition to whiskey in a flask, similar to one found inside the mausoleum. All items, Drew testified, were turned over to Gilbert Perkins and marked for identification.

Surveillance of the downtown post office, Drew continued, occurred from 6:00 p.m. to 11:00 p.m. on February 17, in an attempt to locate the person who mailed the Black Hand letters. The following day, Drew confirmed he returned to Pittsburg.

Frank Williams, sheriff of Venango County, was called and waited on the witness stand as defense attorneys huddled for a short conference before Thomson stepped up to Sheriff Williams.

"Do you know Thomas J. Dempsey?" asked Attorney Thomson.

"Yes, sir."

"How long have you known him?"

"Six or eight years."

"I will now show you a paper marked exhibit 12, under the date of July 30, 1908, and would ask if you were present and saw this paper written?"

"I was."

"Who wrote that paper?"

"I object!" Jordan yelled. "Any further examination of the witness would open an issue which would last for hours."

Jordan turned to Thomson, asking for an offer of proof.

Thomson claimed the purpose was to show the letter as a standard writing for Thomas Dempsey in the belief Dempsey wrote the Black Hand letters to Charles Strong. Jordan argued there was no evidence to show Dempsey wrote the letters, calling the court's attention that the paper presented could not be offered into evidence because it was offered as a standard.

"We offered those four letters as part of a conversation and that is the only way these letters could be introduced," Jordan said before reciting other opinions from prior government cases.

"Now if your honor please and upon the law of Pennsylvania there can be no question that the evidence is not admissible. They have no right to introduce a collateral issue here! What would happen if we should call Dempsey and as a prisoner he could not testify? What position would we be in? It's unfair to us and it places us in a position where we might not be able to defend ourselves," Jordan continued before submitting the laws loudly in relation to expert testimony.

Judge Orr asked Thomson if he had anything to say.

"I believe that in a criminal suit the defendant can not only prove his own innocence, but may show who did commit the offense. We are not injuring the government when we show that some other person commits the crime. We should not be alarmed if the government is surprised when they accuse innocence unjustly," Thomson retorted. "If Mr. Franklin and Mr. Perkins simply confined to their own guilt or innocence in this trial or can we prove who did write these letters and bring the guilty party to justice when we have the evidence in our possession."

Thomson motioned to Perkins and Franklin.

"Is Mr. Franklin and Mr. Perkins simply limited to a denial or can we prove who is guilty? I assert here there is not a scintilla of evidence against Franklin. If Franklin falls out of the case, then Perkins does, too."

A laugh rippled from the courtroom.

Vexed, Thomson waited until the laughter evaporated before continuing: "I think my offer is permitted because, first, as a general proposition, the defendant has a right to deny and prove the guilty party if he can do so; and secondly, this offer is to be followed by the testimony of an expert."

"This has raised a collateral issue and is not permissible," Judge Orr determined, sustaining the objection and sealing an exception for the defense.

Charles Franklin was recalled to identify daily reports from the Perkins Agency dated April 12–19, 1910. After the defense offered the reports as standards of Franklin's handwriting, District Attorney Jordan objected, arguing the papers were selected by the defense and considered self-serving. Judge Orr agreed, and the writings were excluded as standard writings.

The next witness, Dr. Albert Hamilton, claimed many titles when introducing himself. A druggist from Auburn, New York, Hamilton considered himself a chemist and expert in handwriting, fingerprinting, forensic toxicology and microscopy. Hamilton first examined photographs of the Black Hand and standard letters on July 5, 1911, at the Perkins Agency office in Pittsburg, as well as the "Black Hand" letter from Franklin. Attorney Thomson cautioned Hamilton to confine his responses to the case in Erie and Hamilton, nodding in the affirmative. He continued his summary of his examinations, consisting of seven photographs, stating his opinion that he felt several persons were involved in writing the letters, including the Cleveland letter.

"Did you form an opinion as to whether or not the writer of the Black Hand letters and the Cleveland letter was the same as the writer of the four request letters?" O'Brien asked.

Before Hamilton could respond, District Attorney Jordan objected, arguing the government never claimed the Cleveland letter was written by the same person, offering it for other purposes. Judge Orr, viewing the argument as immaterial, sealed an exception for the defense.

Charles O'Brien continued with his argument, claiming nobody saw Franklin write the letters in question. After ten minutes, Judge Orr asked O'Brien how a defendant could choose, at random, such papers as he wanted for samples of his handwriting. Attorney Thomson interjected, seeking to further the defense's point, and was asked to support his argument with documentation. Thomson acknowledged he would present them before the court.

Judge Orr announced he would withhold his ruling until the following morning in case they had law points on the question, which was agreed on by both sides, as court was adjourned for the afternoon.

An eager W.H.S. Thomson opened court on the morning of July 26, 1911, with his argument to enter into evidence Charles Franklin's reports from 1910 and the anonymous Cleveland letter, citing opinions from both the Pennsylvania and U.S. courts justifying the papers' submission unless all papers written by Franklin were offered. Reading from an opinion, Thomson was halted by District Attorney Jordan, who claimed the opinion he referenced was from a civil case and therefore was not applicable.

"Suppose that one hand wrote all the letters, that would be conclusive evidence that Franklin did not write them as one of them is denunciatory of Franklin," Thomson argued. "By the doctrine of exclusion, Franklin could not be guilty of the crime."

Jordan cited a ruling of the Supreme Court in his arguments against changing the procedure and evidence. Jordan again repeated the government was not claiming the Cleveland letter was written by Franklin, and it was therefore not submitted as a standard like Franklin's dictated letters.

"It has not been used as a standard and in any other way for the handwriting. Why should they be allowed to introduce a collateral issue? They have their experts here to examine the standard letters. It would bring in a separate issue."

"The objection to the admissibility of Franklin's letters is sustained, but the objection to the Cleveland letter is overruled," Judge Orr said, allowing the jurors to review the letter as evidence to make their own comparisons.

Following the ruling, Albert Hamilton continued his testimony and was asked by Attorney Thomson if he felt the writer of the Black Hand letters and Cleveland letter was also the writer of the Philadelphia standard letters.

"The writer of the request letters is not the writer of the Black Hand letters and the Cleveland letter. The three black hand letters and envelopes and the Cleveland letter and envelope were written by the same man although there were two alterations."

The standard letters, Hamilton continued, appeared to have been done with normal, natural writing compared to the Black Hand letters, which appeared to be performed with "the influence of the dictator," pointing to what he claimed was erasures and over-writings in the Black Hand letters, with the word *Peach* on the envelope for the first letter, appearing altered, with further strokes in the letter being completely different than Franklin's standard letters. With the naked eye, Hamilton said, the strokes appeared similar, but under a microscope they showed evidence of having been done by a different hand.

The Black Hand letter sent to Chief Wagner, Hamilton continued, showed no alterations. He insisted that the "writer of the black hand letters was a free hand writer," with circular movements, whereas Charles Franklin's writing consisted of sharp points and angles.

Visibly introducing the details from the letters, along with his comparisons, Hamilton informed the jurors altogether they possessed seventy-five characteristics of an individual different from the standard letters. Hamilton's attempt to show photographs of the Black Hand letters earned a rebuke from District Attorney Jordan, who cautioned the defense's witness, leading Hamilton to reconsider and only mention them later on.

Hamilton testified Charles Franklin was a slow, medium-poor writer, both unsteady and wavering, and the Black Hand writer was rapid and efficient with a "firm stroke."

"Franklin writes with a slant which is normal while the black hand writer does not. These are a few of the many reasons upon which I base my opinion that Franklin did not write the black hand letters. The poorer writer cannot disguise better than his writing. That is the condition here and yet the disputed writings contain many fine strokes of penmanship. He cannot disguise beyond his ability."

The Cleveland letter, compared to the Black Hand letters, manifested several instances where Hamilton claimed he was inclined to believe they were written by the same person.

W.H.S. Thomson concluded his questioning, returning to the defense table as District Attorney Jordan rose from his chair, removing his glasses.

"Why are you called doctor? Are you a practicing physician?"

"No, sir," Hamilton smirked. "That is a title accorded to me by the Supreme court because of my skill in detecting cases where the death of a person has been in doubt. It was tacked to me and I cannot help it."

"Are you a registered pharmacist?"

"I am the owner of a drug store. I am a licensed graduate of pharmacy of the Columbia University."

"Have you ever attended any college where they teach handwriting?"

"I do not know of any such college."

"You have given the opinion that the Cleveland letter was written by the same person as the black hand letters?"

"Yes."

"Is it natural or disguised?"

"Both."

"Men writing would naturally try to disguise their writing?"

"They do."

"You called attention to black hand letter number one. Pennsylvania is spelled correctly?"

"Yes."

"Is it not visible that a change was made in the spelling of Pennsylvania?"

"Yes."

"Does not that show that the man remembered that his attention was called to the misspelled word?"

"Well," Hamilton hesitated, "no."

"That shows an effort was made to change it after it was written?"

"Yes, at some time."

"You said it might have been made by another pencil—then by two persons?"

"Yes."

"Then, does it not follow that these two persons were working together?"

"No!" Hamilton protested.

"Objection!" screamed Thomson.

Judge Orr overruled the objection.

"It follows that they were working independently," Hamilton insisted.

"Did you see that through a microscope?"

"No."

Sparse laughter echoed from the spectators gallery. Hamilton said the letters appeared to have been retouched after the government gained possession of Franklin's writings. Jordan then hammered away at Hamilton's examination of the letters, focusing on both similarities and dissimilarities within the letters.

"You have testified that you examined these with great care, yet you say you cannot recall any similarity."

Hamilton remained silent.

"Can you, after the exhaustive examination, point out any others?" Jordan urged.

"That could be answered yes or no and both are correct. If you mean the same type of 'y,' yes; if you speak of relationship of strokes and size of loops, no."

"Answer it," Jordan countered. "Yes or no."

"I can't answer it that way."

Judge Orr interrupted, announcing a recess for lunch.

When court resumed in the afternoon, District Attorney Jordan briefly continued his cross-examination of Hamilton, asking him the dates and locations he observed the letters involved in the case before returning to the government's table.

Webster Melcher, a lawyer and document specialist from Philadelphia, followed, clutching lengthy notes and a large chart underneath his arm, which was soon unfurled, revealing a series of colored lines, strokes, curves and figures from the Black Hand letters.

A member of the bar in Philadelphia, Melcher attested he spent seventeen years testifying in cases throughout Pennsylvania and neighboring states. His examination of all the letters occurred on July 17, 1911. He viewed the photographs first and the original letters later and was of the opinion the writer of the Black Hand letters was the same as the individual who wrote the Cleveland letter. Providing a demonstration based off his examination of the letters as Attorney Thomson aided in manipulating the charts, Melcher spoke "much like a schoolmaster"[34] to the various forms, position and spaces of the letters.

"From the facts that you have detailed could, in your opinion, the writer of the request writings have written the Black Hand and Cleveland letters?" Thomson asked.

"It would have been a physical impossibility for the writer of the request letters to write the Black Hand letters and the Cleveland letter," Melcher said.

"In your opinion was the writer of the Black Hand letters and the Cleveland letter the same man?"

"He was the same person undoubtedly."

David Carvalho, seated next to District Attorney Jordan, whispered suggestions to Jordan before he began his cross-examination,[35] which proved equally as brutal as his confrontation with Albert Hamilton.

"Mr. Melcher I believe you said you were a lawyer in Philadelphia. Are you still on the job as an attorney?" Jordan asked.

"Yes."

"Then you are just taking up this expert handwriting business as a sort of side line?"

"You may put it that way if you like."

"Your entire effort has been to show this jury the dissimilarities between the Black Hand letters and the request writing of Franklin?"

"Far from that."

"You mean to say that you have not been showing the jury the dissimilarities?"

"Not as dissimilarities. I have been making an analysis of the handwriting of the writings. If they are dissimilar it is no fault of mine."

"I want a direct answer, sir," Jordan demanded. "You have been showing the jury the dissimilarities of the request writings and the Black Hand letters?"

"That is false," Melcher snapped back.

"I want that answer struck from the record, and now sir, you answer my question or I will request the court to compel you to. You are a lawyer and know that I have a right to demand an answer."

"That answer must be taken off the record," Judge Orr said to the court reporters before turning to Melcher, "and the witness will answer the question at once."

"I have not."

"Do you wish the jury to understand that you have not been showing them the dissimilarities of the writings?"

"I do not."

"Do you say that the Black Hand letters were not disguised?"

"Only partly."

"Would not the part of the letters that was not disguised be the part that the man would write unconsciously?"

"Not entirely; men often write threatening letters in their natural hand."

"Did you expect to find the Black Hand letters disguised?"

"I had no expectation of finding disguise. I found a whole lot of dissimilarities and have pointed out some of them."

"You are a lawyer and know what you should do, why are you not frank in answering my questions?"

"If you're as frank as I am, you'll be all right."

"One Black Hand letter was written with a forward hand, was it not?"

"I don't call anything forward hand."

"Do you mean to say that you are an expert and do not know what forward hand and back hand writing is?"

"I know what some people call back hand writing."

"Were the Black Hand letters written in the same general style of forward and backhand writing?"

"You will have to define what you mean."

"I am not defining anything for you, sir," Jordan riposted. "You will answer the question or the court will make you answer."

Judge Orr reminded Melcher he testified to knowing back and forward handwriting and should answer the question.

"The letters are written both ways," Melcher reluctantly admitted.

Jordan showed Melcher the first Black Hand letter.

"I ask you if this letter is not written backhand?"

"If you mean that it slants to the left of the vertical, it is backhand. I find both kinds of writing near the bottom."

Jordan followed with the Black Hand letter.

"I ask you if this letter is not written forward hand?"

"If you mean that the writing slants to the right of the vertical, it is forward hand. I find both kinds of writing in it."

"You say that you find two different styles of writing in these letters?"

"I do not mean two different styles of handwriting, but one very wide range of style."

Jordan asked Melcher if he noticed the word *Pennsylvania* in the letters. Melcher acknowledged the word was spelled differently. The remainder of Jordan's cross-examination of Melcher focused on Melcher's time in examining the "Black Hand" letters and the Cleveland letters, which were viewed between July 18 and 22.

After the conclusion of District Attorney Jordan's exhausting cross-examination, court adjourned for the evening.

10

AFFAIRS OF CONSPIRACY

On the morning of July 27, 1911, Professor George Wood, a certified expert accountant and self-described student, teacher, artist and expert since 1891, testified to having performed a careful examination of the Black Hand letters, in person and through photographs, and found them all identical and written by the same hand. The case, Wood said, was different from those usually presented because the papers were disguised.

After earning a stern rebuke from Judge Orr to confine his testimony to his examinations only, Wood explained finding the alphabetical characters distorted and accompanied by displays of symmetrical movement. The standard letters written by Charles Franklin, Wood continued, were different from the Black Hand letters and exhibited irregular curves, limited by restrained methods from the wrist or flexure of the fingers.

"Did your examination of the Black Hand letters include the Cleveland letter?" asked Attorney Thomson.

"I did. The Black Hand letters and Cleveland letter display greater skill than the request writings due to Charles Franklin's physical inability to write them."

With photographs, Professor Wood compared the different strokes in the letters and envelopes, suggesting the long lines were written without any guidelines, which was proof the writer displayed more than ordinary skill with similarities to the Cleveland letter and the Black Hand letters.

"After applying your tests, Professor, what opinion have you of the four letters, was or was not the writer the same?"

"In my opinion, they were written by the same party."

Thomson completed his examination by asking Wood if he noticed changes within one of the Black Hand letters, and Professor Wood told Thomson he had not noticed them particularly.

"Can you make pictures?" District Attorney Jordan asked, approaching Wood.

"I can but I don't do it," Wood replied, saying he felt the Black Hand letters were disguised with forward and backhand writing.

"He would want to prevent detection?"

"I should think so."

"Is the Cleveland letter normal or disguised?"

"It is more nearly normal than the Black Hand letters."

Wood admitted fragments of the letter he considered disguised could be attributed to the writer's habit and experience and considered the Cleveland letter normal.

"Then you are making a comparison of a practically normal letter with the Black Hand letters that are disguised?"

"Yes, but the principles underlying the disguise are the force of habit of the writer."

"You spoke of another characteristic, that was the manner in which the postage stamp was on the Cleveland letter? What bearing has that?"

"Habit."

"You never saw any other envelope on which that man put a stamp?"

"Yes, unless it was the Charles Strong Black Hand letters."

"There are two one-cent stamps," Jordan said, calling Wood's attention to the envelope for the Cleveland letter. "Wouldn't that be the consistent way to put them on?"

"Yes."

"Are those stamps separated?"

"No, sir."

"Why did you say to this jury that because the man put the stamps on that way he wrote the Black Hand letters?"

"I did not say that. I only said it was a thing that attracted my attention."

Jordan then handed the envelopes for the Black Hand letters to Wood, asking if he saw similarities in the placement of the stamps. Wood said no, adding they were all different in respect to relationship of margin. Asked if the paper for the Cleveland letter was different from the Black Hand letters, Wood replied that it was altogether different.

"In the chief of police letter, the first line is clear over to the side of the envelope but the second line is not; how is that?"

"I expect it is because there was no room left for the second line to the left."

"You have seen that all three of the other letters do not have the second line of the address started farther to the left; do you still adhere to your opinion that it is a custom of the writer?"

"I do."

"When did you first see the Black Hand letters?"

"In Erie, last week."

"How much time did you have for the examination?"

"About an hour the first time, and on Saturday of last week I had them an hour and a half or two hours."

"When did you first see the photographs?"

"Early in June at Columbus, in the possession of Mr. Pengelly."

"You took the photographs to copy?"

"Yes, sir."

"Did you give the copies of the photographs to anyone?"

"I did not."

"Were they ever out of your possession?"

"About the middle of June."

"Who got them?"

"Mr. Sayres, attorney for General Miller."

"When at Columbus were you employed by the Perkins Detective Agency?"

"No, sir."

"Didn't you ask to have employment as an expert for the government?"

"Never. I had too many engagements. I wanted to get someone to help me."

"Didn't you get the photographs after you were promised employment by the government?"

"Not at all, sir."

"Did you not in Columbus, in the presence of Inspectors Oldfield, Hutches, and Pengelly, ask what the government was paying for experts, and say that the government had a good case?"

"Never; I am not built on those lines," Wood stammered. "I went to Columbus about other cases. Mr. Pengelly expressed a wish that I be retained and collaborate with him. I met Mr. Oldfield by chance in the lobby of the hotel where we were working. Mr. Oldfield asked me what I was working on. I told him that I had the General Miller letter. He asked me if I would show it to him and I told him that I had not the authority. Mr. Oldfield then asked me if I would accept employment with the government. I told him that I would make any examination that he desired. He took down my address. I never asked employment in this case and never have in any case."

"When was your talk with Inspector Oldfield?"

"Before I photographed the letter."

"When did you become employed in this case?"

"Shortly after July 4th."

"Can't you fix the time exactly?"

"Not any more than it was a day or two after the Fourth of July."

"Have you no record of your employment?"

"I don't count the time that is unnecessary."

"Is there a letter from Mr. Pengelly fixing the date of the return of the photographs?"

"I think there is."

Jordan concluded his cross-examination as Attorney Thomson handed Wood a letter, asking if he recollected the date of the return of the photographs before the defense's final handwriting expert, Hailmer D. Gould, took the stand.

A former faculty member of Mt. Union College in higher mathematics and natural sciences, Gould was previously engaged in the detection of counterfeit money in coordination with the Treasury of the United States, chief of the Secret Service and the Library of Congress in also studying forged signatures through microscopy. Often employed by the government, Gould asserted he was responsible for the discovery of new principles and methods and had testified in various courts throughout the country.

Asked about the "Black Hand" letters and the Cleveland letter, Gould confirmed he had formed an opinion, adding he sought to discover whether the writer of the letters possessed a "gliding touch." Through an examination of Franklin's standard letters, Gould asserted Franklin wrote without lifting his pencil; the reverse, Gould insisted, was true of the writer of the Black Hand letters. To show the relative pressure of the pen on the paper, Gould said the paper's surface was full of "mounds" and "bushes" and the depth of the pen pressure, or ink, could be measured through a microscope.

These observations led Gould to theorize the standard letters were similar on the "up" and "down" strokes, written with a finger movement. This contrasted with Franklin, who had a tendency to lift the pen every three or four letters, different from the finger movement he observed in the Black Hand letters.

Gould argued Franklin wrote with his pen pointing over his elbow, utilizing finger and wrist movements, and the writer of the Cleveland letter wrote with the pen pointing over the shoulder. Questioned about alterations within the Black Hand letters, Gould testified the graphite showed alterations made with a finer pencil.

Asked about his charts, Gould declined to open them, as Judge Orr intended to adjourn until the afternoon. That afternoon, continuing his testimony, Gould unveiled his charts, consisting of different pencil strokes and characters.

Gould professed it would have been physically impossible for Franklin to have written the Black Hand letters and began to argue his point to the jurors when he was halted by District Attorney Jordan.

"Is the witness presenting an argument or testimony?"

Judge Orr flashed a smile, and Gould promptly changed course, arguing the writer of the "Black Hand" letters and the Cleveland letter were the same.

District Attorney Jordan approached Gould's chart, eyeing the illustrations as he glided into his cross-examination, pointing to the illustrations and asking about them. Gould informed Jordan they were made through use of a microscope and then placed onto paper.

"The effect of pen and ink on paper would depend on the kind of pen, kind of paper and kind of ink?" Jordan asked.

"Yes, sir."

"The request letters and the Cleveland letter are the only ones written in ink?"

"Yes, sir."

"The paper is vastly different?"

"Yes, sir, it comes from different factories."

Jordan queried the position to the pen and hand, attempting to discredit Gould's conclusions, calling attention to the texture of the Black Hand letters and the standard writings. Gould contended he could tell by the microscope where the writer stopped to ink the pen or changed his arm movement.

"When did you receive the black hand papers first?"

"July 18th, in this building."

"How long did you have them?"

"An hour or two."

"When did you see the chief of police letter?"

"Same time."

"When did you see the Franklin letters?"

"Yesterday for three-quarters of an hour."

"When did you make these charts?"

"The last one last night."

"Up until you came here you had not seen the original paper and you had these charts here?"

"Yes."

"When did you get these photographs?"

"Middle of June. I did not have the chief of police letter."

"When did you first see the Franklin letter photographs?"

"After I came here."

Asked if two persons worked on the word *Pennsylvania* in the Black Hand letter, Gould affirmed this was true, and the government's cross-examination ended at 2:55 p.m.

Walter W. Perkins, son of Gilbert Perkins and manager of the Perkins Agency office in Indianapolis, testified he was not connected to the agency's work in the mausoleum case and recited the story of his arrest on April 13. When quizzed if his father asked for the return of the envelope or papers, Perkins asserted this was incorrect and confirmed that after bail was secured, both he and his father traveled to the postal inspector's office to request the return of the codicil to his will, but this was denied.

John Ross, bookkeeper for the Perkins Agency in Indianapolis, testified to his work with the mausoleum case and the arrest of Walter and Gilbert Perkins. Under cross-examination from District Attorney Jordan, Ross could not remember if U.S. marshals assisted the postal inspectors but recanted when Jordan singled out the U.S. marshals in the courtroom.

George Henderson, the "General," an operative in the Perkins Agency in Indianapolis, testified about his arrival in Erie with a pair of bloodhounds, confirming he left the same day. Similar to the testimony of Walter Perkins and John Ross, Henderson detailed the arrests at the Perkins office on April 13 but was unable to corroborate whether or not Perkins asked for the return of the envelope.

Following Henderson's testimony, the letter dictated by Annie Strong to Gilbert Perkins was placed into evidence; however, Judge Orr refused to allow the letter written by William Pengelly to Professor Wood. Thomson then attempted to enter into evidence additional items tying the Black Hand letters to Thomas Dempsey, but Judge Orr refused, instructing Thomson to present his proposition in writing and furnish a copy to District Attorney Jordan and the court the next morning and he would issue his ruling. He adjourned court for the day.

At the Reed House that evening, a defiant Gilbert Perkins spoke to the *Erie Daily Times.*

"The Burns agency is to blame for my arrest and trial," Perkins said. "I will show if I can before the trial is over how my work on the McNamara case for dynamiting is to blame for the whole affair. The Burns men did not plant the fragments of paper on me themselves, but hired another man, Detective Thomas J. Dempsey, to plant 'em."[36]

The next morning, typewritten copies of the defense's arguments to enter evidence connecting Dempsey as the writer of the Black Hand letters and Cleveland letter were presented to Judge Orr. Neither the government nor defense argued on the points submitted. District Attorney Jordan repeated his objections on the grounds that any matter involving Dempsey amounted to a collateral issue that could not be presented before the jury.

Judge Orr sustained Jordan's objections and sealed an exception for the defendants.

The defense's strategy had been dealt a death blow.

Attorney Thomson offered a certified copy of Isador Sobel's testimony from Charles Franklin's preliminary hearing, adding Sobel testified the evidence offered in Philadelphia was correct and the defense wished to offer it for contradiction.

Judge Orr argued it did not contradict Sobel's testimony, asserting Sobel's attention was called to it and affirmed as correct. Orr rejected Thomson's motion, indicating there was no need to admit the stenographer's report.

The defense moved on by calling character witnesses who testified to the "good nature" of Gilbert Perkins based on their personal and working experiences, including William Magee, mayor of Pittsburg, and several attorneys and former judges throughout western Pennsylvania.

No character witnesses were called for Charles Franklin.

Professor Wood was recalled and asked about copies of the photograph he made and asked by District Attorney Jordan if the copies were the same used in court.

Gilbert Perkins, cross-examined by Jordan, was asked about his travel to Warren. Perkins testified he left Pittsburg on the night of February 21, reaching Warren the next morning, and departed the following day for Indianapolis, stopping briefly in Erie because his train was late. He left that night and arrived in Indianapolis on the morning of February 23.

Charles Franklin was briefly recalled before the defense rested at 10:35 a.m.

As the government entered the rebuttal stage, William Pengelly testified to District Attorney Jordan that Professor Wood did not have the authority to photograph the letters. Jordan asked Pengelly if Wood asked him (Pengelly) to seek the government's employment on the case. Pengelly confirmed this was true and that Wood asked him to speak to Inspector Oldfield. On June 16, 1911, in the company of Inspectors Oldfield and Hutches, Professor Wood asked Oldfield what the government was paying for experts and said he would like to "get in on the side of the government" and could be of great service to the government's case.

Inspector Oldfield corroborated Pengelly's testimony about his conversation with Professor Wood. Cross-examined by the defense, Oldfield said he and Inspector Hutches were introduced to Professor Wood by Pengelly yet denied telling Wood he might call on him and present a matter before him.

Inspector Edward Hutches corroborated the testimonies of Oldfield and Pengelly about the conversation with Professor Wood. Next, William Pengelly was recalled and shown the Cleveland letter, confirming he examined the letter and did not believe the writer was the same as the individual who wrote the "Black Hand" letters, indicating the Cleveland letter consisted of normal writing using a cramped finger movement with limitations and consistency throughout.

David Carvalho, also recalled by Jordan, was asked about the Cleveland letter and echoed the same opinions as William Pengelly. Asked about allegations that the letters were altered, Carvalho denied seeing evidence of alterations and asserted the letters presented during the trial were in the same condition when in his possession.

Through cross-examination, Carvalho was asked by the defense if the absence of a signature on the Cleveland letter was proof the writer attempted to disguise their identity. Carvalho admitted this was a possibility—however, to him, the writing was not disguised.

District Attorney Jordan offered photographic copies of the three Black Hand letters in addition to the four standard letters by Charles Franklin into evidence, without objection.

At 12:05 p.m., Jordan announced the government would rest.

Charles O'Brien asked to submit three law points with a ruling from the court, handing the document to Judge Orr. The first law point, being under the constitution, indicated postal inspectors had no right to obtain a civil search warrant and violated their authority when they raided the Perkins office in Indianapolis and that jurors should take this into consideration when arriving at their verdict.

Orr refused to read the first point aloud.

The second and third points, that postal inspectors and federal witnesses were subjected to the tests of other witnesses in United States court as to their recollection of occurrences, and the jurors must not bring in a verdict of guilty if they had any reasonable doubt as to the guilt of the defendants, were affirmed by Judge Orr before he announced a recess.

When court resumed that afternoon, both sides would present their closing arguments.

11
INNOCENT BEFORE GOD
AND FELLOW MAN

I t was 2:00 p.m. when W.H.S. Thomson addressed the jury.

"This is a charge of conspiracy," Thomson bellowed, "and a conspiracy must be between two persons. An unlawful combination to do an unlawful set is usually shown by acts. If you lay aside the testimony of the handwriting experts and the finding of the torn papers on Mr. Perkins, I challenge the government attorneys to show a single thing. If Mr. Franklin falls then the government case falls. Mr. Franklin was in Philadelphia attending to his business when called to this city. He did not want to come, but like a faithful soldier, obeyed his superior."

Thomson inched toward the jurors, telling the men the postal inspectors did not "have the manhood" to inform him of his arrest and, after a conversation spanning nearly four hours, gained nothing incriminating from Franklin. "Mr. Franklin made not a statement during that whole time that could be used against him. He left Erie before a single Black Hand letter had been received. The letter from Cleveland was introduced by the government to get away from their desperate case and has proved the golden key that unlocks the mystery and will set Mr. Franklin free."

Thomson criticized William Pengelly and David Carvalho, maintaining their testimony was contradicted by experts for the defense. Carvalho, Thomson said, was no expert but merely "a reader of the form of letters" and chastised his delay in arriving at a "reasonable opinion" in his examination. Professor Gould, Thomson championed, demonstrated through a microscope that Franklin was not the writer of the Black Hand letters.

At least one member of the jury, Thomson surmised, would know more about handwriting than Pengelly, with the handwriting evidence pitting four experts against one, or at best four against one and one-half, because Pengelly, Thomson scoffed, could not be counted on as "being more than half a man."

Quoting former United Kingdom prime minister Lord John Russell, Thomson's voice swelled, "I will not hesitate in doing justice to my clients, though it is necessary to tear down the throne itself."

"I did not know Mr. Franklin until this case started," Thomson said, making his way to Franklin, gently placing his hand on the defendant's shoulder, "but I have been pleased with his frank way and manly conduct. Mr. Perkins is a friend of the old days. I wish I had the power to tear off the mask and show the guilty man who is trying to put this crime on this old man."

As Thomson prattled on, members of the Perkins family sobbed. Even Gilbert Perkins was unable to suppress his tears as they streamed down his cheeks.

"Then if Franklin did not write the letters then some scoundrel did! Now all he had to do when he wrote these letters, all he had to do, was to tear off these pieces and preserve them. How did he mean to establish this? The man who wrote the letters tore off the pieces and preserved them to put on Mr. Perkins!

"Sobel was sworn in Philadelphia to tell the truth, so bear with me for Sobel makes himself very prominent in the case," Thomson asserted. He then read Sobel's testimony from Franklin's preliminary hearing about Sobel's accusations that Perkins believed the Strongs would get letters.

It was plain to see, Thomson argued, the word *Pennsylvania* was altered after Franklin's arrest on April 13, 1911. "Gentlemen, I charge they forged the papers they had in their hands," Thomson howled. "Mr. Perkins denies that he said to this man that pieces of paper would be found on the guilty party when he was arrested."

"Now, all that was necessary to be done. All that was necessary for the man who had these papers in his possession to get them to Indianapolis and have a government inspector plant them on Perkins. Who was this man? It was Woltz!"

"Keep your eye on Inspector Woltz, sitting over there," Thomson gesticulated to Woltz, sitting near the government's table. "I will show you that he is the man who consummated this devilish deed. He was the only man who dared to charge Mr. Perkins with the mausoleum desecration, in that he said that he expected to find the coffin plate in his possession, and the torn pieces of paper. On cross examination he said that he was absolutely certain of this. All they needed was the man to represent the great Burns Detective agency, which is interested in the crushing of the Perkinses, and they had the man. You will be justified in finding that he did not have the papers on his person at all, and the evidence shows that the bold man is absolutely guiltless."

Thomson stepped away and approached Gilbert Perkins, keeping his eyes on the jurors.

"Now the old man swears before God, that he put the cordical [*sic*] of his will on the list of Perkins operators in this envelope but an hour before and that he never saw the papers until they were produced by the postal authorities."

Then Thomson cried out, "The wicked flee, when no man pursues," speaking of the postal inspectors' departure from Indianapolis. "Gentlemen will you convict a man on evidence like that? You must be satisfied of guilt beyond a reasonable doubt before finding a defendant guilty. As far as I am concerned I will leave this case in your hands, certain you will do it justice, as you would have justice done by you."

It was at 3:15 p.m. when Attorney Charles O'Brien began his opening statement.

"Mr. Thomson has covered the case in detail and I shall be as brief as possible as you have been patient in this case. I shall confine my remarks to the things that will show you this is more of a persecution than a prosecution. Last February a heinous crime was committed in this county, when ghouls desecrated the Scott mausoleum and today it still remains a mystery. This case has grown out of the other crime and the government has even suggested that this old man became a ghoul and a vandal, that he might get employment and business. Why these government inspectors have told you they believed they would find in Gilbert Perkins' office in Indianapolis a piece of the copper that was stolen from the tomb here in Erie!"

O'Brien stepped out from behind the table.

"Gentlemen, when these inspectors went to the Perkins' office they did not expect to find any copper plate. They just wanted an excuse to raid the Perkins' office. That warrant was just a shield and pretext. What they were there for was to find incriminatory evidence against Gilbert Perkins. I say gentlemen under the constitution of the United States they had no legal right to search that office. Gentlemen did these inspectors act like men who were acting within the law when they made this search? I say far from it."

O'Brien held his hand out to Inspector Cortelyou, sitting at the government's table.

"Now I would not think I had done my duty if I did not pay my compliments to this wonderful gentleman, Mr. Cortelyou. You have heard Mr. Cortelyou describe how he went to Franklin's office in Philadelphia and told him he had some business with him. He did not have any business with Franklin. He went to get case on him. He did not tell Franklin there was a warrant for him. I am not going to discuss the search of Franklin's office. I am going to call your attention to another peculiar thing in connection with this case. Franklin was 'sweated' for three hours and then they served a warrant on him.

"Gentlemen there is something in that, that is repulsive to any free liberty-loving American citizen. Now they wanted to make some evidence. They build it up. They had a game that they would get a damaging admission and Cortelyou claims he was indicating the so-called request writing and Franklin wrote four from copies Cortelyou held in his hand. Of course the scheme as it was put to you was to get specimens of his writing. A fact occurred out on the street after this three hours' investigation, that Franklin asked him about the paper with the irregular edges.

"You have heard Mr. Franklin's explanation. I say that Franklin was just as frank and truthful about that as anything he did in that office that day. But he was a blockhead, too. I don't think that you or I would give a man the same treatment as he did Mr. Cortelyou, when he asked him to write these letters. His action showed he was free from all guilt and feared no man.

"My time is up and I believe we have gone over the main facts in this case. We believe we have met the government case in all its phases. We believe you have facts before you to convince you that the so-called find of the Reed House envelope was a plant. We believe we have met all of the requirements of this case. The government must have proof that will satisfy you beyond a reasonable doubt." O'Brien paused. "Why there is doubt in every step and on every side of the government case."

"You have learned that Mr. Perkins here has had an excellent reputation throughout life. Keep in mind that character ought to be a shield to a man in a time of trouble. I believe that you will weigh all of the evidence on both sides and will reach a just verdict according to the evidence."

Following a fifteen-minute recess, District Attorney Jordan rose and turned to the spectators behind him before sidestepping toward the twelve jurors.

"All the government wants is a verdict that is warranted by the evidence. There have been several surprises in this case. One of them is that counsel for the defense stated in the beginning that he would fix the blame for the letters and the pieces of paper in Perkins' pocket on Thomas Dempsey and at the close he attempts to fasten the crime upon Inspector Woltz," Jordan said.

"Gentlemen you were present at the opening of this court when the judge called your attention to the fact that the government would be the prosecutor. There is no private prosecutor here. No private prosecutor with malice, as sometimes in the county courts. But a case never comes here that the government is not the prosecutor and no case is brought here until it has been investigated by its proper agents. In the post office department it has its inspectors to run down those who violate the laws of the postal department. The government owes it to the citizens of the United States to run down the violators of the law and punish them.

"I am not asking vengence [*sic*] here. I am simply doing my duty as the prosecuting officer of the court as the judge will do his duty and you your duty," Jordan hesitated as he clutched the indictment in his hand. "We have here an indictment which contains five counts, four of these counts are alike and charge defendants with placing in the post office of the United States for the purpose of carrying out their plot and the fifth count only charges conspiracy. Has it been proved? I am going to show you the truth under the evidence and then ask you if these men are not guilty."

Jordan summarized the case, claiming the motive of Perkins and Franklin was to get as much out of the Strongs as possible. There were the conversations between Perkins and Postmaster Sobel, with a "steady effort" by Perkins to focus on the torn pieces of the "Black Hand" letters predicted to be found on the guilty party when arrested. Jordan paraphrased Perkins's own words.

"His prophecy certainly came true," Jordan said.

Jordan introduced Franklin's role and asked hypothetically, "Don't you think the letters were arranged at that time? Do you suppose Franklin don't know how to spell Pennsylvania, but when he wrote those request letters he misspelled Pennsylvania, he wrote it 'Pennsylvainia'?"

Charles Strong. His wife, Annie. Strong's secretary, Stephen Walker. Police Chief Edward Wagner. All their testimonies, Jordan said, corroborated Perkins's forecast that torn, threatening letters would be sent.

"There were five people that he told this to, and he said he thought the Strongs had better offer a reward that was the way they got the other fellows. Isn't it a remarkable thing that when the same kind of a letter was mailed to the chief of police, Gilbert Perkins was in Erie for an hour on his way to Indianapolis?" Jordan asked. "They make much ado about the letter Mrs. Strong sent to Gilbert Perkins, thanking him for his work. Why, gentlemen, she knew nothing then about these charges coming up against Gilbert Perkins. Inspector Oldfield had no feeling in this matter. He didn't know Perkins. He was ordered here by the government and he came to do his duty and find the writer of these letters. He gathered around him other inspectors. They went out to Indianapolis because Gilbert Perkins was there. He had predicted that the papers would be found on the person of the writer when arrested and they took him at his word."

Jordan took one of the Black Hand letters and its corresponding torn piece of paper on a piece of pasteboard.

"They arrested Gilbert Perkins and they found the papers," Jordan emphasized, showing the completed letter.

Following the raid of the Perkins office in Indianapolis, Jordan painted a picture of how he believed Perkins concocted the rest of his plan, preserving the torn pieces of paper.

"The plot was skillfully and adroitly painted," Jordan said, again fusing the Black Hand letter and torn piece of paper, his voice intensifying. "I ask you now if you think it would be possible to tear that sheet of paper that way unless with design? It would have been impossible for Oldfield to have torn a paper to fit the letter.

"You have the testimony of a newspaperman here in Erie named Crane. He asked Franklin about sending out a certain story and Franklin told him not to, but added, 'You know I hate these people.' It shows the venom in the man. He went to the chief of police and told him, 'Well, chief, I'm here on this mausoleum case but you know how damned little use I have for the Strongs.'"

Jordan next ridiculed the handwriting experts for the defense.

"Perhaps they thought they were smart," Jordan said, dismantling Hailmer Gould's microscopic examinations. "He did not tell you if they were letters or clotheslines."

It was William Pengelly and David Carvalho whom Jordan placed the greatest confidence in out of all the experts, particularly Carvalho.

"He told you on the witness stand why he hesitated. It was because he was a friend of Gilbert Perkins. The defense cannot even venture to say that he testified against them because he had any malice in his heart. In fact he loved Gilbert Perkins. Perkins was his friend and he hated to give the evidence against him.

"That man did not want to testify for the government against his old friend, Gilbert Perkins—but he did go on that witness stand and told you the truth, because justice is justice, and because God is God." Jordan hesitated before glancing at a nearby clock. "Gentlemen, it is growing late and you have been extremely patient in this case. I will not detain you longer, but will leave this case in your hand. Far be it from me to ask you to lay aside your sympathy, but remember this, justice comes first, then sympathy. I will leave this case in your hands, believing that after you have carefully considered all of the evidence, you will return a verdict against both of the defendants of guilty in manner and form as indicted."

Jordan concluded his closing arguments at 6:20 p.m., and court was adjourned.

That evening, F. Bourgeois of the Burns Detective Agency office in Pittsburg scoffed at Gilbert Perkins's accusations.

"The insinuation about the copper plate was made to impress the public that we tried to plant it in a Perkins office," Bourgeois told a reporter. "The fact of the matter is that a dozen witnesses know that a copper plate was found in the mausoleum after the desecration was discovered and that it was secured from A.P. Burton's undertaking establishment at 12 o'clock noon instead of in the night. It was taken to Pittsburg to have it tested with a view of determining what sort of tools was used to break it."

John Jordan's closing arguments were roundly praised by the morning editions of dozens of newspapers on July 29, 1911.

The *Erie Evening Herald* wrote:

> *He took the four experts of the defense and by as neat a line of satire as has been heard here for some time, riddled their testimony and made them a laughing stock. Like a drama, fiendish in its plot and conception, Mr. Jordan portrayed the happenings since the mausoleum desecration and characterized the principals in it.*

When court opened that morning, Judge Orr wasted no time in presenting his charge of the jury: "Gentlemen of the jury, the defendants Gilbert Perkins and Charles Franklin, stand indicted for violation of two sections of the criminal code of the United States. The first section provides that whoever devises any scheme to defraud, shall for the purpose of executing such scheme, place or cause to [be] placed in any post office of the United States or authorize, or shall cause to be delivered by mail to the direction thereon, any such letter, shall be punished."

Judge Orr explained each of the counts against Perkins and Franklin in detail and their connection to the case before defining reasonable doubt and addressing the character witnesses called for Perkins, adding that although none were called on behalf of Franklin, this should not impugn his character.

Orr explained he would not address the actions of the postal inspectors.

"It is apparent that certain facts are not disputed, to-wit: The fact that these detectives were connected with the Perkins agency; that they were summoned to Erie for work; and finally, relieved from this employment. After they arrived in Erie letters began to arrive at the Strong home. The defendants are charged with mailing these letters. The use of the mails is the charge against them. The theories of both sides have been set forth to you at length, so I will not go into the details unless there is some special request. If you find the defendants schemed to defraud the Strongs and mailed or caused to be mailed the Black Hand letters, you may find them both guilty. If you find they mailed but the first, then you may find them guilty under the first and third counts. But if you find they wrote the second and not the first, you may find them guilty under the second or fourth counts. If you find they conspired, but did not send the letters, you may find them guilty of the fifth. If you find one guilty and not the other, you can acquit one of the defendants. If you have a reasonable doubt you can acquit both of them."

Judge Orr concluded his charge twenty-seven minutes later after reading the two law points asked by defense attorneys, and minutes later the jurors were placed in charge of the tipstaves and escorted from the room.

Charles Franklin turned to newspaper correspondents at the press table.

"That was certainly a fair charge," he smirked.

As the crowd receded from the courtroom, newspaper correspondents jockeyed to downtown telegram offices and wired the latest news in the case as those involved in the government and defense lingered around downtown, preparing for a long day.

One hour and fifty minutes later, at 12:20 p.m., the tipstaff announced a verdict had been reached.

Judge Orr arrived within several minutes. The courtroom was sparsely populated, with a majority of the spectators unaware of the verdict. Court officially resumed as each of the jurors, stern in feature and downcast in expression, entered with a steady tread. An expressionless Charles Franklin entered and took his seat while Gilbert Perkins sat on the other side of the defense table, supported by his daughter, Gertrude Adams, who was consoled by W.H.S. Thomson's wife.

Gilbert Perkins's expression, wrote the *Herald*, changed "in an instant." His bright confidence as he strolled the corridors of the federal building during the jurors' deliberations had evaporated.

A "tense stillness" blanketed the courtroom as the envelope containing the verdict was handed to Judge Orr. Orr read the verdict without saying a word before passing it to Clerk Lindsey.

Lindsey's voice boomed: "We find the defendants, Gilbert Perkins and Charles Franklin, guilty as indicted."

Gertrude clasped her father's side as her brother, Harry, flung his arms around the frail Perkins, who looked as if he had been struck by a "bolt of lightning from a clear sky," nearly falling from his chair.

George J. Arrison, foreman of the jury, asked that extreme mercy be shown Perkins.

Charles Franklin stared ahead, unmoved.

Excited voices tore through the crowd as Gertrude Adams suddenly fainted. Men rushed to her aid as a nearly inconsolable Gilbert Perkins clenched the hand of his son Walter between sobs.

"My boy, my boy," Perkins moaned. "I'm innocent!"

District Attorney Jordan asked that the sentence be handed down. Judge Orr assented but temporarily delayed until a physician administered medicine to Gilbert Perkins and removed his daughter from the room. His composure regained, Perkins, joined by Franklin and flanked by their attorneys, approached the bench.

"Gilbert Perkins, is there any reason why the sentence of this court should not be passed upon you?"

"I am an old man," Gilbert Perkins said, his voice fracturing. "I am innocent before my God and fellow man. I did not do this. I am not guilty. I ask the mercy of the court."

Orr looked to Charles Franklin.

"Charles Franklin, is there any reason why sentence of this court should not be passed upon you?"

"None, except that I didn't do the job."

"The verdict of the jury is no surprise to the court. The offense for which you have been found guilty is a grave one against the United States and society. It is not alone for the reformation of the individual that sentences are imposed, but for an example to others and as a protection to society. I can conceive of few offenses graver and more destructive of social life than those for which you have been found guilty. It is my duty to pronounce judgment upon you."

"It is painful for me, as I have known Mr. Gilbert Perkins for a number of years," Judge Orr said, removing his eyeglasses. "I would impose both a fine and an imprisonment upon you, but a fine often brings hardship to a family. Therefore I will not impose a fine in this case. Therefore, that the ends of

Front page of the *Erie Evening Herald* on July 29, 1911, announcing the guilty verdicts. *Author's collection.*

justice may be obtained in the case of the United States against Gilbert B. Perkins and Charles H. Franklin, the sentence of Charles H. Franklin shall be five years in the United States penitentiary at Leavenworth, Kansas. The sentence of Gilbert Perkins shall be three years in the United States penitentiary in Leavenworth, Kansas."

Judge Orr slightly turned away as an emotionless Franklin returned to his chair. Perkins, tears rolling down his face, remained still.

"Your Honor," Perkins said, "was that two or three?"

"Three," Orr responded, scarcely above a whisper.

W.H.S. Thomson motioned for a new trial, with Judge Orr advising he would give the matter consideration.

Harry Perkins reentered the courtroom, and arrangements for bond were made, fixed at $5,000 each, pending the decision of the Circuit Court of Appeals. As the courtroom gradually emptied, Perkins's operatives and family did their best to console those who stayed behind, including Gilbert Perkins's wife, Sarah, who remained by his side.

At 6:30 p.m., Perkins and his wife departed the federal building, locked arm in arm.

Charles Franklin lit a cigar and chatted lightly with friends, only remarking to reporters that "the contest had only begun," predicting neither he nor Perkins would spend a day in prison.

"The truth," Franklin prophesized, "as it must come out, sooner or later."

As newspapers announced the conviction, W.H.S. Thomson started preparations for an appeal, focusing on Judge Orr's refusal to allow evidence against Thomas Dempsey, firmly declaring that if a new trial was refused the defendants were prepared to carry the case before the U.S. Circuit Court of Appeals in Philadelphia.

At the Reed House, Gilbert Perkins, surrounded by his family and attorneys, ate a hearty dinner in the dining room. Having "shed his mournful skin observed earlier in the courtroom,"[37] Perkins appeared hopeful and determined.

On the other side of the dining room, Charles Franklin sat alone.

Speaking to the *Pittsburg Press*, Perkins believed he would never serve a day in prison, and his "quick resumption to veritable youthful confidence has caused amazement."

The next morning, Charles Franklin departed for Philadelphia. Gilbert Perkins, joined by his family and detectives, left that evening for Pittsburg. Attorney Charles A. O'Brien remained optimistic.

"I can say that I was never more hopeful," O'Brien remarked to the *Erie Daily Times*. "We have just started to fight this thing."

12

WE HAVE JUST STARTED TO FIGHT

On July 31, 1911, U.S. Attorney John Jordan confirmed members of the U.S. Secret Service were pursuing active leads in the Scott mausoleum case, including potential indictments against two or more persons, telling reporters, "We shall sift this thing to the very bottom and if the evidence warrants it these suspects, too shall have their day in court."

After seven months, the investigation had amassed thousands of documents, including files obtained from the Perkins offices in Pittsburg, Indianapolis and Philadelphia, in addition to the physical evidence recovered by Perkins operatives in February 1911. Jordan refused to confirm the identities of the suspects, only remarking the government believed three to five men were involved whose identities were known to government authorities.

Such revelations following the Perkins-Franklin trial highlight the hesitance of Inspector Oldfield and his inspectors, who refused to reveal the source of their evidence against Perkins and his agency.

With the feverishness in Erie dwindling, Charles and Annie Strong hosted an elaborate dinner for Inspector Oldfield at their mansion. The year 1911 only reinforced the belief among the family that they would forever be at risk of harm because of their social status and wealth, and they extended an offer to Oldfield to become director of security for the family. The financial compensation, ten times his government salary, allowed Oldfield free rein. He could work for any client he wished, as long as it did not interfere with the Strongs' business, guaranteeing Oldfield's work would never again be domineered by government bureaucracy.

Oldfield, who grew to admire the Strongs, was flattered. He promised to give the offer serious consideration.

On August 4, 1911, Judge Charles Orr denied the defense's motion for a new trial, and the defense attorneys immediately filed an assignment of errors before the U.S. Circuit Court of Appeals in Philadelphia. Gilbert Perkins and Charles Franklin remained free on bond.

In Erie, the mausoleum case faded from public view. On August 5, 1911, thousands gathered in Erie for the annual outing of the Odd Fellows Orphan Home of Meadville as they celebrated their annual picnic at Waldameer. Railroads ferried crowds in special coaches to the city from nearby towns, and the roads leading into the city were congested.

"Gathered along the streets were thousands of Odd Fellows and their ladies," wrote the *Erie Daily Times*, "and they applauded when the orphans from the great home of the order at Meadville rode by, led by stirring music and followed by Cantons in their shimmering regalia and Odd Fellows with badges and banner."

The following week, delegates from the Knights of Pythias arrived in preparation for the annual state convention, expecting to draw twenty thousand tourists to the Gem City. As throngs of delegations arrived aboard crowded trains day and night, factions of the fraternal organization lodged at Camp Reichard and other locations within the city.

With the influx of visitors, Erie was again overburdened—its hotels and boardinghouses were filled. A camp, laid out with military precision, expanded to three hundred tents set in regular squares, with the expectation of two thousand or more near Waldameer. According to the *Erie Daily Times*, this provided the "most picturesque and pleasing delight of Waldameer, and where they are removed from the active bustling of camp life."

In downtown Erie, the Masonic temple, where the convention would take place, was "equipped with stenographers, typewriters, telephones, flags, badges, pennants, and programs" with messenger services installed throughout the city, urging visitors to stay throughout all eight days of the convention.

Thousands of Pythians swarmed Erie's streets on the morning of August 17, 1911, as thousands of onlookers witnessed a grand parade including delegations from Union City, Meadville, Cambridge Springs, Waterford, Corry and Titusville, in addition to delegations from towns in Ohio and New York.

"All have come to take part in or look on the grand parade," boasted the *Erie Daily Times*. "It was a sight worth coming the distance to see."

Top: Members of the City of Erie Police Department prior to the parade for the Knights of Pythias on August 18, 1911, on State Street in downtown Erie. *Ed Kindle Collection.*

Bottom: The Knights of Pythias, photographed at Camp Reichard near Waldameer. *Ed Kindle Collection.*

Following a perilous flight in high winds, famed aviator Harry Atwood landed on the circus grounds of upper Peach Street, south of Erie, during the early morning hours of August 19, 1911, where he was greeted by nearly eight hundred people. After receiving a round of applause, Atwood departed for the Reed House in Mayor Liebel's automobile and planned to depart later that afternoon.

Crime, however, continued to flourish in Erie, including a holdup of four men at the Cascade Street railroad crossing and a brief gun battle between two highwaymen and Lieutenant William Beiter of the Pennsylvania Railroad Police, with authorities believing some of those involved were part of the gang responsible for the attempted robbery of the Philadelphia & Erie express train on the night of June 30, 1911.

On August 28, 1911, Thomas Dempsey appeared at the Mercer County Courthouse in Franklin, Pennsylvania, for trial. Despite the *Erie Daily Times* claiming Inspector Oldfield and others would be present, prosecutors instead appeared asking for a continuance after being unable to locate important witnesses. The case was continued to the November term with many doubting it would ever materialize.

Commemorating the ninety-eighth anniversary of Commodore Oliver Hazard Perry's victory at the Battle of Lake Erie, the Erie Yacht Club requested all watercraft in Presque Isle Bay take part in a procession on Sunday, September 11, 1911, requesting participants decorate their boats "with flags and bunting," in an event predicted to lure sizeable crowds to Erie's harbor.

It was the arrival of President William H. Taft that created mass excitement in Erie on September 16, 1911, the first time a sitting president was to be entertained in the city overnight. That evening, as the city waited for the president's arrival, streets along the planned procession route were cordoned off leading to the Majestic Theater, which was transformed "into a handsome banquet hall,"[38] with "beautiful and appropriate"[39] decorations. Sixty police officers, joined by the U.S. Secret Service, worked in coordination to prevent crowding on the platform of the Union Depot to protect the president and those in his party.

"Long before the time for the train to arrive, the streets were thronged with a surging, seething mob of humanity. Rich and poor jostled together alike, all; anxious to pay respect to the head of the nation and to see the leader of the people. All stood for more than an hour awaiting the arrival, while police, naval militia, National guards and sailors from the Wolverine held back the crowds as best as they could," wrote the *Erie Evening Herald*.

"Never before in the history of Erie has there been such a crowd on the streets as was assembled last night."

Lingering on the platform of the Union Depot were Chief Wagner and Captain Detzel, joined by those who would take part in President Taft's procession, including Charles and Annie Strong, Samuel Drown (president of the chamber of commerce), Judge Emory Walling, William J. Stern and Congressman Arthur Laban Bates.

Around 9:00 p.m., "a crowd surged across the tracks and under the gates and the gates, in lowering, nearly injured several who were standing close by,"[40] and several minutes later watched as the switchman swung his lantern indicating the arrival of President Taft's train. Police officers pushed back against the crowd, who, according to the *Herald*, "became hilarious" as "one woman insisted on remaining without the lines."

President Taft's train emerged from the darkness, decreasing speed through waves of hissing smoke and grinding gears as it hauled the president's private car, two compartments, a dining coach and a baggage car. At the crossing the train groaned to a halt as newspapermen rushed to the rear platform of the train, shadowed by two Secret Service men. Members of the reception committee excitedly rushed to the platform but were restrained by the Secret Service.

Under the dim glow of an electric light on the rear of his illuminated rail coach, President Taft exited with his infectious smile, fluttering his hat to the crowd, and was greeted by a thunderous roar from roughly twenty-five thousand people.

As the vehicle procession crawled onto State Street, the band struck up "The Star-Spangled Banner." Downtown, crowds grew in both size and enthusiasm "packed on the housetops and the porches and every available place along the route"[41] to see the president.

"You can't make me believe Erie is a city of only 70,000 population," remarked the president's physician, Dr. Thomas C. Rhodes. "Erie looks like a city of 360,000."

As the president arrived at the Majestic Theater, members of the National Guard and police formed a phalanx through which the automobiles passed. Inside the theater, occupants rushed to the windows and fire escapes of the building as President Taft and his party arrived through the stage entrance. Following the banquet, Taft and his party were driven to the home of Charles and Annie Strong and entertained with a small dinner.

The next morning, President Taft attended the Unitarian church for worship and listened to a sermon from Reverend Thomas Byrnes, with those

President William H. Taft standing next to the Strongs' granddaughter, Thora Ronalds, on the front steps of the Strong mansion. *Erie County Historical Society at the Hagen History Center*.

in attendance allowed with the admittance of a ticket. A luncheon followed at the Strong home, with the table being "extremely handsome in its pretty and simple decorations of mauve orchids and lilies of the valley, the bisque table setting making it practically one mass of white."[42]

That afternoon, President Taft was driven to Charles Strong's private estate, where he and members of his party were quietly served dinner at Strong's log cabin before returning to the Strong home that evening, where Postmaster Isador Sobel and Congressman Arthur Bates paid their respects. It was during his stay at the Strong mansion that President Taft, weighing in excess of three hundred pounds, became stuck in one of the private bathtubs and needed to be assisted by Charles Strong and his secretary, Charles Hilles.

During the early morning hours of September 18, 1911, Taft departed Erie for Detroit, Michigan.

On September 21, at the Henry Hotel in Pittsburg, Charles Franklin spoke to a reporter for the *Erie Daily Times*, insisting he was engaged in that city to look after his own interests. Jovial during his interview, Franklin lugged around the lengthy transcript from his trial.

President William Taft photographed at the Strong Mansion. *From left to right*: President Taft, Thora Strong Ronalds, Charles Strong, Charles D. Hilles, Thora Ronalds, Annie Strong and Major Archibald Butt. *Erie County Historical Society at the Hagen History Center.*

"This is the most laughable affair that I ever came across," Franklin said. "I have not been worrying very much because my conscience is clear and I know that in the end everything will turn out all right. The writer of those letters is laughing up his sleeve. It is not going to do them any good to send me to prison. In fact, if I really thought for a moment that I would have to serve I would just be willing to start my sentence right away. I was 500 miles away when those letters were written."

Gilbert Perkins, confined to his home in Hazelwood and diagnosed with nervous prostration, continued to correspond with various acquaintances and family, including Guy Jordan, a friend from Waterford, Pennsylvania. Perkins wrote:

My Dear Friend:
Your letter of 17ᵗʰ inst, is duly at hand today, and I heartily thank you for the kind words you expressed therein. I also thank you for giving me the impression of my old-time friends in Waterford, namely, that none of them believe I am guilty of the charges brought against me at Erie. The defense

that we made there was, in the mind of any fair man, enough to acquit, nevertheless we were convicted.

The shock that I experienced, and to know that an innocent man could be convicted upon false testimony and jobbery, is sad to realize to say the least, and I can pledge you, as well as to my friends in Waterford, and before my God, that I never wrote or caused to be written any Black Hand letters to the Strongs or anyone else. I further proclaim and declare, before Almighty God, that I never knowingly had in my possession, or in any of our offices, the fragments of any Black Hand letters, or any knowledge of any of these fragments that were introduced at that trial as coming from my possession, were jobbery and perjury and unreasonable.

It is awful to think how wicked and desperate the villains must have been to resort to such a conspiracy, for they have wrecked our business, our homes and thus far branded me as a convict. It is a sin and a wicked one, for these conspirators to shoulder and sooner or later God will pick their conscience and there will be no end of their trouble.

I am keeping up under this strain as well as any one can do, and I trust that my God will deliver me soon from the hands of these conspirators.

Our case has been carried to the U.S. court of appeals, which convenes in Philadelphia on the 9th of October. It will be argued there before three U.S. circuit judges—Judge Gray, of Delaware; Judge White, of Philadelphia, and Judge Buffington, of Pittsburg, and I trust in God that these judges will look into this matter carefully and justify and set aside the verdict and give us a new trial at Pittsburg.

Again I thank you for your letter, and ask that you convey to all of my friends in Waterford my earnest and utmost thanks for the kind feeling displayed by them in this my hour of trouble.

I may say that wherever I go, the sentiment appears to be in my favor, and all, like my good friends in Waterford, are ready and willing to extend a helping hand should it become necessary to ask for a pardon and seek executive clemency.

With best wishes for all, I am,

Yours very truly,

G.B. PERKINS.

In Erie, the gradual rise in crime continued to spark concerns from the public.

"Erie has had its grave robbery, its black hand letter writers, its murders, its open red light district and open gambling dives, one and all running

194

without restraint," wrote the *Erie Daily Times*. "But while we have all this, Erie isn't going to the devil."

Before the end of the month, Charles A. O'Brien and W.H.S. Thomson had filed their sixty-six-page appeal before the U.S. Court of Appeals, claiming ten assignments of error and attacking the conviction:

> *The testimony had scarcely a scintilla of corroborative evidence. The mutual dislike existing between the Strongs and Franklin amounting to nothing in itself and the only other scrap of evidence viz: the question asked Cortelyou by Franklin as to the irregular edged paper, being a tracing from which the former dictated was indisputably answered by the production of the tracing itself, which showed the irregular edge: As to Franklin this was the government's case.*

The relationship between Charles Franklin and Gilbert Perkins, however, fractured by mid-October. Franklin loudly protested his prison sentence, insisting it was "unjust to give him the longer term," and vowed to fight at the first opportunity.

On October 21, 1911, Walter and Harry Perkins appeared before the U.S. Court in Pittsburg and requested the bail pieces for Franklin, later withdrawing his bond. Within the following hour, Franklin was arrested and escorted to the Allegheny County Jail and dispensed in the jail lobby to Deputy Warden John McNeil, who offered to store Franklin's valuables in a safe place.

"I will lock that diamond stick pin in the safe for you. It will be better than wearing it in your cell."

"All right, I appreciate your position and that you must be strict with all who come into the jail," Franklin said, removing a diamond stickpin from his scarf. "Here is also a gold nugget that I prize highly as a pocket piece. I will give you all my valuables to put in the safe for me with your kind permission."

Franklin was also given the opportunity to send telegrams to associates in Erie, Philadelphia and other cities in an attempt to find a bondsman. That night, Franklin was resigned to the fact his friends had deserted him.

"I'm a victim of circumstances," Franklin said, almost sobbing.

Franklin's melancholy was short-lived, as he was later observed smiling defiantly, believing his release was imminent. His imprisonment, though, ignited concerns from federal officials questioning the legality of his commitment to the county jail and questioned who would be responsible for the incurred costs and expenses.

On October 23, 1911, John Jordan filed his response to the defense's request for an appeal, arguing:

> *It is a matter of surprise that counsel for appellants, in their printed argument make light of testimony upon which the defendants were convicted. They certainly did not view it in that light at the time of the trial. The evidence of the government was so strong and convincing that counsel for defendants as well as the jury were strongly impressed with the strength of the government's testimony and recognized that it was a proper case for the jury to pass upon.*

Soon, another surprise emerged.

And it came from Charles Franklin.

On the morning of October 24, 1911, Charles Franklin appeared before Judge Orr and was remanded to jail following his formal surrender. After the hearing, Franklin was accompanied by U.S. marshals to the office of Postal Inspector James Cortelyou. Before entering Cortelyou's office, Franklin spoke candidly to a reporter.

"I was unjustly convicted," said Franklin, "and I was simply dragged into this case without having ever seen or heard anything of the [Black Hand] letters. I had nothing to do with them and only saw them for a few minutes at the counsel table at Erie when the Perkinses were not looking. Immediately after the trial I commenced a diligent search for evidence which would show who wrote the letters, for I was a victim of a scheme and a plot. I spent all the money I had, about $1,500, and could easily have spent a lot more. I came to this city recently to clean the case up and was just about to do so, when I was surrendered by my bondsmen."

Asked why he was meeting with Cortelyou, Franklin said, "I shall tell all I know. I'll name the man, the guilty man. Since I have been released I have secured photographic plates made from the original letters and I have all the evidence to convict the man who wrote them."

Refusing to reveal the identity of the "guilty man," Franklin predicted revelations would be "one of the biggest sensations of the day. Would not I be a fool to do five years for another man's account?"

The meeting in Cortelyou's office lasted nearly an hour, with Franklin treated to a light lunch by U.S. marshals before returning to the jail, his every movement closely shadowed by a half-dozen Perkins operatives.

U.S. Attorney John Jordan later confirmed Franklin was informed by Cortelyou there were no promises given on immunity. Although refusing to discuss Franklin's statement, Jordan did hint that Franklin confirmed additional parties were involved in the mausoleum desecration but stopped short of naming those involved.

"If Franklin would make a clean breast of the whole affair," Jordan said, "it would be acted upon by the government, but what he told yesterday was not enough."

On November 15, 1911, John Oldfield resigned from the Postal Inspection Service, ending a thirteen-year career, deciding to engage in work as a private detective. News of Oldfield's resignation reached Erie two days later, with the *Erie Daily Times* proclaiming Oldfield's work in the Strong–Black Hand case being "the crowning effort of his career with the post office department." Erie wished Oldfield "the greatest success in his business venture."

Unbeknownst to those in Erie, the first case he worked as a private detective was hunting down those responsible for the desecration of the Scott mausoleum, supported by the extensive work performed by Detective Sergeant Jack Welsh of the City of Erie Police Department.

In the days after his retirement, Oldfield met with Welsh, speaking at great lengths about the evidence in the case. Oldfield listened intently as Welsh laid out the facts, having first suspected something was amiss with Perkins's agency when he tailed him to 725 West Eighteenth Street, the home of Mortimer Hall, a relative of Perkins through his maternal side of the family. Welsh felt Perkins's movements were suspicious and decided to keep a close eye on him.

The night after the mausoleum was discovered broken into, when he was on guard near the mausoleum's entrance around 2:00 a.m., Welsh observed three men standing on the corner of Cherry and West Nineteenth Streets, watching the cemetery. As he inched closer in the darkness, Welsh watched the men as they stood under a streetlight. Welsh was certain one of the men was Mortimer Hall.

Confiding his suspicions to fellow officer Richard Dundon, Welsh asked Dundon, who lived two blocks from Hall's home and knew those he associated with, to keep a close eye on him. Within a day, Dundon furnished more evidence to Welsh, who enlisted the assistance of Detective Sergeant Richard Crotty.

Visiting the mausoleum in person, Oldfield observed Welsh reenacting the main events from the investigation, gesturing to the mausoleum doors, where he concluded the edges were damaged from tools used by a mechanic. Hall, Welsh told Oldfield, was a tinsmith and used such tools.

Above: View in the Erie Cemetery looking in the direction of one of the pair of footprints. The Scott mausoleum is to the left, out of frame. *Author's collection*.

Opposite, top: Looking toward the intersection of West Nineteenth and Cherry Streets where Detective Sergeant Welsh spotted the three suspicious men. *Author's collection*.

Opposite, bottom: West gate of the Erie Cemetery on Cherry Street near Brown Street. The Scott mausoleum is barely visible through the trees to the right. *Author's collection*.

Besides Perkins and Franklin, Welsh theorized three men were involved, pointing to the footprints he found in the snow on the morning of February 9, 1911. When Oldfield asked how many times he believed the vandals visited the tomb, Welsh summarized two, possibly a third had the mausoleum not been found broken into. Evidence showed, Welsh said, that one of the visits occurred on January 27, 1911.

The footprints, Welsh continued, indicated a trail leading from a gate on Cherry Street, with the two sets of footprints coming from West Nineteenth Street, with those footprints having been made in an attempt to obliterate other footprints; however, at some point, someone "stepped out of line," leaving a visible print from a size 9 men's shoe.

Welsh also brought about the concerns with the bloodhounds, brought by Perkins's men. Officers at the cemetery later told Welsh the bloodhounds attempted to venture beyond the cemetery but were stopped by Harry Perkins. Welsh believed that had the dogs been allowed to continue, the trail would have led to Mortimer Hall's home.

All this evidence, Welsh argued to Oldfield, was enough in his mind to approach Chief Wager and the Strongs, but he was removed from the case before he could do so.

Oldfield's investigation pointed to five men within the Perkins Union Detective Agency responsible for plotting and carrying out the desecration of the Scott mausoleum in an attempt to extort a bribe from the Strong family and, if needed, kidnap the Strongs' granddaughter for a hefty ransom. Perkins and his men then conspired to plant the torn pieces of paper from the Black Hand letters on Thomas Dempsey, charging him with using the U.S. mails for improper purposes in sending threatening letters to Charles Strong.

Because the plot did not involve charges being leveled by the federal government, Perkins planned to utilize the services of Thomas Cochran of Franklin to help prosecute the case, ensuring the agency and those involved would be handsomely rewarded for their services. Perkins's plot, however, backfired with the interference of the U.S. Postal Inspection Service, which intercepted the torn pieces of paper on Gilbert Perkins before the conspiracy could be fulfilled.

Oldfield delivered his results to both John Jordan and the Erie County district attorney, and it was decided to delay the arrests pending the outcome of Perkins and Franklin's appeals.

On December 4, 1911, William Stern took the oath of office as mayor in Erie, all but guaranteeing the culmination of Edward Wagner's disastrous tenure as police chief. Captain William Detzel was appointed chief of police and Jack Welsh promoted to captain. Newspapers praised Detzel's promotions within the department, with the *Erie Daily Times* calling Welsh "one of the ablest officers on the force."

Two days later, U.S. Attorney John Jordan appeared before the U.S. Court of Appeals for the Third Circuit in Philadelphia, attacking the defense's arguments, including handwriting testimony introduced at trial. Acknowledging it was inadmissible as evidence under federal statutes, Jordan argued an objection had not been raised by defense attorneys.

Although newspapers criticized Jordan's arguments, he defended his actions: "The papers were not offered as standards of comparison or test papers, but as evidence for other purposes. The government then called two experts to examine the Franklin papers, also the Black Hand papers. There was no objection on the part of the defendants to this evidence. Counsel for the defendants cross-examined these expert witnesses and looked upon the matter of their testimony being admitted as proper."

On January 25, 1912, Judge Joseph Buffington of the U.S. Court of Appeals in Philadelphia denied a motion for a new trial and, in his opinion, scribed: "I have carefully reviewed the whole case and in my opinion Judge Orr made no error in excluding the evidence offered by the defense and which was objected to by Mr. Jordan. The court finds no reason for disturbing the verdict of the jury."

"THERE IS LITTLE I can say regarding the case," Jordan said, "except that I am satisfied."

A defeated Charles O'Brien told reporters, "There can be no appeal and we must accept the ruling as final, as it comes from the United States court of appeals, and the case cannot be taken to any higher tribunal."

Gilbert Perkins was visiting his son Walter when he learned his appeal had failed and hurried to his home next door, where he broke the news to his wife. She sank into a chair and cried as a despondent Gilbert Perkins wailed, pacing the floor, "I am innocent! As God is my witness, I am innocent!"

When visited by a reporter later in the day, Perkins maintained his innocence.

"I can't understand it. I hope I may not live another second if I am not an innocent man. Before God I am innocent. Oh, how could they ever do this to an innocent man. If only there was one grain of guilt it would not be so hard, but for an innocent man to be punished. It is hard, hard."

Charles Franklin, photographed on March 13, 1912, upon his arrival at the U.S. Federal Penitentiary at Leavenworth, Kansas. *National Archives.*

Because of Perkins's frail condition, Senator John Kern of Indiana corresponded with Attorney General George Wickersham in a last-ditch effort to issue a stay of sentence, claiming Perkins's health was so critical, "a prison sentence may contribute to his death."

Wickersham communicated with U.S. Attorney John Jordan, but after an extensive review of the case, Jordan refused to stay Perkins's sentence. On March 13, 1912, Charles Franklin and Gilbert Perkins were delivered to the U.S. Penitentiary at Fort Leavenworth, Kansas, and assigned prisoner numbers 7896 and 7897.

As Perkins and Franklin began their prison sentences, John Oldfield held a lengthy conference with Erie County detective John Sullivan in Erie, later visiting the home of local alderman Edward Hayes. There, Oldfield swore on allegations against Gilbert Perkins, Charles Franklin, Harry Perkins, John McCain and Mortimer Hall for the desecration of the Scott mausoleum.

13

EVIL MINDS AND DISPOSITIONS

I t was just after midnight on March 14, 1912, as John Oldfield, joined by County Detective John Sullivan and Captain Jack Welsh, waited inside the City of Erie Police Department, nestled in the bowels of Erie City Hall. Peering outside, Oldfield could spot the darkened silhouette of the Strong mansion across the street.

The sixty-seven-year-old Sullivan, one of Erie's most recognizable citizens, was a former captain with the police department until 1883, when he was appointed county detective, a position he held until 1902 before rejoining the department as chief. Sullivan resigned three years later, becoming an agent for the Northwestern Pennsylvania Humane Society before being reappointed as county detective in January 1912 by newly elected district attorney J. Orin Wait.

Oldfield, full of energy and determination, spoke to Sullivan and Welsh after swearing an affidavit the evening before. Five arrest warrants in hand, he was ready to proceed. Sullivan and Welsh later concurred no arrests should occur in Erie until confirmation was received from Pittsburg that Harry Perkins and James McCain were in custody. Believing a call would not come until the morning, Sullivan and Oldfield retired for the night. Welsh remained on duty.

At 2:30 a.m., Welsh received a telephone call notifying him Harry Perkins and McCain had been located but objected to their arrests because the warrant had not been forwarded to Pittsburgh. A frustrated Welsh implored those within the department to hold both men while he spoke to County Detective Sullivan. After being informed by Welsh about the update from Pittsburg, Sullivan phoned the department there, asking the superintendent to make information against John McCain, who was planning to flee to Gibraltar, charging him with being a fugitive from justice. Unsure of the legality of the procedure, they informed Sullivan they would keep both men under surveillance.

Sullivan asked Captain Welsh for an officer to assist him to Pittsburg. Welsh detailed Detective Sergeant Lambertine Pinney, and soon both men were scheduled to depart aboard the first train that morning to deliver the warrants in the smoky city.

Captain Welsh then phoned Oldfield at the Reed House, announcing he and his men were ready to proceed and inviting

Erie County detective John P. Sullivan. *From the* Erie Daily Times.

Oldfield to meet him at the home of Mortimer Hall on West Eighteenth Street. Assisted by Richard Dundon, Captain Welsh departed for West Eighteenth Street.

At 5:00 a.m., while most of the city still slumbered, the sun barely crested the horizon to the east as Welsh arrived at 725 West Eighteenth, finding Oldfield already waiting. Together, the men approached the front door, warrants in hand for Hall's arrest and search of his home. Officer Dundon thumped his fist against the door. In a muffled voice, Mortimer Hall spoke from the other side, inching the door open as Dundon announced himself. Rubbing his eyes, Hall asked if they could wait until he was dressed and minutes later appeared with his wife, Maude.

Captain Welsh suggested Hall step outside, and after Hall descended the steps, the captain read the warrant for his arrest. As Dundon stepped forward to handcuff Hall, his wife screamed, attracting the attention of neighbors from their nearby porches. After Hall was placed in the custody of Detective Sergeant Crotty, Dundon, Welsh and Oldfield handed a warrant to Maude Hall to search her home, as the men sought to locate a roll of copper and name plates from the Scott mausoleum.

By 6:30 a.m., Mortimer Hall had been transported downtown to headquarters and placed in a cell, with much of the city awakening to the breaking news.

"Arrest Three in Scott Tomb Case; Warrants Out for Perkins and Franklin" was the headline on the morning edition of the *Erie Daily Times*. By then a second search of the Hall residence had been completed, including partial excavations in the cellar. Nothing of value was ever located.

Speaking to the *Times*, Maude Hall defended her husband.

> *They have found nothing here for there has been nothing. During the investigation which the Perkins men made here in Erie Marty received a special delivery letter from old man Perkins asking him to call at the Reed house to meet all the Perkins men working on the case. The detectives who have been searching the past few weeks knew of this letter and they went through the writing desk several times trying to find it. I told them that the letter had been torn up as it was thought of no consequence and not worth preserving.*

"The credit goes to Capt. Jack Welsh and Patrolman Dundon," John Oldfield announced as he was encircled by reporters. "Welsh started this case and has had the evidence for a long time. He was the first man to get on the right track."

Asked about County Detective Sullivan and Detective Sergeant Pinney, Oldfield said they were due to arrive in Pittsburg before noon and were expected to return that evening with Harry Perkins and John McCain in custody. Oldfield also confirmed arrest warrants were sworn out for Gilbert Perkins and Charles Franklin despite their incarceration. After his interview, Oldfield left for the Strong mansion, where he briefed Annie Strong throughout the day, keeping in constant communication with County Detective Sullivan.

In his office in Pittsburg, Harry Perkins calmly smoked a cigarette as he spoke to reporters. When told newspapers wrote he was under arrest and en route to Erie for his involvement in the desecration of the Scott mausoleum, Perkins chuckled, "Why, it's absurd. Erie papers have announced for almost a year that a warrant was sworn out for my arrest and I haven't been arrested yet."

Perkins looked outside as the sun sparkled through the windows.

"Nothing has happened yet, and here it's almost eleven o'clock."

Around noon, John Sullivan and Lambertine Pinney arrived in Pittsburg and met briefly with Pittsburgh police, confirming both men were kept under close surveillance and continued to refuse to submit to arrest without a warrant. At the office of Robb & Seymour, the detectives met with attorneys representing Harry Perkins and John McCain, in a nearly four-hour-long meeting, with Perkins's and McCain's attorneys insisting both men had the right to give bail before a magistrate in Pittsburg before attending a preliminary hearing in Erie.

Sullivan firmly objected, insisting only a valid bond could be drawn upon conditions of the statute, which required an appearance in Erie County. Attorney Robb, courteous yet obdurate, insisted the form of bond he held both men to ensured he, not the detective, was correct. Sullivan declared if the law proved he was incorrect he would acquiesce, as he believed he was acting within proper legal grounds and could return to Erie with the bonds valid to surety.

Further legal consultation confirmed Sullivan was correct in his assessment of the law, and bail bonds were conditioned for the appearance of Perkins and McCain, with bail given before a local alderman and sureties qualifying to Sullivan's satisfaction, and after bail was arranged, both men returned to Erie.

As reporters and onlookers clamored outside of his office, Erie County district attorney J. Orin Wait explained the five men were charged with conspiracy because of the possible lengthier sentence. Because the desecration law in Pennsylvania was passed after the Scott mausoleum's desecration, it could not be applied to the case.

"We will fight this case through to the finish," Wait said. "I have looked over the evidence hurriedly and feel certain that convictions are sure for all the men under arrest. The charges were not made until we were sure the evidence was satisfactory and in such shape as to leave no question before a jury."

That afternoon, in being interviewed by the *Herald*, Mortimer Hall was described as "a tall, thin man of lithe build, light hair and light eyes" and wearing a "soft collar and sweater coat."

Mortimer Hall vehemently maintained his innocence.

"I have no knowledge whatever of the crime nor the offense. I declare I had nothing to do with it. In fact I know as little about it as anyone."

"What is your relationship to Gilbert Perkins?"

"He is an uncle of mine. His wife is a sister of my father."

"Did you not receive a check of $5.85 from Perkins since the affair happened?"

"Yes. It was a few days after they were called here and had brought the bloodhounds here. I worked for Perkins two days and he gave me a check for $5.85."

"Did not Perkins call on you frequently while here?"

"Yes. He had written me a letter and the next morning before the letter reached me he came down to the shop to see me about working for him. I have worked at Patterson & Sterling's shop and also for the Jewel Electric Sign Company."

Hall refused to comment further.

The *Erie Daily Times* again had scooped the *Dispatch* and *Herald* when it reported on the arrests in the mausoleum case, releasing an extra edition a half hour before the *Herald*. An article about the incident did not appear in the *Dispatch* until March 15. The *Erie Daily Times* sold all copies within minutes.

Mortimer Hall was escorted to the office of Alderman Hayes on the morning of March 18, 1912, by Chief Detzel. Near city hall, a *Times* staff photographer took a photo of Hall, who smiled in response.

"Did you get a good one?" he asked the photographer.

When Hall arrived, he was greeted by County Detective Sullivan and the arraignment began, with Alderman Hayes reducing Mortimer Hall's bond to $1,000. Asked if he secured bail, Hall said he had not but was expecting to and, upon the conclusion of the hearing, was remanded back to the Erie County Jail.

Evidence in the investigation continued to leak to the public, including private detectives shadowing Mortimer Hall's family in the city of Titusville and the gathering of eyewitnesses who placed some of the men in the Erie Cemetery in early to mid-January 1911. In the district attorney's office, preparations continued for trial, including special drawings of the cemetery.

On March 23, 1912, the preliminary examination for Harry Perkins, John McCain and Mortimer Hall was scheduled at Alderman Hayes's office, with large crowds forming in front of the building. A constable guarded the door, admitting only witnesses or those having an interest in the case.

"As a consequence the throng was disappointed," wrote the *Erie Daily Times*, "but men and boys hung out resolutely, determined to get a look at the principals in a charge of an incident which has become worldwide."

At 2:00 p.m., Mortimer Hall entered and was greeted affectionately by his father, who broke into tears as he wrapped his arms around his son before conversing with his attorney, Miles B. Kitts. Harry Perkins arrived twenty minutes later accompanied by attorney John Robb. Perkins greeted his cousin

Mortimer Hall is escorted by Chief of Police William F. Detzel. *From the* Erie Daily Times.

and the district attorney. John McCain, temporarily delayed, appeared, and the hearing began.

Following the start of the hearing, District Attorney Wait asked for a continuance, claiming new evidence had impelled the prosecution to request a delay, which was agreed on by all parties and rescheduled for April 16, 1912, at 2:00 p.m. Mortimer Hall then posted bond and was released after his father appeared with Guy Judson, of Waterford, who qualified as a bondsman to the satisfaction of the district attorney.

In the coming weeks, John Oldfield sought out witnesses instrumental to the prosecution's case, only to have difficulty in locating them. Others recanted their evidence. Using astute tactics learned as a postal inspector, Oldfield tried in vain to ensure the case would proceed to trial.

On April 16, 1911, the defendants appeared before Alderman Hayes. District Attorney Wait and attorneys Uriah P. Rossiter and Louis Rosenzweig, retained by the Strongs, were alongside John Oldfield and Postal Inspector James Cortelyou in a cramped room lined with extra chairs and tables. The large iron railing that graced the front of Hayes's office was removed to ensure enough room for witnesses.

An unsteady District Attorney Wait stood as the hearing began.

"We will offer no evidence," Wait declared.

Shocked whispers rippled throughout the room.

"Under the circumstances there is nothing left for me to do but discharge the prisoners," Hayes remarked, eyeing the defendants before congratulating the men. Harry Perkins, maintaining an "air of perfect composure," cracked a smile as he was congratulated. Mortimer Hall and James McCain, relieved of all tension, turned to family and friends. Within minutes, Harry Perkins, John McCain and Mortimer Hall—shadowed by attorneys, family and friends—departed Hayes's office as free men and vanished from view.

"And thus endeth another chapter of the famous mausoleum desecration case," wrote the *Erie Daily Times*.

The abrupt end to the case was barely noticeable in the press, overshadowed by a much greater, sensational tragedy: the sinking of the RMS *Titanic*. Again, the case proceeded outside public view, forgotten until March 13, 1914, when Mortimer Hall filed a civil suit against Annie Strong, alleging he was wrongfully imprisoned and suffered humiliation, sickness and damages totaling $100,000, following his arrest in 1912.

Stirring details of the mausoleum case and the trial of Gilbert Perkins and Charles Franklin were resurrected extensively in the pages of the *Erie Daily Times*.

That same afternoon, Harry Perkins filed three additional civil suits, separately against Charles Strong and Annie Strong, and another suing the two of them together, claiming damages of $150,000. When he was seen leaving the Erie County Courthouse, the once convivial Harry Perkins ignored reporters. As these were considered the largest civil suits filed within Erie County's history—and believed to be the most important civil actions brought in the state—speculation reigned in local newspapers, promising a sensational hearing if the cases went to trial.

The civil suits languished from numerous postponements and delays until December 1915, when the civil cases brought by Harry Perkins were heard before Judge Emory Walling, only to be non-suited. Mortimer Hall's case was also non-suited.

Never again would the desecration of the Scott mausoleum be brought before the courts, and those responsible for the despicable deeds were never brought to justice. The story then faded into legend, and in the decades that followed, those associated with the case passed away.

Occasionally the story of the mausoleum and its thrilling sensationalism would resurface through local newspaper articles. In 1949, John G. Carney, local historian and columnist for the *Erie Daily Times*, wrote about the case, including it during his speaking engagements about Erie's history. In 1956, when the *Erie Daily Times* wrote a collection of articles titled "Famous Erie Crimes," the case was briefly featured.

Since then, especially around the autumn months—Halloween in particular—the case has enjoyed a smattering of regurgitation, woven through neatly summarized articles outlining elementary facts of the case. Though they were interesting enough, they never delved into the arrests following the convictions of Gilbert Perkins and Charles Franklin, with no mention of John Frank Oldfield and Jack Welsh, who sought to bring those responsible to justice.

Now, over 112 years after it was horribly broken into, the Scott mausoleum still has not revealed all of its secrets, most probably forever lost to history. Officially, the case remains unsolved.

The war of yellow journalism between the *Erie Daily Times*, the *Erie Dispatch* and the *Erie Evening Herald* continued long after the mausoleum case. Annie Strong continued to direct the management of the *Herald* until it was renamed the *Erie Daily Herald* in 1920 and before its merger with the *Dispatch* in 1922, becoming the *Erie Dispatch-Herald*, lingering on until its merger with the *Times* in 1957. The *Erie Daily Times*, now the *Erie Times-News*, has outlived every competitor in its 135-plus-year history.

Sometime between March 1912 and 1914, Charles and Annie Strong hired John Oldfield to recover their granddaughter Thora Ronalds, who had been kidnapped. Oldfield recovered Thora and returned her to family, and the identities of those responsible were lost to history, as the incident occurred without attracting the attention of newspapers. The only indications of this event are brief notations within Annie Strong's correspondences to John Oldfield, in which she expressed her gratitude for his services to the Strong family.

Charles and Annie Strong's strained marriage deteriorated in the years that followed, and by 1918, the couple had separated, with Charles permanently residing at his log cabin and Annie remaining in their home on West Sixth Street. In May 1928, after years of steadily declining health, Annie's condition grew worse and she was confined to her home, with her last public appearance on the morning of May 17, 1928, as she thanked a group of boys from the St. Joseph's Orphanage who serenaded her on the front lawn. Annie's graciousness, according to reporter Tom Sterrett, had a lasting effect on the boys: "The orphan boys went away very happy. They had seen, and had met face to face, and had been addressed by Mrs. Strong, and had found her kindly and motherly, and not at all the proud, grand, haughty lady their minds had fancied."

That morning, she suffered a stroke and never recovered. At 6:30 a.m. on May 19, 1928, Annie Strong passed away at the age of sixty-nine, with her daughter and granddaughter at her side. After a sermon at St. Paul's Episcopal Cathedral, a private affair with strict admittance, Annie's remains were interred inside the family mausoleum at the Erie Cemetery, with a delegation of police officers acting as pallbearers and a special cordon of police assigned to the Strong home and the mausoleum during the services.

Writing about Annie Strong's interment in the mausoleum, *Times* reporter Jay James scribed, "When the bronze doors clang shut, the final chapter in the life of Mrs. Charles H. Strong will have been recorded."

Charles Strong, now a widower, would later be seen walking alone on the grounds of his estate.

"He was kind of a loner, I think," Irene Brown Ritter, niece of Thora Strong's bodyguard, Charles Storch, later recalled. "If he'd go by us, he'd nod. Once he tipped his hat at me. I was so thrilled. My aunt told me he did that when he liked you."

Strong continued making generous contributions to the community—contributions that still benefit Erie to this day, including the donation of land for the construction of the Zem Zem Hospital for crippled children on

Charles Strong relaxes on the porch of his Somewhere estate. *Erie County Historical Society at the Hagen History Center.*

West Eighth Street, a portion of his estate gifted to the Erie Day School and land for the Erie County Historical Society to construct its headquarters and museum. He also remained instrumental in his support for Hamot Hospital.

Though he was once an active member in the Erie University and Kahkwa Yacht Club at the university; Manhattan, Yale and Delta Kappa Epsilon clubs of New York City; and the Skull and Bones Society, as Charles Strong advanced in age, his eyesight began to diminish. This did not deter him from his persistent interest in business affairs or activities, and despite being an avid reader, he was often informed by a secretary of world events and politics from newspapers. With his failing health, he "guarded himself scrupulously against colds."[43]

Strong's daily rides in his automobile through the city and countryside, usually in the late afternoon and night, ceased during the fall of 1936 as bronchial and heart ailments confined him to his cabin. On the afternoon of November 8, 1936, Charles Strong suffered a heart attack at his log cabin and passed away at the age of eighty-three.

"Condolences poured into the office of the Erie County Electric Co. from throughout the country,"[44] when news of his death was learned.

On November 12, 1936, the Erie County Electric Company office closed at 11:00 a.m. for the remainder of the day out of respect for Strong, and after a service at St. Paul's Episcopal Cathedral, his casket was transported to the Erie Cemetery, where it was carried by employees of the Erie County Electric Company and *Dispatch-Herald* serving as pallbearers. He was interred in the Scott mausoleum.

Matilda "Thora" Ronalds married Clyde Bemus Leasure in Manhattan, New York, in 1917. Lacking a desire to remain in Erie like her parents, Thora resided in New York City before returning to Erie and in 1924 lived in a Tudor-style brick home on upper State Street with her daughter, also called Thora, choosing to entertain guests there instead of the mansion. On April 13, 1939, at the age of fifty-five, Thora Ronalds passed away at her home in Erie and was interred in the family mausoleum.

When her mother passed away, Thora Scott-Ronalds was thirty-one years old. Her father, Reginald Ronalds, had died in 1924, and with the passing of both of her grandparents, she inherited what remained of her grandparents' legacy and estate.

Charles Strong's casket is loaded by pallbearers at his funeral. *From the* Erie Dispatch-Herald.

Lacking affection for Erie, Thora forged her own path. After the outbreak of World War II, Thora became active with the Red Cross in London, England, in 1943, and several years later she married Donald Arthur McElroy of Erie in Bedford, New York. Although the marriage never produced children, Thora traveled the world with her husband, choosing to stay clear of the public life, yet occasionally visited Erie and kept in contact with several persons.

In time, the estate of her grandfather Charles Strong was diminished to just forty-seven acres, with the grounds and buildings remaining desolate under the supervision of Strong's longtime secretary Grace Morton Virture and Strong's cabin remaining empty and abandoned since 1939. Portions of the estate were gradually

Thora Ronalds-McElroy. *Erie County Historical Society at the Hagen History Center.*

piecemealed until what remained was sold at auction in December 1969 to Zurn Industries, with plans to develop the property into a townhouse complex. The holdings that once encompassed Erie's west side had disappeared, too, including large swaths of land stretching east of Peninsula Drive to Sommerheim Drive, gifted by Thora in 1974.

In 1975, a permit for the demolition of Charles Strong's cabin was issued by the city, despite opposition and outcry from the public, although it was rumored $500,000 would be required to restore the cabin to its former glory. Before the cabin was torn down, an interior decorator stripped its interior for salvaging, including a gold-lined toilet bowl, hand-hewn stones, wooden beams and other furnishings.

Today, the only traces of the "Somewhere" Estate are a series of the stone walls that lined the property, now housing LECOM Bayfront and South Shore Place, a thirty-acre waterfront neighborhood.

The Scott mansion remained vacant after Annie Strong's death until it was sold to Bishop John Mark Gannon in March 1941 and later became part of Gannon College, now Gannon University. Since then, it has undergone several renovations to preserve its interior. Today the building is known locally as "Old Main," and it serves as administrative offices for the university.

On October 15, 1990, Thora Ronalds-McElroy passed away at her home in Bedford, New York, at the age of eighty-two, and she was buried in the Sleepy Hollow Cemetery in Sleepy Hollow, New York, alongside her husband, extinguishing the lineage of her family tree.

During John Frank Oldfield's stint as a private detective, some of America's wealthiest families were his clients. Utilizing his expertise and connections with law enforcement agencies throughout the country, Oldfield was in high demand.

In 1914, during the oil boom in California, Oldfield was one of several Ohioans who invested in George Metcalf's Coalinga fraudulent oil scheme in Fresno County, California. Oldfield later secured an indictment against Metcalf and obtained a promissory note to repay his original investment of just over $10,000.

In 1915, plagued with recurring stomach problems, Oldfield underwent an operation at Johns Hopkins in Baltimore, where tumors were removed from his stomach. Returning to Athens, Ohio, for recovery, Oldfield later embarked on a six-month-long trip across the country with family and close acquaintances. The tumors removed from Oldfield's stomach, however, were malignant, and his stomach issues resurfaced. During the winter of 1916, Oldfield's health deteriorated as he continued to lose weight.

On May 25, 1916, at the age of forty-nine, John Frank Oldfield passed away from cancer. After his death, his collection of letters and evidence, including weapons used in the cases he investigated, was secured in six large steamer trunks. Because of the infamous nature of Oldfield's work, his widow, Margaret Galena, forbid any of their sons to discuss his legacy or speak of the items within the steamer trunks.

Hearing of Oldfield's passing, Annie Strong wrote to Margaret Galena, conveying her condolences and heartbreak. After the passing of Margaret Galena in 1946, the legacy of John Oldfield, stored in those six steamer trunks, was passed down to his son William Hamilton Oldfield. When the banks of the Hocking River flooded the grounds near William Hamilton Oldfield's home, five of the six trunks were lost. What could be salvaged has miraculously been preserved by Oldfield's great-great-grandson William Hamilton "Hammy" Oldfield.

After his admission to the U.S. Penitentiary at Fort Leavenworth, Gilbert Perkins was placed in the hospital for observation, with the physician stating, "Upon his admission to this Institution, March 14th, 1912, Perkins was in a very feeble condition, evidently due either to a recent attack of illness or mental strain or both. He was emaciated and anemic and the least exertion caused him to manifest symptoms of marked exhaustion."

Despite extensive treatment, Perkins's condition declined; he suffered from repeated attacks of vertigo, insomnia, arteriosclerosis and a double inguinal hernia. "Perkins," the physician later wrote, "was in worse physical condition than upon his arrival."

A letter to Senator John Kern in October 1912 illustrated the grim assessment of Perkins's condition: "He is visibly aged, is more feeble and is not standing confinement well, and if not soon released will die in prison."

Senator Kern continued fighting for Perkins's release, going so far as to contact the Department of Justice and other agencies, including writing to President William H. Taft.

It was not until after January 1913 that it appears Perkins's health started to improve, as he performed duties in the penitentiary chaplain's office and library. When not corresponding with others, Perkins read copies of the *Erie Daily Times* and the *Kansas City Journal* and wrote to his wife and children weekly.

In April 1913, William S. Ryan, an attorney from Indianapolis, wrote to Robert W. McClaughry, warden of the federal penitentiary in Leavenworth, Kansas:

> *I have advised Perkins—upon the suggestion of Attorney General McReynolds in person—to apply for a parole, with the assurance of the Attorney General that Perkins' enemies would not be allowed to use the machinery of the government to his unjust injury if he should be paroled. I will thank you for kindness to poor old Perkins in this emergency as he seems in every way quite helpless, like all detectives, who themselves, get into trouble.*

McClaughry responded to Ryan, stating he would "see that he has every opportunity to have his case considered before" the board of parole. Although eligible for parole in March 1913, Perkins instead petitioned for a pardon of his conviction and was released on July 1, 1914.

Perkins returned to Pittsburgh and lived a quiet life until February 1925, when he and his wife relocated to Waterford and operated the Green Goose Inn, formerly the Camp Inn, with Perkins's son Walter acting as manager of the establishment while Gilbert remained involved "in a minor capacity." Perkins's other sons, Harry and Gilbert Jr., were also reportedly involved in the inn's management, with Harry operating a tire and repair business as well as the LeBoeuf motion picture house.

"Today these same Perkins are conducting a tea room during the summer months in their former home at Waterford," wrote the *Erie Daily Times*.

In February 1926, Gilbert Perkins fell and fractured his femur, which exacerbated exhaustion and, supplemented with ongoing senility, contributed to his death on February 9, 1926, at the age of eighty-three. A military burial was provided for the once proud Civil War veteran within the grounds of the Waterford Cemetery.

Charles Franklin remained in contact with his wife and daughter through letters as he engaged in manual labor in the laundry, bathroom and barbershop inside the federal penitentiary. After his parole on March 28, 1914, Franklin arrived several days later in Erie and lodged at the Reed House before continuing to Philadelphia, where he planned to rejoin his family.

In 1917, Franklin filed for a pardon to restore his civil rights, which were eventually restored, and worked as a manager for a successful broom manufacturing company in Philadelphia until the 1930s, when he gained employment as an auditor for the City of Philadelphia in the City Tax Receiver's Office. Franklin steered clear of the public for the rest of his life, keeping a clean record until his death on November 4, 1944, at the age of seventy-two from heart failure.

Although he publicly maintained his innocence, it was clear on several occasions that Charles Franklin expressed a desire to speak about his role in the case, although only for personal gain. Following the dismissal of charges against Franklin and the four others for their roles in the mausoleum desecration, on April 20, 1912, U.S. Attorney John Jordan wrote to the warden of the federal penitentiary in Leavenworth, Kansas, informing him Franklin was willing to communicate with John Oldfield:

Charles Franklin and his wife, Mary, pictured here in Atlantic City, New Jersey, in the years after his release. *Descendants of the Franklin family.*

Mr. Franklin has lately written to counsel employed in this matter that he would give any and all information within his possession on this subject, and Mr. Oldfield has been directed by Mr. Rossiter, the counsel to whom the letter was written by Franklin, to go to the prison at Leavenworth and have an interview with Franklin.

Like most documents and reports in the case, details of Oldfield's interview with Franklin have not survived, and despite privately confirming to government officials his involvement in the Scott mausoleum desecration case, Charles Franklin went to his grave publicly protesting his innocence.

The Perkins Union Detective Agency continued under the leadership of Harry Perkins while his father was incarcerated. After his return to Waterford, Pennsylvania, in the 1920s, Harry Perkins continued managing the agency until his death in 1963. His son Harry H. Perkins Jr. operated the agency until 1967, when a judge in Pittsburgh ordered the agency to cease business following the expiration of its license.

Annette Thomas remained a stenographer in Pittsburgh until her death in 1930 at the age of fifty-five.

John McCain returned to Erie and worked as a carpenter. While visiting a home in May 1938 to fix a furnace, McCain plunged headfirst down a stairwell, fracturing his skull, resulting in his death at the age of sixty-eight.

Mortimer Hall continued working as a tinner for Patterson & Sterling in Erie after his release. By 1920, he and Maude had relocated to Titusville, Pennsylvania, before moving to Deland, Florida, where he worked in the construction industry until his retirement in 1945. He passed away in 1958 at the age of eighty-four.

Edward Hutches retired from the Postal Inspection Service and worked as a sewing machine salesman, passing away in 1950 in Painesville, Ohio, at seventy-nine.

James Woltz served as the safety director for the Youngstown Sheet and Tube Company in Youngstown, Ohio, for twenty-five years after leaving the U.S. Postal Inspection Service. After his retirement, Woltz returned to his hometown of Parkersburg, West Virginia, where he was the treasurer and vestryman of the Trinity Episcopal Church until his death in 1945.

William Ela was prominently involved in the 1926 case of Gerald Chapman, a notorious robber from New Britain, Connecticut, convicted in the murder of a policeman, before his retirement from the Postal Inspection Service. He passed away in 1944.

After retiring as a postal inspector, William Cleary worked as a commercial salesman before entering the Oriental Lodge No. 500 of Indianapolis, passing away in 1945.

Water Cookson relocated to Los Angeles, California, and, after a twenty-one-year career as a postal inspector, released a book, *The Art of Financing*, in 1923. He later became a broker and passed away in Maryland in 1953.

Following his departure from the Postal Inspection Service, James Cortelyou served as the chief of county detectives for the Philadelphia city detective service. Cortelyou frequently returned to Erie until his death in 1927 from pneumonia.

Harry Ulery of the Indianapolis Police Department figured in many sensational arrests in that city until stricken with spinal meningitis, succumbing at the age of thirty-seven on January 20, 1915. Keller DeRossette remained a detective with the Indianapolis Police Department until an illness forced his retirement in 1930. He passed away at the age of sixty-eight in 1935.

Judge Charles Orr remained a senior member of the bench of the District Court for Western Pennsylvania in the years following the Perkins-Franklin trial. A former vice president of the Pennsylvania State Bar Association and member of the Duquesne club and Pittsburgh golf club, Judge Orr died at the age of sixty-four following heart trouble.

John Jordan served as U.S. district attorney for the Western District of Pennsylvania until 1913 and returned to private practice in his hometown of Bedford, where he died from bronchial pneumonia in 1932 at the age of eighty-three.

Charles O'Brien remained solicitor for the City of Pittsburg until 1921. During World War I, while his sons served in the military, O'Brien became actively engaged in the city to help support the war and remained active with his law firm until suffering a fatal heart attack at his home in 1928 at the age of seventy-four.

W.H.S. Thomson was nominated by President Woodrow Wilson to the Western District of Pennsylvania following the death of Judge James Young and was confirmed by the Senate on July 21, 1914. He served on the bench for seventeen years before retiring as senior judge. After several years of health problems, Thomson died in 1932 at the age of seventy-five.

William Pengelly continued working as a handwriting expert and was employed with the U.S. Department of Justice and War as a special examiner of documents for the intelligence department of the British government and gained recognition when called as an expert in the infamous case of Alfred

Dreyfus in France. Pengelly died at the age of seventy at his home outside of Columbus in 1935.

David Carvalho remained a handwriting expert until his death in 1925 at his home in New Rochelle, New York, and is regarded as one of the pioneering experts in the study of handwriting examination in American history.

Dr. Albert Hamilton would provide his opinions in various criminal cases, examining firearm evidence in the Sacco-Vanzetti case after both defendants filed an appeal for a new trial. He would return to Erie in May 1930 to present testimony as a defense witness during the trial of Edna Mumbulo, Erie's infamous "Wicked Stepmother."[45] Over the years, Hamilton's work has come under intense scrutiny, with his legacy widely regarded as the work of "an incompetent charlatan."[46] Hamilton passed away in 1938 at the age of seventy-eight.

Hailmer Gould passed away in 1924 at the age of seventy-six in Cleveland, Ohio.

Jack Welsh remained a captain within the City of Erie Police Department until Edward Wagner returned to the department, resulting in his demotion to the rank of lieutenant, lasting until Wagner was appointed county detective. Finding his role as county detective undesirable, Wagner returned, again, to the department, and Welsh found himself assigned to the rank of lieutenant of the newly formed vice squad.

Following Edward Wagner's death in 1922, Welsh returned to the rank of captain. Declining health forced him to be absent from his duties for a considerable period of time, which culminated with a stroke, resulting in his demotion to the rank of patrolman and ending Welsh's twenty-nine-year career.

Because of his long and self-sacrificing service to the city, under direction of then Mayor Joseph Williams, Welsh remained on the payroll for the department as a sign of gratitude. After visiting his daughter in Detroit, Michigan, in an attempt to convalesce, he collapsed in her home and died from a heart attack there on May 14, 1926.

"He was a fine officer and a splendid man," Mayor Williams told the *Times*. "I counted Captain Welsh a very good friend of mine, and I am deeply grieved by his death."

Detective Sergeant Lambertine Pinney was later demoted to the rank of roundsman in 1916, although two years later he again assumed the rank of detective sergeant, followed by lieutenancy in 1927, overseeing pawnshops throughout the city to monitor stolen goods. An intestinal obstruction suddenly ended Pinney's life in 1937 at the age of seventy-nine. Considered the oldest officer in the department, Pinney's career spanned forty-five years.

Richard Crotty remained a detective sergeant and investigated many important cases in the department's history. "It was said of Detective Crotty," wrote the *Times*, "that he never, or at any rate, almost never, had used handcuffs on any of his prisoners."

Crotty died in 1926 at the age of sixty-nine.

John Sullivan returned to his former position as a probation and parole officer and later as a court crier. Despite his failing health, Sullivan continued his duties until he was confined to his bed in June 1926, passing away several months later at the age of eighty-one.

"John Sullivan was a man of sterling character," eulogized the *Erie Daily Times*. "He was a man of great intellect, of exceptional ability and he gave freely of that intellect and ability to serve his city and his county."

After leaving the police department in 1912, Edward Wagner worked for the Bessemer Railroad as a detective and was stationed during the summer at Conneaut Lake Park. Following Lambertine Pinney's demotion in 1916, Wagner returned to the department as a lieutenant and several months later was promoted to captain.

After the passing of County Detective Frank H. Watson, Wagner was appointed to that position by then district attorney C. Arthur Blass, a role he would remain in until his health forced his resignation and return to the police department as captain. A severe case of appendicitis caused his death in December 1922 at the age of sixty-four.

Isador Sobel would serve as postmaster for Erie for sixteen years and later remained active in local politics. He was later elected president of the Erie County Bar Association, serving nine consecutive terms. Known as a prominent and influential man of Jewish faith in America, Sobel founded the District No. 3 B'nai B'rith Home for Children in Fairview, Pennsylvania, serving as president from 1912 until his death in 1939.

After defaulting on his bail, Thomas Dempsey was briefly imprisoned in October 1911 in Franklin, although the charges against him in the Black Hand case there were later dismissed. In 1912. he filed a civil suit against General Charles Miller, seeking recovery for damages from his arrest. Two years later, the civil case was non-suited in the Mercer County courts.

The writer of the Black Hand letters in the city of Franklin was never apprehended, and Dempsey continued his work as a private detective until appointed as a special policeman in 1916 with the City of Erie Police Department, filling in for officers absent from duty or ill. Like much of his life, his tenure with the department was marred by scandal when, in May 1916, Dempsey communicated with questionable characters in Erie's criminal underworld, telling them to contact him should they get in trouble.

The next month, Dempsey was promoted to the rank of patrolman and later special detective for the city solicitor's office, to assist with the city's civil cases. Dempsey's ailing health, plaguing him since his service in the Spanish-American War, contributed to his death on October 28, 1917, at the age of forty-eight.

A.H. "Hutze" Knoll remained a fixture in Erie's art scene until the 1920s, when he retired and moved west, passing away in San Diego, California, at the age of seventy-five, in 1932.

Those responsible for the bombing of the R.S. Battles bank in Girard were never apprehended and the reward of $1,000 never claimed.

The writer of the Black Hand letters to Horace N. Thayer of Erie also remains a mystery to this day.

Burglaries of churches in the city of Erie and neighboring towns, believed to be connected to the desecration of the Scott mausoleum, remain unsolved. Although its brick edifice was later coated in white, St. John's the Baptist Church still serves mass, despite a dwindling Catholic congregation.

William Ott, Arthur Richter and Clarence Cantor all served in the U.S. military during World War I. After the war, William Ott was later employed as a bookbinder for Ashby Inc. and passed away in 1963. Arthur Richter later moved to Lincoln, Wisconsin, where he was self-employed as a tour guide until his death in 1973, and Clarence Cantor worked at the American Meter Company for over forty years, passing away in 1975.

The railroad tracks of the New York Central Railroad that used to traverse West Nineteenth Street are long gone, and with them some of the accompanying buildings from Little Italy to the north of the Erie Cemetery. This includes the home of Mortimer Hall, which has been long razed, where now only a patch of overgrown grass and earth remains.

Amassing seventy-five acres, the Erie Cemetery remains one of the oldest in Erie County. After 1911, the cemetery endured other cases of vandalism. Perhaps one of the most infamous incidents occurred in July 1952, when vandals damaged roughly sixty tombstones and monuments, causing $60,000 in damages. Despite a vigorous investigation by the City of Erie Police Department, those responsible were never found.

Following the desecration of the Scott mausoleum, the marble slabs that formerly held the names of those buried within the crypts were removed

The Scott mausoleum as it appears today in the Erie Cemetery. *Author's collection.*

in an attempt to conceal the present-day locations. The bodies of Richard Holmes Townsend and his daughter, Anna, were later removed from the mausoleum and today are interred in the Townsend mausoleum, located in the Rock Creek Cemetery, Washington, D.C.

The interior of the Scott mausoleum continues to remain a closely guarded secret in accordance with the wishes of the estate of Annie and Charles Strong and is guaranteed to fuel conspiracy theories, supplemented with bloodthirsty ghouls, missing corpses and what-ifs for years to come.

Yet for those who pass through the Erie Cemetery on a bitter February evening, just as darkness creeps over the edges of the earth, perhaps one can hear the echo of the vandals from inside the mausoleum, engaged in their ghastly deed for all eternity.

APPENDIX
CASE-RELATED DOCUMENTS AND LETTERS

The following documents are just some of a few thousand pages involved in the research for this book. This collection of documents includes some items never printed before for the general public, such as microfilm scans of the original "Black Hand" letters, correspondence from the prison records of both Gilbert Perkins and Charles Franklin and other items of historical interest.

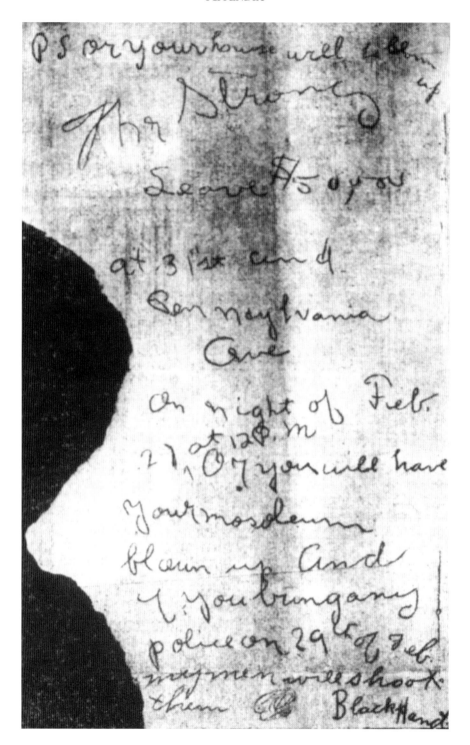

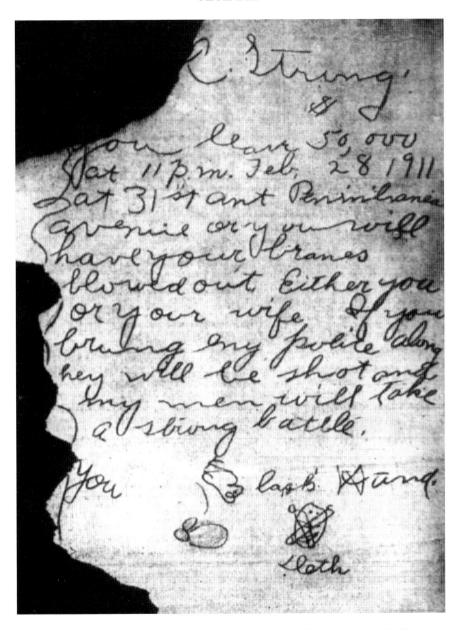

Opposite: The first Black Hand letter sent to Charles Strong on February 13, 1911. *From the* Erie Evening Herald.

Above: The second Black Hand letter sent to Charles Strong on February 15, 1911. *From the* Erie Evening Herald.

APPENDIX

TRUSTY PRISONER'S AGREEMENT.

Name _Gilbert B Perkins_ , No. _7897_ , Color _White_

Crime _Using the Mail to Defraud_

Sentence _Three_ ; Years _—_ , months _—_ , days _—_

Date of Sentence _July 29-1911 (Began March 10)_ Sent from _Pittsburgh Pa._

Full term expires _March 10-1915_ , Short term expires _July 1-1914_

Received at Penitentiary _March 13-1912_ , Occupation _Detective_ , Age _40_

Reasons for being made a Trusty prisoner

Is the above-stated name your right name? _Yes_

If not, what is your right name? _—_

Give a full history of the crime for which you were sent here. _I was charged at Erie Pa. with_ [State fully the nature of the crime. Persons injured physically, financially, or otherwise. State when and where the crime was committed. Name of persons with you when the crime was committed and what was done with him or them. State the reason why the crime was committed and whether or not you plead guilty at the trial.] _using the mails to defraud it being alleged that I together with one Charles Franklin who was in my employ did conspire, by means of letters, which were sent to one Charles Strong of Erie Pa, to obtain the sum of $50,000.ºº We both plead "Not Guilty," but were both found a Guilty and I received sentence as above and Franklin received sentence of five years in this Penitentiary Reg No 7896_

With whom do you correspond? _Mrs S E Perkins Pittsburg Pa. (Wife)_
Mr H. H. Perkins " " (Son)

Where and by whom were you arrested? _At Indianapolis Ind. by P.O. Inspector_

Are you married? _Yes._ Number of Children? _Five._

Name and P.O. address of parents, _Both deceased_

Name and address of wife, _Mrs S E Perkins Pittsburg Pa._

Have you ever served sentence in Penitentiary, Reformatory, Work House, or Jail before? _No_ [State under what name, when, and where.]

Do you own any real estate? _No._ [State where located and the value of it.]

In consideration of being made a Trusty prisoner, I, _Gilbert B Perkins_ , No. _7897_ a prisoner in the United States Penitentiary, Leavenworth, Kansas, do hereby pledge my word that I will not attempt to escape from said Penitentiary or Penitentiary Reservation, and will serve faithfully the unexpired part of my sentence.

[Signature.] _Gilbert B. Perkins_

Reg. No. _7897_

Remarks: _Ed. S. Wright, 846 Western Ave North side Pittsburg_
Hon. Wm. A. McGee, Mayor of Pittsburg Pa.
Albert Lieber, Indianapolis Ind

Trusty Prisoner's Agreement for Gilbert Perkins while incarcerated at the United States Penitentiary at Leavenworth, Kansas. *National Archives.*

Gilbert Perkins's fingerprint card from his prisoner file. *National Archives*.

APPENDIX

TRUSTY PRISONER'S AGREEMENT.

Name: Charles Franklin   No. 7896   Color: White

Crime: Using mails to defraud and conspiracy

Sentence: 5   Years — , months — , days

Date of Sentence: July 29th. 1911.   Sent from W.Dist, Penn, Pittsburg

Full term expires: March 10th 1917   Short term expires: November 16th, 1915

Received at Penitentiary: March 13th, 1912.   Occupation: Detective   Age 45

Reasons for being made a Trusty prisoner

Is the above-stated name your right name?   Yes.

If not, what is your right name?

Give a full history of the crime for which you were sent here. It was alleged that I used the mails to
defraud one, Charles Strong, at Erie, Penn. in February 1911. No financial loss
to any one. I was associated in the scheme with G.B.Perkins, now incarcerated
in this penitentiary.

       I plead "NOT GUILTY"

With whom do you correspond?   Wife.

Where and by whom were you arrested? Philadelphia, Penn., by P.O.Inspector Marshall.

Are you married? Yes   Number of Children? One

Name and P. O. address of parents. Deceased

Name and address of wife. Mrs. Mary E. Franklin, 460 West 4th, St., Erie, Penn.

Have you ever served sentence in Penitentiary, Reformatory, Work House, or Jail before? NO.

Do you own any real estate? NO.

In consideration of being made a Trusty prisoner, I, Charles Franklin   No. 7896
a prisoner in the United States Penitentiary, Leavenworth, Kansas, do hereby pledge my word that I will not attempt to escape from said
Penitentiary or Penitentiary Reservation, and will serve faithfully the unexpired part of my sentence.

[Signature] Charles Franklin

Reg. No. 7896

Remarks: Conrad Klein, c/o Reade House, Erie, Penn.
F.K.Bassett, 828 State St., Erie, Penn.

Trusty Prisoner's Agreement for Charles Franklin while incarcerated at the United States
Penitentiary at Leavenworth, Kansas. *National Archives.*

230

Charles Franklin's fingerprint card from his prisoner file. *National Archives.*

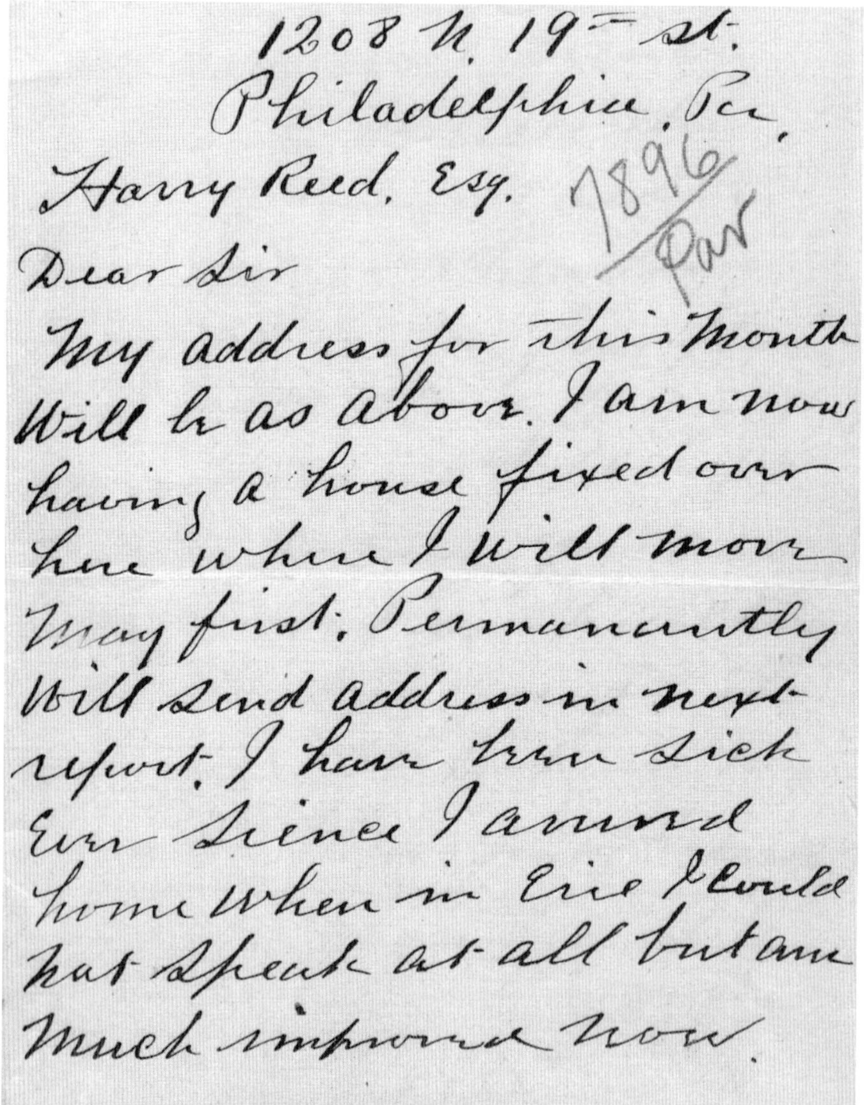

1208 N. 19= st.

Philadelphia, Pa,

Harry Reed, Esq.

1896
Pav

Dear Sir

My address for this month
will be as above. I am now
having a house fixed over
here where I will move
may first, Permanently
will send address in next
report. I have been sick
ever since I arrived
home when in Erie I could
not speak at all but am
much improved now.

First page of a letter written by Charles Franklin updating his address to government authorities after his release. *National Archives.*

All I have done since here is to oversee the alterations and repairs on house. When done. I will have a fine place and will start to work. about May 1st. perhaps before. hoping you are improved in health and thanking you for the interest you took in my behalf. I am Yours Sincerly

Chas Franklin

(7896)

1208 N. 19th St.
Philadelphia Pa.

Second page of a letter written by Charles Franklin updating his address to government authorities after his release. *National Archives.*

NOTES

1. Ghouls

1. "Ghouls Desecrate Scott Tomb," *Erie Daily Times*.
2. Garvey, *Erie, Pennsylvania Mayors*.
3. Ibid.
4. "Erie's Most Magnificent Wedding," *Erie Daily Times*.

2. Tyrannical, Unlawful and Exacting Practices

5. "Charles H. Strong Gives Theory," *Erie Daily Times*.
6. "It's a Joke," *Erie Daily Times*.

3. Rivalries Renewed

7. "Calls Perkins 'Vulture,'" *Cleveland Plain Dealer*.
8. "Secret Service Men Working Here," *Erie Daily Times*.
9. Born in Louisville, Kentucky, Campbell moved to Ridgway, Pennsylvania, in his youth, where he later worked in the lumbering and manufacturing business before attending the Pennsylvania Military Academy in Chester, where he obtained a degree in engineering. Campbell relocated to Erie and worked with the Erie City Iron Works as an engineer before becoming an executive with the Hays

Manufacturing Company. Campbell established the Campbell Brass Works, which operated until its dissolution in 1918. Campbell would later become a well-known local architect when he was instrumental in the construction of the Ariel Building in downtown Erie. Following his retirement, Campbell retreated from public life to his farm, which was constructed on ten acres of property off the Waterford Pike, on a knoll overlooking the Erie Institute of Aeronautics Airport in Kearsarge. A noted recluse, Campbell met a tragic end when his battered body was found by his daughter, Ruth Van Cleve, on Sunday, August 5, 1945. An investigation by the Pennsylvania State Police spearheaded an inquiry that would spread across several states and into Canada, and on August 20, 1945, John Darius West and Robert Pepperman of Williamsport, Pennsylvania, confessed to Campbell's murder. Both men were returned to Erie, where they pleaded guilty and were sentenced to death. West and Pepperman were executed on March 25, 1948.

4. A Pitched Battle

10. Thora Scott-Ronalds was seen frequently on the streets of Erie accompanied by a female nurse and two bodyguards. One of the many rumors at the time, which was reported on by local Erie papers and others, such as the *Cleveland Leader*, focused on the possibility that those who broke into the Scott mausoleum and desecrated its interior had done so as a personal attack against the Strong family, with the intent of potentially kidnapping Thora. Other rumors, such as reported by the *Leader*, claimed that attempts were made to question Reginald Ronalds, the estranged son-in-law of the Strongs and Thora's father, but that repeated efforts were unsuccessful, with rumors indicating Ronalds had left for London to reside with his mother.
11. "Fear Ghouls May Take Tiny Heiress," *Cleveland Leader*.
12. "Have Detectives Abandoned Hunt?" *Erie Daily Times*.
13. Oldfield and Bruce, *Inspector Oldfield and the Black Hand Society*.
14. Ibid.
15. Ibid.
16. "Bill to Stop 'Black Hand' Letter Sending," *Erie Daily Times*.
17. "Working at Scott Mausoleum," *Erie Daily Times*.
18. Between articles appearing in the *Erie Daily Times*, the *Erie Evening Herald* and the *Erie Dispatch*, there are inconsistencies in describing the

placement of Mackey's apartment, with some claiming he lived directly above the bank and others indicating he resided on the second floor, next to the bank.

19. Pinkerton agents were able to conclude a rough estimate of the number of cottages broken into after confirming the most recent dates the properties were tended to by the cottage owners.

5. Crawfishing

20. "Detectives Arrested," *Erie Daily Times*.
21. "Times Extra Told the Story," *Erie Daily Times*.
22. Ibid.
23. "Trying to Put Erie Letters on Thomas Dempsey," *Erie Daily Times*.

6. Sensational Affairs

24. "Sunday Campaign in Erie Drawing to a Close," *Erie Daily Times*.
25. "Case Against G.B. Perkins and Franklin," *Erie Daily Times*.
26. "Perkins and Franklin Both Indicted," *Erie Dispatch*.
27. Also known as a bill of indictment, a true bill refers to a grand jury's decision to indict a criminal defendant.

7. A Desecration Revisited

28. Legal term meaning to suppress or extinguish summarily and completely.
29. "Trump Card in Black Hand Trial," *Gazette Times*.
30. "Witnesses Tell of Blackhand Letters," *Erie Evening Herald*.
31. Ibid.
32. Despite the majority of newspaper articles, including those in Erie, reporting the testimony from Isador Sobel consistently, *mausoleum* is clearly misspelled in the original letter. It is possible Sobel's testimony or words were misconstrued.
33. "Detective Tells of the Raiding," *Erie Evening Herald*.

9. The Scapegoat

34. "Experts Clash with District Atty. Jordan," *Erie Dispatch*, July 27, 1911.
35. Ibid.

10. Affairs of Conspiracy

36. "Perkins Blames Burns Agency," *Erie Daily Times*.

11. Innocent Before God and Fellow Man

37. "G.B. Perkins Convicted," *Pittsburg Press*.

12. We Have Just Started to Fight

38. "Erie Will Open Wide Its Arms," *Erie Evening Herald*.
39. Ibid.
40. "Thousands Lined the Streets," *Erie Sunday Herald*.
41. Ibid.
42. "Nation's Executive Says Good-Bye," *Erie Evening Herald*.

13. Evil Minds and Dispositions

43. "Charles H. Strong Dies," *Erie Daily Times*.
44. "C.H. Strong Funeral Rites Will Be Held," *Erie Daily Times*.
45. Mumbulo and her then common-law husband, Ralph Mumbulo, were both charged and indicted for the March 22, 1930 death of Ralph's eleven-year-old daughter, Hilda. Hilda's death was originally reported as an accident. Several days following her death and the removal of her body to New Berlin, New York, Ralph Mumbulo and Edna, then under the surname DeShunk, eloped and were married several days later. It was only after Dan Hanley, coroner of Erie, received complaints about the Mumbulos' behavior that the case was reopened, followed by a scandalous investigation and subsequent trial that spring. Edna Mumbulo was later found guilty of second-degree

murder and sentenced from ten to twenty years at the Industrial Home for Women in Muncy, Pennsylvania. Mumbulo's sentence was commuted in December 1938, and she rejoined her husband, Ralph, who was never prosecuted for the crime.

46. *Jim Fisher True Crime*, "Albert Hamilton: Courtroom Charlatan," May 20, 2023, http://jimfishertruecrime.blogspot.com/2012/02/albert-hamilton-one-of-americas-first.html.

BIBLIOGRAPHY

Books

Carvalho, Claire, and Boyden Sparkes. *Crime in Ink*. New York: Charles Scribner's Sons, 1929.

Chamberlin, Thomas. *History of the One Hundred and Fiftieth Regiment, Pennsylvania Volunteers, Second Regiment, Bucktail Brigade*. Philadelphia: F. McManus Jr. & Co., Printers, 1905.

Claridge, John R. *Lost Erie: The Vanished Heritage of City and County*. Erie, PA: Erie County Historical Society, 1991.

Dombrowski, Justin. *Murder & Mayhem in Erie, Pennsylvania*. Charleston, SC: The History Press, 2022.

———. *Wicked Erie*. Charleston, SC: The History Press, 2023.

Erie Cemetery: A Hand Book, Historical Biographical and Descriptive. Erie, PA: Herald Printing and Publishing Co., 1903.

Erie County Bar Association. *Memoirs of the Erie County, Pennsylvania, BENCH and BAR*. Vol. 2. 1st ed. Erie, PA: Erie County Bar Foundation, 2000.

Garvey, William. *Erie, Pennsylvania Mayors: 150 Years of Political History*. Erie, PA: Jefferson Educational Society, 2017.

Kruszewski, Sandra. "Some Information About the Gannon Administration Building—Known as the Strong Mansion." Unpublished manuscript: Gannon University Archives, 1975.

Oldfield, William, and Victoria Bruce. *Inspector Oldfield and the Black Hand Society: America's Original Gangsters and the U.S. Postal Detective Who Brought Them to Justice*. New York: Touchstone, 2018.

Rust, Albert E. *History of Erie County Electric Company: 1884–1932*. Erie, PA: A-K-D Printing Company, 1932.

Walling, Judge Emory A. *Memoirs of the Erie County Pennsylvania Bench and Bar*. Erie, PA: Erie Printing Company, 1928.

Criminal Cases and Official Records

Commonwealth of Pennsylvania v. Carl Penetzke, John Costa and Earl McBride. Erie County Court of Common Pleas, No. 35, May 1909.

Inmate Casefile, U.S. Federal Penitentiary, Leavenworth—Charles Franklin. (1912–1914) *The National Archives*.

Inmate Casefile, U.S. Federal Penitentiary, Leavenworth—Gilbert Perkins. (1912–1914) *The National Archives*.

United States v. Gilbert B. Perkins and Charles Franklin. District Court of the United States for the Western District of Pennsylvania. No. 1. July Term, 1911.

Newspapers

Bangor Daily News. "Ghouls Rob Family Vault." February 10, 1911.

Buffalo Evening News. "Grave Is Robbed of Woman's Body." February 9, 1911.

———. "Country-Wide Search for Tomb Despoilers." February 10, 1911.

Cleveland Leader. "Ghouls Stole Scott's Body, Family Fears." February 10, 1911.

———. "Bloodhounds Seek Trail of Tomb Vandals." February 11, 1911.

———. "Hunt for Erie Tomb Vandals Called Off, Is Openly Hinted." February 12, 1911.

———. "Shadow Reporters in Scott Mystery." February 13, 1911.

———. "Fear Ghouls May Take Tiny Heiress." February 14, 1911.

———. "Strong Letter Put at Franklin's Door." July 22, 1911.

Cleveland Plain Dealer. "Ghouls Seen at Work." February 11, 1911.

———. "Keeps Erie Police from Scott Tomb." February 11, 1911.

———. "Man 'Higher Up' Hired Ghouls to Rob Scott Tomb." February 11, 1911.

———. "Finger Prints Leading Clew in Ghoul Hunt." February 12, 1911.

————. "Search Cites for Man 'Higher Up.'" February 13, 1911.

————. "Ghoul Suspects Escape at Night." February 14, 1911.

————. "Drop Erie Ghoul Case." February 15, 1911.

————. "Detectives Seized in Erie Tomb Case." April 14, 1911.

————. "More Detectives Will Be Arrested." April 15, 1911.

————. "Key in Cleveland to Erie Mystery?" April 16, 1911.

————. "Threatens Millionaire." May 14, 1911.

————. "Charges P.O. Conspiracy." May 24, 1911.

————. "Perkins Accuses Detective Burns." July 8, 1911.

————. "Releases Fraud Witness." July 8, 1911.

————. "Sleuth's Trial Opens Today." July 17, 1911.

————. "Erie Tomb Case Testimony Opens." July 19, 1911.

————. "Tells About Raid on Tomb Sleuths." July 20, 1911.

————. "Relates Arrest in Tomb Fraud Case." July 21, 1911.

————. "Bare Defense Plan in Trial at Erie." July 22, 1911.

————. "Brings New Name into Strong Case." July 25, 1911.

————. "Perkins Is Guilty, Says Jury at Erie." July 30, 1911.

————. "Calls Perkins 'Vulture.'" July 31, 1911.

Conneautville Courier. "Something to Crow Over." September 16, 1881.

Erie Daily Times. "A $35,000 Mausoleum." November 25, 1889.

————. "Silent Vigils." October 21, 1891.

————. "Of Doubtful Truth." October 10, 1894.

————. "Incendiary Fire." July 17, 1895.

————. "A Former Erie Man Died in Philadelphia Yesterday." January 20, 1898.

————. "The Late Lieut. Van Cullom." January 21, 1898.

————. "Mrs. W.L. Scott Died at Atlantic City Yesterday." May 20, 1898.

————. "The Remains." May 21, 1898.

————. "Death of Mr. Townsend." November 28, 1902.

————. "Society & Personal." November 29, 1902.

————. "Death of Mrs. McCollum." December 21, 1904.

————. "Mrs. McCollum's Funeral." December 22, 1904.

————. "Funeral of Mrs. M'Collum." December 23, 1904.

————. "Burned to Death in Sleeping Room." August 26, 1905.

————. "Another Opium Joint Is Raided." December 26, 1905.

————. "Stolen Fish Nets." January 2, 1906.

————. "Stole Silk." January 19, 1906.

————. "Silk Stealings." January 24, 1906.

————. "For Stealing Brass." February 20, 1906.

————. "Hotel Gossip." February 24, 1906.

———. "Erie's Most Magnificent Wedding." February 24, 1906.

———. "Ronalds-Strong Wedding." February 24, 1906.

———. "Want's Franklin's License Revoked." March 19, 1906.

———. "Detective Franklin's Mistake." March 19, 1906.

———. "Mr. Franklin Files Answer." March 25, 1906.

———. "Franklin Gives His Side of Case." March 26, 1906.

———. "Editorial." April 11, 1906.

———. "The Court Revokes Franklin's License." April 23, 1906.

———. "Detective Franklin Working for Lake Shore." May 9, 1906.

———. "Detective Franklin Goes to Cleveland." July 12, 1906.

———. "Reward of $1,000 Offered for Capture of the Blackmailers." April 9, 1909.

———. "The Blackmailers Are Still at Large." April 10, 1909.

———. "Blackmailers Arrested." April 12, 1909.

———. "Admits It Is a Side Issue Pure and Simple." April 13, 1909.

———. "Blackmailers Are Committed to Jail." April 13, 1909.

———. "The Blackmailers." April 14, 1909.

———. "Unlawful Use of United States Mail." April 21, 1909.

———. "Blackmailers Plead Not Guilty." April 23, 1909.

———. "Blackmailers Plead Guilty." May 11, 1909.

———. "Sentences Imposed by Judge Walling." May 25, 1909.

———. "Charles H. Strong Gives Theory in Interview with Cleveland Leader Reporter." February 10, 1911.

———. "Detectives Find Woman's Body in Crypt of the Tomb." February 10, 1911.

———. "Erie Case Like Theft of Body of Millionaire Stewart in 1878." February 10, 1911.

———. "Ghouls Desecrate Scott Tomb; Steal Woman's Body." February 10, 1911.

———. "It's a Joke." February 10, 1911.

———. "Milkman Tells Gruesome Story of a Night Prowler Who Saw Men with a Corpse." February 10, 1911.

———. "Strip Altar of Its Articles of Gold and Silver." February 10, 1911.

———. "Vandalism the Work of Men Familiar with the Interior of the Magnificent Mausoleum." February 10, 1911.

———. "Four Bodies Placed in New Caskets Today." February 11, 1911.

———. "Mrs. Strong Feared Father's Body Taken." February 11, 1911.

———. "Mrs. Thora Scott Ronalds Grants Times an Interview." February 11, 1911.

———. "Rival Detectives Differ as to Crypt in Which Body Was Found." February 11, 1911.

———. "Theory That Ghouls Were Directed in Their Work by Some Outside Party Substantiated." February 11, 1911.

———. "Casket Lid Missing; Detectives Puzzled." February 13, 1911.

———. "Three Boys Find Stolen Article." February 13, 1911.

———. "Have Detectives Abandoned Hunt for the Vandals?" February 14, 1911.

———. "Scott Mausoleum to Be Under Guard Day and Night." February 17, 1911.

———. "Black Hand Letters Sent to Mrs. Charles H. Strong Said to Be the Cause of the Pinkertons Here." March 3, 1911.

———. "Bills to Stop 'Black Hand' Letter Sending." March 8, 1911.

———. "Connect Dynamiters with Tomb Desecration." March 11, 1911.

———. "Trimmings of Coffin Were Not Found." March 13, 1911.

———. "Editorial." April 14, 1911.

———. "Times Extra Told the Story to Erie Readers." April 14, 1911.

———. "Yeggs Who Did Girard Bank Job to Be Nabbed." April 14, 1911.

———. "Erie Is Center in Perkins Case Says U.S. District Atty." April 15, 1911.

———. "Franklin Arrested at Philadelphia Office." April 15, 1911.

———. "Girl Jails Sleuths in the Perkins Case." April 15, 1911.

———. "Secret Service Men Working Here." April 15, 1911.

———. "Movements of the Secret Service Men Covered Up in Erie." April 17, 1911.

———. "J.F. Oldfield Working Here on Perkins Case." April 18, 1911.

———. "Chas. Franklin Alleged to Have Written Letters." April 29, 1911.

———. "Perkins and Franklin to Be Tried in Erie Latter Part of July." April 29, 1911.

———. "Bullet Hole Through Window at Edison Plant." May 3, 1911.

———. "Arrest Man on Serious Charge." May 17, 1911.

———. "Hutze Knoll Bound Over to July Term Court." May 17, 1911.

———. "Erie Manufacturer Threatened by Black Hand Letter Writers." May 23, 1911.

———. "Alleged They Stole Silver." May 24, 1911.

———. "Looking for Black Hand Letter Writers." May 24, 1911.

———. "Sleuths Accuse P.O. Inspectors." May 24, 1911.

———. "Blunders of Wagner Are More Apparent in Black Hand Case." May 25, 1911.

———. "Can't Scare the Times by Such Methods." May 25, 1911.

———. "Wagner Not Competent to Head Police Force." May 26, 1911.

———. "The Perkins Detectives Are Hopeful." June 15, 1911.

———. "Perkins Has a Bad Opinion of P.O. Inspectors." June 28, 1911.

———. "Dempsey Claims the Perkins People Caused His Arrest in Effort to Vindicate Themselves." July 3, 1911.

———. "Franklin Here Preparing for Trial on July 17." July 8, 1911.

———. "Trying to Put Erie Letters on Thomas Dempsey." July 11, 1911.

———. "Charged with Conspiracy Against the Perkins Agency." July 15, 1911.

———. "Case Against G.B. Perkins and Franklin Before the U.S. Grand Jury." July 17, 1911.

———. "Trial of Perkins and Franklin Taken Up Before Judge Orr in United States Court." July 18, 1911.

———. "Scott Tomb Desecration Reviewed in Testimony of Mrs. C.H. Strong." July 19, 1911.

———. "Defense in Black Hand Case to Produce Writer of Letters Before Court." July 20, 1911.

———. "Case Against A.H. Knoll Ignored by Jury." July 20, 1911.

———. "Hotels Jammed." July 20, 1911.

———. "Franklin Wrote the Letters Say Expert." July 21, 1911.

———. "Post Office Inspectors Tell of Investigations Leading to Arrest of Perkins Detectives." July 21, 1911.

———. "Martz Taken Back; May Not Be Called Against G.B. Perkins." July 22, 1911.

———. "Defense on in Blackhand Case—Expert Tells of His Friendship for G.B. Perkins." July 24, 1911.

———. "Dempsey Issue Ruled Out of Case Against Detectives." July 25, 1911.

———. "Gilbert Perkins on Witness Stand." July 25, 1911.

———. "Defense Scores Point in Admission of Cleveland Letter." July 26, 1911.

———. "Pittsburg Expert Testifies Franklin Could Not Have Written Letters." July 27, 1911.

———. "Perkins Blames Agency for His Arrest." July 28, 1911.

———. "Black Hand Case in the Jury's Hands." July 28, 1911.

———. "Burns Agency Comes Back at the Perkinses." July 29, 1911.

———. "Perkins and Franklin Guilty; Sentenced to Leavenworth Prison." July 29, 1911.

———. "Prepare Reasons for New Trial in Franklin-Perkins Case." July 31, 1911.

———. "May Indict Two in Perkins Affair." August 1, 1911.

————. "Federal Authorities May Have Tools Used in Tomb Desecration." August 3, 1911.

————. "Odd Fellows Throng City—Thousands Gather for Annual Midsummer Outing." August 5, 1911.

————. "Pythians to Have Keys to City Next Week—The Program." August 12, 1911.

————. "Franklin Not Worrying About 5 Years in Pen." September 22, 1911.

————. "G.B. Perkins' Letter." September 22, 1911.

————. "Erie Isn't Going to the Devil." September 23, 1911.

————. "Perkins and Franklin Fighting for New Trial." September 30, 1911.

————. "Jordan Files His Answer to the Appeal." October 23, 1911.

————. "Franklin Tells of Mausoleum Job to U.S. Inspector?" October 24, 1911.

————. "No Immunity for Franklin." October 26, 1911.

————. "J.F. Oldfield Has Resigned." November 17, 1911.

————. "Perkins' Appeal Hearing on Today." December 6, 1911.

————. "Perkins' Appeal." December 8, 1911.

————. "Jordan Says Reports Were Exaggerated." December 13, 1911.

————. "Arrest Expected in Scott Tomb Mystery." January 15, 1912.

————. "Perkins and Franklin Must Go to Leavenworth Prison." January 25, 1912.

————. "Innocent! Wails Perkins in Great Agony." January 25, 1912.

————. "Erie the Center of News Stories One Year Ago Now." February 7, 1912.

————. "Evidence Has Been Secured Tomb Mystery." February 16, 1912.

————. "Seeks Respite for Gilbert B. Perkins." February 26, 1912.

————. "Arrest Three in Scott Tomb Case; Warrants Out for Perkins and Franklin." March 14, 1912.

————. "Warrant Served by J.P. Sullivan." March 14, 1912.

————. "Will Bring Perkins and M'Cain to Erie." March 15, 1912.

————. "Perkins and M'Cain Here Next Saturday." March 16, 1912.

————. "Hall Recommitted for Hearing on Saturday." March 18, 1912.

————. "Put Off Hearing Scott Tomb Case." March 23, 1912.

————. "Jurors for Most Important Term." April 4, 1912.

————. "Important Jury Has Been Drawn." April 9, 1912.

————. "Hearing of Tomb Case Next Tuesday." April 13, 1912.

————. "Perkins, M'Cain and Hall Were Discharged at the Hearing Today." April 16, 1912.

———. "Sues Mrs. Strong for $100,000; Mortimer H. Hall Asks Damages." March 13, 1914.

———. "Strong's Sued for $250,000 in Four Separate Actions." March 14, 1914.

———. "Plaintiffs File Claim in $150,000 Damage Suit Against Mr. and Mrs. Strong." July 18, 1914.

———. "Postpone Trial of Strong Cases." February 22, 1915.

———. "Cases Brought Against Strongs Are Postponed." June 7, 1915.

———. "Case of H. Perkins vs. Strongs May Not Start Till Friday." December 7, 1915.

———. "Story Tomb Desecration to Be Retold in Damage Suit of Harry H. Perkins." December 10, 1915.

———. "P.O. Inspectors Here for Trial of Strong Case." December 10, 1915.

———. "Tomb Mystery Is Being Aired in Courts of Erie Co." December 11, 1915.

———. "Perkins Resumed His Testimony at Opening of Court." December 13, 1915.

———. "Strong Case Non-Suited by Court; Jury Discharged." December 14, 1915.

———. "Hall Case Non-Suited by Walling." December 15, 1915.

———. "Some of the Facts Connected with Police Affairs." November 26, 1917.

———. "New Philadelphia Safety Director Well Known Here." December 18, 1919.

———. "Famous Scott Mausoleum Case Recalled as Perkinses Take Over Green Goose Inn." February 10, 1925.

———. "Dundon Named Captain of Police." April 29, 1926.

———. "Pneumonia Fatal to F.E. Crane, Editor of the Times." December 20, 1926.

———. "Hear Echo of Scott Mausoleum Desecration as J.T. Cortelyou Succumbs in Philadelphia." April 15, 1927.

———. "Keeping Up with the Times." August 10, 1936.

———. "Wandering." November 19, 1936.

———. "Bunny Berigan to Play Here." April 17, 1939.

———. "Keeping Up with the Times." August 29, 1939.

———. "Keeping Up with the Times." August 6, 1945.

———. "Fabulous 60-Year-Old Scott Will Finally Settled." September 16, 1950.

———. "Desecration of Scott Mausoleum Recalled." February 16, 1955.

———. "Desecration of Mausoleum Was Shocking." February 7, 1956.

———. "Erie History." December 23, 1958.

———. "Keeping Up with the Times." April 12, 1963.

———. "Grave-Robbing Scandal Remains an Erie Mystery Even after 70 Years." October 29, 1981.

———. "Erie Daily Times Celebrates 97th Birthday—Never Looked Better." April 12, 1985.

———. "English Carve Erie Settlement Out of Wilderness." June 12, 1988.

———. "From Boss Tweed to Mrs. Strong." February 18, 1995.

Erie Dispatch. "Arson Charged." July 17, 1895.

———. "Suspected Fire Bug Arrested." July 17, 1895.

———. "The Fire Caused Trouble." July 18, 1895.

———. "Tangled Up with the Law." July 22, 1895.

———. "Franklin Way of Settling." March 10, 1906.

———. "Franklin Way of Settling." March 17, 1906.

———. "Franklin's Methods to Be Aired." March 20, 1906.

———. "License Has Been Revoked." April 24, 1906.

———. "Result of Franklin's Methods." April 24, 1906.

———. "Blackmailers Demand $500." April 9, 1909.

———. "Black Hand Letter Gang Under Arrest." April 13, 1909.

———. "St. John's Church Offers $500 for Thief's Capture." February 11, 1911.

———. "Three Boys Find Articles Stolen from St. Johns." February 12, 1911.

———. "Perkins and Franklin Both Indicted by Federal Grand Jury." July 18, 1911.

———. "Connect Desecration of Mausoleum with Threatening Letters." July 20, 1911.

———. "Franklin Is Implicated in Note Writing." July 21, 1911.

———. "Expert Picks Franklin as Letter Writer." July 22, 1911.

———. "Resume Perkins Case; Hand-Writing Expert Testifies in Morning." July 25, 1911.

———. "Defense Makes Broad Denial of All Charges." July 25, 1911.

———. "Judge Rules Against Plan of Perkinses." July 26, 1911.

———. "Perkins On Stand Denies Knowledge of Black Hand Letters." July 26, 1911.

———. "Defense Allowed to Put Cleveland Letter and Others in Evidence." July 27, 1911.

———. "Experts Clash with District Atty. Jordan." July 27, 1911.

————. "Defense Expert Says Franklin Could Not Have Written Letters." July 28, 1911.

————. "Black Hand Letter Testimony Concluded in Morning Session." July 29, 1911.

————. "Perkins Case Goes to the Jury Today." July 29, 1911.

————. "Perkins and Franklin Get Prison Terms." July 30, 1911.

————. "Franklin Without Bail Last Night; Still Imprisoned." October 22, 1911.

————. "Officials Question Franklin Commitment." October 23, 1911.

————. "More Revelations Are Expected from Detective Franklin." October 27, 1911.

————. "U.S. Attorney Jordan Admits Error Points in Perkins Hearing." December 8, 1911.

————. "Bail Furnished by M'Cain and Harry Perkins." March 15, 1912.

————. "Perkins and M'Cain to Get Preliminary Trial Here March 23." March 16, 1912.

————. "Will Admit Hall to Get Bail for Hearing." March 17, 1912.

————. "Hall Fails to Get Bail for Hearing." March 19, 1912.

————. "Preliminary Trial in Mausoleum Case Is Set for Today." March 23, 1912.

————. "Find New Evidence in Mausoleum Case; Put Over Hearing." March 24, 1912.

————. "Hearing of Mausoleum Case Is Up Tomorrow." April 14, 1912.

————. "Perkins, Hall and M'Cain Discharged in Mausoleum Case." April 17, 1912.

————. "Suit of Harry H. Perkins Begun Before Judge Walling." December 12, 1915.

————. "Asks Non-Suit in Perkins Case; Decision This Morning." December 14, 1915.

————. "Jury Is Called in Mortimer Hall Case." December 15, 1915.

————. "Non-Suits Case of Harry H. Perkins." December 15, 1915.

————. "Non-Suits Case of Mortimer H. Hall." December 16, 1915.

Erie Evening Herald. "Detective Franklin—Petition to Have His License Revoked Was Presented in Court." March 19, 1906.

————. "Make Out a Strong Case." April 3, 1906.

————. "The Judge Will Decide." April 10, 1906.

————. "License Revoked." April 23, 1906.

————. "The Franklin Case." April 24, 1906.

————. "He May Be Prosecuted." April 24, 1906.

———. "Black Hand Letters Sent to Mr. C.H. Strong." April 9, 1909.

———. "Black Hand Letter Writers Are Caught." April 12, 1909.

———. "The Blackmailers in Jail Awaiting a Trial." April 13, 1909.

———. "No New Charges Have Been Made." April 14, 1909.

———. "Were Held for the U.S. Court." April 23, 1909.

———. "Up for Trial Next Week." May 4, 1909.

———. "Murder Trial May Be Taken Up Tomorrow." May 11, 1909.

———. "The Judge Passed Sentences Today." May 25, 1909.

———. "The Prisoners Taken to Pen." May 26, 1909.

———. "Body Taken from Scott Mausoleum." February 9, 1911.

———. "St. John's Catholic Church Entered by Bold Robbers." February 10, 1911.

———. "Facts About Scott Tomb Desecration." February 11, 1911.

———. "Boys Find Stolen Loot." February 12, 1911.

———. "Yeggs Blow Up Girard Bank." March 10, 1911.

———. "Charge Detectives with Writing Threatening Letters." April 14, 1911.

———. "Thieves Visit Summer Homes." April 15, 1911.

———. "Surprises Are Promised in Perkins Case." July 14, 1911.

———. "Perkins' Cause the Arrest of Government Witness." July 15, 1911.

———. "Detective Perkins and His Son Arrive in Erie; Black Hand Letter Case to Begin Monday." July 16, 1911.

———. "Federal Court Starts Perkins Case." July 17, 1911.

———. "Federal Grand Jury Is Taking Evidence." July 17, 1911.

———. "Letters Received by Mr. Strong Threatened Death." July 18, 1911.

———. "Witness Tells of Blackhand Letters Sent Strong Family." July 19, 1911.

———. "Detective Tells of the Raiding of Perkins Indianapolis Office." July 20, 1911.

———. "Defense Tries to Show Raid Illegal." July 20, 1911.

———. "Detective Franklin's Connection with Case Is Brought Out by Chief Inspector Cortelyou." July 21, 1911.

———. "Experts Point Out Similarity in Writings of Black Hand Letters." July 21, 1911.

———. "Postal Inspectors Did Not Work with Burns Men Says Mr. Oldfield." July 21, 1911.

———. "Perkins Still Keeps His Life of Defense a Secret; Many Conferences Are Held." July 23, 1911.

———. "Dempsey Wrote Letters and Planned Conspiracy Says Defense." July 24, 1911.

———. "Franklin Takes Witness Stand to Explain His Side of the Case." July 25, 1911.

———. "Gilbert B. Perkins Denies All Federal Authorities Have Charged Against Him." July 25, 1911.

———. "Judge Orr Rules Dempsey's Name Out of Letter Case." July 25, 1911.

———. "Defense Denied the Right to Bring Dempsey into the Case." July 26, 1911.

———. "Defense Expert Says Two Men Worked on Blackhand Letters." July 26, 1911.

———. "Perkins' Son Tells of Raid in Indianapolis." July 27, 1911.

———. "Counsel for Defense Makes Bold Charge to the Jury." July 29, 1911.

———. "Both Found Guilty by Jury." July 29, 1911.

———. "Deny Perkins New Trial." August 4, 1911.

———. "Dempsey Wins His Release." October 25, 1911.

———. "District Attorney Files Answer in Perkins Case." October 25, 1911.

———. "Franklin Says He's Innocent." October 25, 1911.

———. "Still Probing Letter Case." October 27, 1911.

———. "Perkins' Appeal Is Heard Today." December 6, 1911.

———. "Appeal Unlikely Says Mr. Jordan." January 25, 1912.

———. "Conviction of Perkins and Franklin Upheld by Court." January 25, 1912.

———. "Perkins and Franklin Present New Appeal." February 26, 1912.

———. "Arrests in Mausoleum Case." March 14, 1912.

———. "District Attorney Wait Says the Evidence Is Conclusive." March 14, 1912.

———. "Harry Perkins Denies He Is Arrested as Suspect." March 14, 1912.

———. "Information Issued in the Mausoleum Desecration." March 14, 1912.

———. "Perkins and M'Cain Held; Bail Fixed at $1,000 in Pittsburg." March 15, 1912.

———. "Grant Perkins and J. M'Cain Hearing Soon." March 16, 1912.

———. "Hall's Bail Reduced by the Alderman." March 17, 1912.

———. "Reduce Bail of Mortimer Hall to $1,000." March 18, 1912.

———. "Continue Hearing of Perkins, Hall and Jas. M'Cain Until April 18." March 23, 1912.

———. "Mausoleum Case Comes to End Suddenly." April 16, 1912.

———. "Perkins Damage Suit Is Started." December 11, 1915.

———. "Perkins on Stand Tells His Story." December 12, 1915.

———. "Testimony of Harry Perkins Was Concluded." December 13, 1915.

———. "Afternoon Session of Perkins Trial." December 13, 1915.

————. "Non-Suit Is Granted in Perkins Case." December 14, 1915.

————. "Compulsory Non-Suits Are Rare in Erie Co. Court." December 14, 1915.

————. "Hall Case Is Non-Suited in Civil Court." December 15, 1915.

Erie Morning Dispatch. "Scott-Strong." September 9, 1881.

Gazette Times. "Perkins and Franklin Arraigned at Erie in Strong Black Hand Letter Case." July 19, 1911.

————. "Trump Card in Black Hand Trial." July 20, 1911.

————. "Woman Says U.S. Attorney Made Threat." July 23, 1911.

Lake Shore Visitor. "One of Erie's Most Historic Homes Was Purchased by Bishop Gannon in 1941." July 27, 1979.

Los Angeles Times. "Ghouls Break Into Mausoleum; Body Taken Held for Ransom?" February 10, 1911.

New York Times. "Says Blackhanders Forced Scott Tomb." February 10, 1911.

————. "Held as Black Hand Writer." April 29, 1911.

————. "Strong Blackmail Case Up." July 18, 1911.

————. "Trial of Detectives Begun." July 19, 1911.

Pittsburgh Gazette Times. "Jury in Perkins' Case Reports Today." July 18, 1911.

————. "Cortelyou Tells About Franklin." July 21, 1911.

————. "Writing Expert Tells of Letters." July 22, 1911.

————. "Fight of Experts in Black Hand Trial." July 24, 1911.

————. "Perkins Springs Sensation at Trial." July 25, 1911.

————. "Judge Orr Rules Out Dempsey Issue." July 26, 1911.

Pittsburg Post. "Testifies Franklin Blundered." July 21, 1911.

Pittsburg Press. "Some Local Detective Stories: A Rush Order." October 26, 1902.

————. "Richardson Tells Who Put Up $70,000." December 2, 1906.

————. "Perkins Sleuth Is Attacked." July 20, 1911.

————. "Perkins Defense Is Shaken." July 21, 1911.

————. "Perkins Case Develops New Theory as to Form of Plot." July 22, 1911.

————. "Perkins Case Battle Is Growing in Fierceness." July 23, 1911.

————. "Handwriting Expert Makes Points Plain." July 24, 1911.

————. "Perkins Testifies in His Own Behalf." July 25, 1911.

————. "Courtroom Scene in Perkins Trial Was Dramatic." July 30, 1911.

————. "G.B. Perkins Convicted, to Fight On." July 30, 1911.

ABOUT THE AUTHOR

J USTIN DOMBROWSKI is a well-respected and noted historian from Erie, Pennsylvania, specializing in local criminal, legal and historical records. An alumni of Mercyhurst University, he can usually be found searching for his next historical adventure or spending time with his family. This is his fourth book with The History Press.

ALSO BY JUSTIN DOMBROWSKI

Murder & Mayhem in Erie, Pennsylvania
Erie's Backyard Strangler: Terror in the 1960s
Wicked Erie